W9-CIA-210

THE
REPORTER
READER

Edited by MAX ASCOLI

Editor of THE REPORTER

A Fortnightly of Facts and Ideas

Doubleday & Company, Inc., 1956

Garden City, New York

CONTENTS

Far Away

Not So Far Ahead

And Still the Orient

A Few Jingles

That Man

Comment on the Arts

In Africa

A Little Business

A Way for America

A PRINCIPLE OR TWO

Some Negative Thinking
about Norman Vincent Peale

BY WILLIAM LEE MILLER

I've been thinking negative thoughts, which Dr. Norman Vincent Peale, America's most successful Protestant minister, says we should never think. What's worse, my negative thoughts have been about Dr. Peale himself.

Dr. Peale believes in the Power of Positive Thinking. He says "only positive thoughts get results." What results? you ask. Success, happiness, money, health, friends, relaxation, peace of mind, power, self-confidence, vacations on Waikiki Beach, and, what is to me a truly frightening prospect, "Constant energy."

The results Dr. Peale himself has achieved by following the "Magic Formula" of Positive Thinking are impressive indeed. His weekly network TV show, "What's Your Trouble?", gets upwards of five thousand letters a week; his articles, such as the famous "Let the Church Speak Up for Capitalism" in the *Reader's Digest,* appear in popular magazines by the dozen; his own magazine, *Guideposts,* is one of the "fastest-growing inspirational publications in the country"; he himself has been the subject of many lyrical articles, including a cover story in *Newsweek* and "The Power of Norman Vincent Peale" in *McCall's;* his printed sermons ("How to Stop Being Tense," "No More Gloomy Thoughts") and his self-help booklets ("Spirit-Lifters," "Thought-Conditioners") are mailed around the world by his own publishing outlet, Sermon Publications, Inc., of Pawling, New York; he speaks regularly to large national gatherings, especially of business groups; he has a regular network radio show, "The Art of Living," and appears often on radio and TV in such special appearances as a one-night substitution for his Pawling neighbor, Lowell Thomas; Christmas cards bearing a cheery message from him are sold throughout the land; he has a weekly syndicated newspaper column carried "in nearly one hundred dailies"; and now he has a regular question-and-answer page in *Look.* Of the *Look* feature, the press

1

release said, "Norman Vincent Peale will add new millions . . . to his already colossal audience. . . . He will answer the questions of *Look* readers on social and moral problems. In his first article, Dr. Peale gives *Look* readers his advice on such problems as debt, falling in love with someone else's husband and the H-Bomb."

Somewhere in between Dr. Peale finds time to preach in the Marble Collegiate Church of New York City, where there are overflow crowds at two services each Sunday. The worship bulletins of the church dutifully record, in column after column, the far-flung enterprises of the minister, with dates, times, and prices. And the "lounge" of the church serves as a salesroom: thirteen of Dr. Peale's sermons on LP records, $4.50; a subscription to *Guideposts*, $2; "maroon, gold-lettered binders" made to hold "a year's supply" of Dr. Peale's sermons, $3.

And then there is his book *The Power of Positive Thinking* (Prentice-Hall, $2.95). This product of Dr. Peale's constant energy has already sold nearly a million copies, and the publishers are said to have a goal of two million; it is available on records in an RCA album ("You can hear the inspiring talks of Dr. Norman Vincent Peale *right in your own home!*") and now there is an edition for young people ("Your market—every parent among the millions who have read this inspirational best seller. . . . Specially rewritten by Dr. Peale and adapted to the needs and interests of young people. . . . Backed by major national advertising, special juvenile market advertising, and all-out Christmas advertising"). For 112 weeks, as of this writing, *The Power of Positive Thinking* has been on the *Times's* best-seller list, a far longer time than any other current book, and for most of that time it has been the nonfiction leader. For 1954 it will undoubtedly duplicate its performance of 1953, when, according to Prentice-Hall, it sold more copies than any other book—fiction or nonfiction—except the Bible. It is now being readied, apparently, to pass that one last competitor, for a "new Deluxe Pocket Edition" ($3.95) has been placed on the market, "Bound handsomely in genuine Sturdite . . . stamped in gold with flexible binding . . . wrapped attractively in cellophane . . . ideal for carrying in pocket or purse . . . printed on fine white Bible paper."

2

I have just read *The Power of Positive Thinking*. In addition, I have read Dr. Peale's other books: *A Guide to Confident Living* ($2.95), *You Can Win* ($1.50), *The Art of Living* ($1.50), and those of which he is co-author, *Faith Is the Answer* ($2.95) and *The Art of Real Happiness* ($2.95). Let me say, in the unlikely event that anyone else would undertake this redundant inspirational feat, that it isn't necessary. If you have read one, you have read them all. There are no surprises in Dr. Peale. The chapters of his books could easily be transposed from the beginning to the middle, or from the end to the beginning, or from one book to another. The paragraphs could be shuffled and rearranged in any order. The swarms of examples, which alternate successful business executives and successful athletes, with successful military figures thrown in for variety, could be transposed to support one point or another interchangeably.

As a result of reading Dr. Peale's one point in every simple, easy book, chapter, and paragraph, I am so full of "confidence-concepts," "faith-attitudes," and "energy-producing thoughts," of "thought-conditioners" and "spirit-lifters," of "10 simple, workable rules," "8 practical formulas," "7 simple steps," "2 fifteen-minute formulas," and a "3 point program," of "proven secrets," "true stories," and "actual examples," of "healing words" ("tranquillity," "serenity") and "magic words" ("Faith Power Works Wonders"), so adept at "Imagineering" and "Mind-drainage" (also "grievance-drainage") that I have the Confidence, Faith, Vigor, Belief, Energy, Efficiency, and Power to write an article criticizing Dr. Peale. Believe me, Dr. Peale, without you I never could have done it.

"The secret of a better and more successful life," according to Dr. Peale, "is to cast out those old dead, unhealthy thoughts." "To make your mind healthy," says Dr. Peale, "you must feed it nourishing, wholesome thoughts." The trouble with a fellow like me, he claims, is that my "mind is literally saturated with apprehension, defeat thoughts, gloomy thoughts." But my problem is not only that I find that there are real things in the world about which we legitimately can be apprehensive, negative, unhopeful, and even gloomy from time to time, but that one

3

of the surest causes of such negative thinking, in me, is Dr. Peale's own kind of "Religion."

The key to the immense success of that "Religion" is its message. In this, Dr. Peale differs from other heroes of the current popular religious revival. In a way Dr. Peale is the rich man's Billy Graham, furnishing the successful and those who yearn to be so something of the same excitement, direction, and reassurance with which Mr. Graham supplies his somewhat less prosperous and more fundamentalist followers. But there is an important distinction to be made. As Mr. Graham surely would admit, his own message is essentially similar to that of hundreds of other evangelists, past and present, rising from a fundamentalist background; the key to Mr. Graham's special success is not in any distinctive message but in his personality and his virtuosity as a performer. But Dr. Peale's attraction lies somewhat less in personal charism than in his constantly reiterated single theme. Mr. Graham's success depends almost entirely upon his personal presence, but Dr. Peale has been as successful with the written as with the spoken word.

This is not to say that Dr. Peale's personality and speaking ability are unimportant. He is an effective master of an audience, full of jokes and anecdotes, buoyant and confident. But it is his message that explains his unique success. One comes away from Billy Graham impressed not so much with anything that has been said as with Billy Graham; from Dr. Peale, one comes away with a vivid awareness of the one thing he said. It is an idea that has made Dr. Peale.

The idea is that affirmative attitudes help to make their own affirmations come true. Dr. Peale takes the obvious but partial truth in this idea and builds it into an absolute law; he erects on it a complete and infallible philosophy, psychology, and religion, so that he can solve every problem just by denying it really exists and promise that every wish can be fulfilled just by "thinking" it: "Expect the Best and Get It"; "I don't believe in defeat"; death is "not Death at all"; "Change your thoughts and you change Everything."

All this is hard on the truth, but it is good for the preacher's popularity. It enables him to say exactly what his hearers want to hear. He can say it constantly, confidently, simply, without qualification and with the blessing of God. He need say nothing that might cut across his hearers' expectations, challenge the adequacy of their goals, or make demands of them. Instead, he can affirm and reaffirm that it is simple to be exactly what they want to be, to have exactly what they want to have.

Dr. Peale's idea thus allows him to go completely over into that situation of which liberal Protestantism always is in danger, where the desires and notions of a traditionless congregation determine absolutely what gospel shall be preached. In this again, Dr. Peale differs from other leaders of the popular religious revival. Someone like Bishop Fulton J. Sheen has obligations to Catholic dogmas that prevent him from fashioning his message entirely according to popular preference; Billy Graham, too, has some restraint upon him from the more or less fundamentalist gospel to which he is committed. But Dr. Peale is apparently free of obligation to any intellectual tradition or framework of interpretation antecedent to that which he works out to correspond exactly to the climate of opinion and desire in which he preaches. It is quite difficult to find any place where the more profound claims of historic faith have affected his vigorous, beaming, eminently successful, and resolutely cheerful message.

Though I have said that Dr. Peale's books are all alike, yet there is this one qualification: The later books are worse. The earlier ones, in which Confident Living and Positive Thinking were plainly foreshadowed, nevertheless spoke the message in something nearer to the ordinary preacher's tones. The word was already self-help, but the voice was more like that of an ordinary liberal pastor, with his three points, usually in alliteration, with homely examples, some passages from the Bible, a rhetorical flight or two, a few quotes from Tennyson or Shakespeare, and some spaces through which a word greater than any words of the preacher might manage to make its way to some hearer. But in *The Power of Positive Thinking* such spaces are pretty well sealed; every quotation from the Bible is cut, clipped, and interpreted to make just Dr. Peale's point; the rhetoric of the sermon has been replaced by the short punchy sentences and atrocious jargon of the advertisement; the three points of the preacher have been supplanted by the Five

Things You Can Do of popular psychology; and Tennyson's place has been taken by Eddie Rickenbacker.

Dr. Peale is good at what he does. He has the ability —and the nerve—to fit his message precisely to the exacting requirements of mass popularity. His discoveries parallel those of the composers of singing commercials. For example, he extols, and assiduously practices, "repetitious emphasis." He is willing to use without flinching the most blatant appeals and to promise without stint. The advertisements of his book explain, with remarkable candor, the basis of its appeal: "ARE *You* MISSING THE LIFE OF SUCCESS? Norman Vincent Peale's great best seller . . . is GUARANTEED to bring it to you! Make people like you. . . . Increase your earnings. . . ."

Like other success salesmen, Dr. Peale numbers his points and fixes them in the mind with memorable new words; his "formula" for solving problems through the power of prayer, for example, is "(1) PRAYERIZE, (2) PICTURIZE, (3) ACTUALIZE." He is careful to avoid the slightest hint of anything that would be definite, determinate, or different enough to offend anyone; and above all he requires not the slightest effort either to understand or to act upon his message. As Dr. Peale says elsewhere, "Don't doubt. Doubt closes the Power flow."

Dr. Peale's idea and his ability to present it might enable him to be popular in any place at any time, but it seems to work especially well in America now. The importance of studying Dr. Peale lies in what his enormous success means about our present situation in this country.

The American roots of Positive Thinking are not hard to find. They include most of those characteristics which observers are always identifying as typically American: our self-confidence and optimism, our worldly practicality, and our individualism and striving for success, concerned more with private career than public problems. They include, more particularly, that special combination of these characteristics which places its practical, individual confidence in the triumphant power of "mind" or "faith" over all external limits. This combination appears in the peculiarly American religion of Christian Science, in the "mind-cure" movement of the turn of the century, which William James discusses in *The Varieties of Religious Experience,* and in many a "mental science" type of religion since. Perhaps these themes, especially the last, are characteristic more of middle- and upper-class America than of the nation as a whole, but they do seem to appear both in our serious literature and in our popular culture, as in the Horatio Alger stories of another day and the "How to" books and newsstand self-help of today. What Dr. Peale has done is to take these themes, which represent much of what is sound and also much of what is not so sound in American life, and reduce them to a unity, stating them in their simplest, baldest, extremest form. What was sound has pretty well been lost in the process.

But Dr. Peale's statement of his simplified version of these old American themes may be extremely popular right now just because they no longer seem self-evident. His success may be partly explained, ironically, by the fact that we no longer automatically believe what he is saying; we need to be reassured. Disturbing events have intervened, and so we listen a bit desperately to this voice which insists, more confidently than ever, that what we always believed is still true and that things *will* turn out all right, they will, they will. Just write it on a card and repeat it ten times a day.

The absolute power that Dr. Peale's followers insist on granting to their Positive Thinking may betray, however, a note of desperation. The optimism is no longer the healthy-minded kind, looking at life whole and seeing it good, but an optimism arranged by a very careful and very anxious selection of the particular bits and pieces of reality one is willing to acknowledge. It is not the response of an expanding epoch when failure, loneliness, death, war, taxes, and the limitations and fragmentariness of all human striving are naturally far from consciousness, but of an anxious time when they are all too present in consciousness and must be thrust aside with slogans and "formulas," assaulted with clenched fists and gritted teeth, and battered down with the insistence on the power of Positive Thinking.

The success striving is different, too. The Horatio Alger type seems to have had a simple, clear confidence in getting ahead by mastering a craft, by inventing something out in the barn, or by doing an outstanding job as office boy. The Peale fan has no such confidence and trusts less in such solid realities as ability and work and talent than in the ritual repetition of spirit lifters and thought conditioners written on cards and on the determined refusal to think gloomy thoughts.

The "individualism" of the message is of that "personalized" kind which, having lost a genuinely personal relation, tries now to recapture it by contrivance, which thinks it overcomes standardization by stamping the buyer's initials on the product, or which, by adding "and I do mean YOU," pretends to be speaking to an individual instead of to a microphone and a Hooper rating. Dr. Peale's works are "personalized" with the same insistent YOU the Uncle Sam on the recruiting poster used, sternly pointing his finger at the YOU, who is everybody and nobody. The drugstore I went to this morning had a new sign tacked to the screen door: "Norman Vincent Peale Solves YOUR Personal Problems—in Look Magazine." *My* personal problems? In *Look* magazine? No, thank you.

The effort to regain by devices what cannot be regained by devices is especially evident in Dr. Peale's "power," "energy," and "vitality." The feeling of the loss of those powers must be very deep. Every chapter seems to promise "power": prayer power, creative mind power, faith power. This "power" is not control over the world so much as over oneself. That which should be natural —vitality, vigor, animal energy—is here the subject of "spiritual" manipulation. Human powers are not evoked by revealing some true center of interest and excitement in the world outside, but are exhorted to rise by the sheer mesmerism of "repetitious emphasis." There is no real *content* to Dr. Peale's preaching, in the sense of some vivid objective interest: a job to be done, a cause to be joined, a truth to be understood. The transaction is entirely within the reader. There is a complete absence of any really concretely interesting and exciting world, which might bring out the reader's vital responses (and overcome his boredom, which must be immense). There is no such world because to see it, to be interested and excited by it, and to respond to it would require effort, and Dr. Peale's "amazing results" never require any effort.

This is a striking difference between Dr. Peale's themes and those in the American heritage to which his are related: His optimism and practicality are "easy"

8

and "simple." There is never the suggestion that hard work might be involved in achievement. There are no demands upon the reader. This is not the sturdy practical guide whose maxims have to do with the shoulder and the wheel, the nose and the grindstone; there is no pushing and grinding to be done.

The master motif is that of the formula. The promised results are to be achieved by the contrivances and devices that are spoken of on every page, the "methods," the "secrets," the "formulas," the "techniques" that flood through the books by the hundreds. All of them, of course, are "scientific." The Bible is scientific, in fact: It is ". . . a book which contains a system of formulas and techniques designed for the understanding and treatment of human nature. The laws are so precise and have been so often demonstrated . . . that religion may be said to form an exact science." Christianity is "a simple yet scientific system of successful living that works."

Many of Dr. Peale's techniques come from the famous and successful men with whom he is intimate. In Dr. Peale's books these men turn out to talk just like Dr. Peale. There is a continually recurring episode in the books that goes like this: Peale meets Great Man; Peale humbly asks Great Man for his secret (his formula, technique); Great Man tells Peale strikingly Peale-like secret (formula, technique) upon which Peale then expatiates. Something like this occurs in *The Power of Positive Thinking* on page 105 ("dynamic man at the height of his power"—secret is to repeat Mark 9:23), page 117 ("outstanding newspaper editor, an inspiring personality"—secret is card in wallet with words to effect that successful man is successful), pages 150–151 (Howard Chandler Christy, artist—secret is spending fifteen minutes filling mind full of God), page 229 (a Member of Congress—secret is be relaxed), page 212 ("outstanding man in his line"—secret is don't think defeat), page 223 ("a famous businessman who handles important affairs and varied interests"—secret is quiet period in living room with wife after breakfast).

Everything in this maze of formulas and techniques is "workable," even the teachings of Jesus. We are referred to "competent spiritual experts" and to Dr. Peale's own "How Cards." Dr. Peale takes all of our worship of the practical and the technical unabashedly into the realm of the spirit. But nothing much that could be called spiritual remains. In place of any Holy of Holies there is the bathroom mirror, on which you are to paste the latest slogan.

About the current book there is a faintly blasphemous promise, for a religious book, of a money-back guarantee. The message is endorsed throughout by satisfied users; it is PROVED, it has WORKED, it is TESTED. In fact, Dr. Peale's book is not much else than an extension of the advertisements of that same book, telling again between the covers, with further testimonials, what we have already been told, with testimonials, on the jacket and in the ads: This method WORKS. One might give prospective buyers of the book the tip that since the book is "repetitious emphasis" of positive thinking, one can achieve exactly the same effect—and save money—simply by reading and rereading the advertisements.

But to do that might be to miss what is beyond doubt the most remarkable of all the multitudinous examples of the power of Positive Thinking that appear in Dr. Peale's best seller, the incredible story of the Mustard Seed Remembrancers. For those who are too busy, or too negative, to read the book I now pass on this truly heart-warming story.

A couple named Flint were failing, broke, and full of negative thinking. They read a condensation of Dr. Peale's *A Guide to Confident Living*. The Flints, on reading Dr. Peale, were particularly impressed with the section on "Mustard Seed Faith." Though living in Philadelphia, they drove each Sunday to New York to hear Dr. Peale and continued to do so, says Dr. Peale, "even in the most inclement weather."

In an interview, Dr. Peale told Mr. Flint that if he would "utilize the technique of faith, all his problems could be solved."

One day Mr. Flint said to his wife that this powerful recommendation would be easier to follow if he had some tangible reminder of faith. They looked for a mustard seed. His wife fished something out of a pickle jar and he carried it around with him. But the seed was small and he lost it, and, since he had already begun to think positively, he got the idea that it might be put in a plastic ball. Mr. Flint asked Dr. Peale if he thought

10

the resulting object could be merchandised, and after consulting a businessman ("one of the greatest executives in the country"), the gadgets went on sale in a department store in New York. The initial ad said: "symbol of faith—a genuine mustard seed enclosed in sparkling glass: makes a bracelet with real meaning." Dr. Peale adds, with the glint of Positive Thinking in his eye, "These articles sold like hot cakes."

The Flints now have a factory in a Midwestern city producing Mustard Seed Remembrancers, the perfect ending to the story of Positive Thinking. However, there is one unfortunate negative note at the end of Dr. Peale's account: "So popular and effective is it that others have copied it, but the Flint Mustard Seed Remembrancer is the original." That's the trouble with Positive Thinking; other Positive Thinkers come along and try to cut into your territory.

The suspicion that there is danger in all this is strengthened by a look at what Positive Thinking means in specific areas like psychology and politics.

Dr. Peale has been concerned with psychology and psychiatry throughout his career. He was one of the first ministers really to take seriously the contributions of these studies, before the relation of religion and psychiatry became the fad it is now. He joined in founding the American Foundation for Religion and Psychiatry, and his church continues to provide its chief financial support.

Some of Dr. Peale's early books were written in collaboration with psychiatrist Smiley Blanton. Dr. Peale has gone on, independently, to use a few words and ideas of popular psychology for his own easy, simple, and successful operation. Men who are working to relate psychiatry to pastoral counseling say he has set their work back many years. The heart of the criticism is that Dr. Peale short-circuits the difficult processes of psychological healing; he promises quick, painless, and complete "solutions" to problems which may be deep and complex, and which may require real discipline and professional treatment. Moreover, he tends to encourage the weak, sick, and confused to depend not upon the agencies of their own local community but upon himself and his books.

The basis for the criticism that serious counselors

make of Dr. Peale becomes obvious in this episode from his TV program: A child has been frightened by the stories of the new bombs, and worries and loses sleep. Dr. Peale, scarcely waiting for the problem to be voiced, pats the child on the head and says, Don't be afraid; God will take care of you; no H-bomb will fall on New York.

This is Positive Thinking, all right, following the counsel of his book: "Never mention the worst. Never think of it." But how long does it last, to repress those worries on the affable assurance of the preacher? And what does it do to one's maturity? And what happens if an H-bomb *does* fall on New York?

A woman with a real problem, once a fan of Dr. Peale's, now says in disgust, "He told me I didn't have any problem." Certainly Positive Thinking can help when a problem rests in some unjustified pessimism or lack of confidence. But sometimes our problems are real, aren't they? And then Dr. Peale's message is a dangerous counsel that we not face them. Dr. Peale's rejection of "negative thinking" may be a rejection of any real thinking at all, for serious thought necessarily involves the confrontation of all the elements of problems. Dr. Peale's message tends to reinforce the anti-intellectualism of the times, for any serious thought is bound to appear somewhat negative to the bland outlook of the Peale follower.

The social and political meaning of this message is clear in its immense admiration of power figures and big names. These admired persons are all successful in the most immediate and worldly sense: military men like Douglas MacArthur, for whose faith book Dr. Peale wrote an introduction, businessmen, and athletes. No professors, no serious writers or serious artists, no thinkers or critics, no one whose life enterprise has a different goal than success.

"Executives" as a class are special favorites of Dr. Peale's. As the comedian Henry Morgan once said of *The Power*, "This book isn't for me, I'm not an executive; nobody in this book but executives." What the book can mean to executives is made plain in this advertisement: "EXECUTIVES: Give this book to employees. It pays dividends!" The most unsettling part of this proposal is not just that this "religious" book is justified at the cash register ("It really pays off in dollars and cents!" says

12

William A. Cole of Toms River, New Jersey) but that the profits are obtained by the executive buying the book in lots to use on his employees, quieting their complaints, making them enthusiastic for their firm, and increasing sales. Salesmen are said to have "Renewed faith in what they sell and in their organization" (apparently regardless of what the product or the organization may be). The book brings "Greater efficiency from the *office staff*. Marked reductions in clock-watching. . . ."

Positive Thinking also makes politics much easier and more efficient. In 1952 Dr. Peale proposed a "prayer plan" to select the President, a plan which seemed to encourage its users to regard their choice as an absolute and divinely inspired selection of *the* man God wanted.

God seems regularly to answer Dr. Peale's own prayers with the Republican candidates. His (Dr. Peale's, that is) most startling political act was his letter to ministers in New York State suggesting that they support Joe Hanley for Lieutenant Governor because he had once been an ordained clergyman. In 1952 he said that though ordinarily ministers should stay out of politics, when there was a *moral* issue involved they should speak up, in this case for Eisenhower and Nixon.

And so what does the Peale phenomenon mean? It means that an old, wrong answer to our new American problems is very popular, and that we have a hard choice to make. We are a people accustomed to simplicity and success and unprepared for tragedy, suddenly thrust into mammoth responsibilities in a complex world and a tragic time. In the face of hard and unexpected facts we can rise to a new maturity, or we can turn instead to those who pat us on the head and say it isn't so at all, like the Reverend Doctor Norman Vincent Peale.

Christmas 1954

BY MAX ASCOLI

It is appropriate, I think, that the question of what Christmas means in our day and country be asked not only from the pulpit but also on the editorial page of a magazine that is concerned with but not obsessed by politics. Wherever Christmas is observed and people wish each other merriment, they ought to find out what they should be merry about—lest this day be the culinary, bibulous culmination of a shopping spree.

The massive character of the Christmas celebration in our country, the Christmas trees alight, with all their trimmings, in such an overwhelming number of American homes, the "Adeste Fideles" heartily sung by men and women who are anything but *fideles*—all this by itself constitutes a phenomenon of imposing proportions. There must be some other reasons for it, aside from social conformity and the frantic advertising campaigns of department stores anxious to clear their inventories. The fact is that in the western world and probably well beyond its boundaries, it is difficult to find many civilized human beings whose hearts remain coldly unaffected by the anniversary of that birth—no matter whether they consider it a myth or historical reality.

Indeed, it is difficult to think of that birth as plain unquestionable history, but it is equally difficult to see it as a sheer legend—one of the many, many legends that the religions of the world have transmitted to us. For the Christian, that event 1954 years ago is the point of confluence and irradiation of countless miracles. For the non-Christian and the doubter, that legend and what came out of it is still the most extraordinary success story, the most durable piece of fictionalized theology, the history of mankind has ever known.

Certainly in the countries of western civilization both the believers and the nonbelievers who to any extent are stirred by painting or by music cannot help associating that birth with the accounts they have received from such artists as Giotto and Handel, to mention only two. Truly, there are no greater masterpieces in all the arts than those designed to make men relive the birth—or the crucifixion—of Christ.

Yet this is only part of the truth about the meaning of Christmas, for it concerns only a part or a section of mankind. Modern times have contributed something even more important and decisive than all the paintings of the Madonna and all the Christmas oratorios. Democracy and industrialism have proved to be extraordinarily

14

contagious forces of literally universal appeal. They have brought to men of all races and religions the notion that no matter how abject their lot may be, they too can improve it if they only learn how to use the tools of modern technology and of self-government. Both sets of tools have become at the same time extraordinarily complex and extraordinarily easy to handle—if the very moderate price for apprenticeship is paid.

There are very few savage tribes left in our world where human beings have not been reached by the knowledge that they can establish communities of their own and defend a certain amount of personal privacy within them. The patterns for both community and national life and for the individual and his rights are easily available.

These patterns have been shaped during centuries of struggle and hard work by what can be called, to use a shorthand expression, Judaeo-Christian civilization. Actually, everything created on or near the shores of the Mediterranean during thousands of years which proved to be a force for enduring social cohesiveness went into the making of that civilization: The Jewish idea of the one universal God went into it, the disciplined thinking of Greek philosophy, the rules of conduct in practical affairs codified in that old testament of business called Roman law, and much more.

When the tumultuous fusion of all these component elements finally ended, and individualism both for the well-rounded human being and for independent nations emerged with the Renaissance, a period of explosive creativeness started that still proceeds at an ever-increasing pace.

But not one of the great explosive events of modern times can even be compared to the one where the idea of "rendering unto Caesar" was first announced—if for no other reason than because all the other revolutions, including the one which started rolling fourteen centuries later, can be traced back to the unto-Caesar principle. By becoming subject to two separate allegiances, to God and to Caesar, the human person was at the same time sanctified and fissioned.

Part, but only part, of man owes obedience to the temporal powers that be; the other part cannot be touched by those powers, and has a right to criticize and resist them. This realm of the spirit, this half of man

15

which according to the Christian principle belongs to God, makes man responsible during the span of his life for the fraction of divinity entrusted to him. At the same time it establishes the dependence of men upon one another, as children of God, in a fundamental relationship of equality irrespective of personal worth or achievement.

The fission and the conflict between these two elements in man, no matter how called—Emperor and Pope, rights of kings and human rights, authority and freedom —has fantastically energized the human adventure, but gives little chance for relaxed, animal quiet to the human breed. No wonder the Jews have been the object of such unrelenting, revengeful hatred, particularly in our times: They are held responsible not for the death of Christ but for His birth.

Our modern civilization is so deeply rooted in Christianity that it can sometimes afford not to consider itself Christian—particularly since the patterns it has created have been so eagerly adopted by peoples untouched by the Christian experience. Yet the nations that still call themselves Christian should not be allowed to forget that the ideals they live by are more or less veiled translations or secularizations of Christian principles. Perhaps these principles had better remain translated and secularized to avoid the curse of clericalism and theological dispute. But how can we be oblivious—at least at Christmas time—of the fact that the principle of freedom, sometimes called liberalism, is nothing but a translation in abstract terms of the Christian idea of man as the temporary responsible bearer of divine creativeness?

In our days, the most savage attempt to outlaw the "unto-God" part of man is being conducted. Our nation is uncompromisingly against that attempt. But how can our rulers claim to fight Communism if they impose on those citizens whose work is most needed in that fight unquestioning, indeed enthusiastic loyalty to that new idol called security? Do our rulers ignore that their vaunted respect for the rights and freedom of the human person is only an abstract, secularized way of expressing that resistance unto Caesar which is made imperative by man's allegiance unto God? Yet, after all their pious sermons, they go on acting like fretful little Caesars.

16

If we citizens forget all this, then we can be merry just the same on Christmas Day. But let us not pretend that we are celebrating the divinity—or the dignity—of man. Let us just go on a big binge that will leave us with a heavy head and a belching stomach the morning after.

The Small Band Is Dwindling

BY ERIC SEVAREID

Mr. John W. Davis was buried the other day at the age of eighty-one. Another of that dwindling group of towering Americans from a past age of event is gone—great men like Henry Stimson, who never achieved the pinnacle of public life, the Presidency, when lesser men did; men whose dedication to their country was whole-souled, nevertheless, and for whom the supreme frustration of personal ambition never deflected them away from public services of a monumental nature.

The small band of true elder statesmen is dwindling still smaller, their counsel will one day soon be entirely lost, and sometimes one wonders how and when they are to be replaced. This may be illusion, but it always seemed to me they represented an influence in our public affairs fundamentally different from the mental and emotional promptings of most men now of the prime and middle age. The minds of men like Davis and Stimson—one could add others, like Learned Hand or the poets Sandburg and Frost—were formed in a quite different era.

Their views of life were rooted in the long American past, anchored in what seemed to be rock. Their principles of conduct and action, their faith in the American vision, were matured before the First World War, which began the present process of anarchy in personal and public principle. Nearly all who have matured since that first world slaughter matured in doubt and the short-term view. *They* matured in faith and the long view. On behalf of their eternal principles of the free mind, they would join no hasty rationalizations in the misused name of security. They would today, I think, in the face of possible war in Asia, look to the lessons of history, not to the compulsions of strategy, where so many lesser men direct their eyes.

There were eternal verities for a man like John W. Davis, and one was the meaning of the American Constitution. He was probably the greatest Constitutional lawyer of his time; and he would, if his verities were involved, defend a so-called security risk other men would shun, or even an acknowledged Communist.

Always, the principle was the thing, not the individual, not the pressing needs of the harried present nor the fleeting charms of popularity. Knowing the majority can be wrong, such men would not bow to the icons of public opinion. One cannot quite imagine them scrutinizing the public-opinion polls, sending careful trial balloons into the air to see where safety lay, or surrounding themselves with ghost writers, weighing each calculated word to offend no possible pressure group. They proceeded from principle and hoped the needs of the moment would fit; they did not proceed from the needs of the moment, inventing or adjusting principle as protective coloration.

Such men had a positive effect on their country's course, beyond, sometimes, the influence of those who had taken the great offices in their stead. One wonders, sometimes, what the course of Reconstruction would have been, that period of public disease, had Horatio Seymour not lost the Presidency to General Grant, so vastly inferior to Seymour in intellect and vision. One wonders what would have been our course through the frantic 'twenties, ending in the depression collapse, had John W. Davis not lost the Presidency to Calvin Coolidge, who sat on the White House porch and rocked, impervious to a new idea . . . Those are the might-have-beens of history, indication in themselves of how wrong the majority can be.

But Davis's life and works were not might-have-been in themselves. Private life did not frustrate the great lawyer; his works were many and important, and the country is the better for his long and enviable life.

(*From a broadcast over CBS Radio*)

Comrade Joe and the V.F.W.

BY ROBERT BINGHAM

When President Truman talked about "scaremongers and hatemongers" during a radio address not long ago, Senator Joseph R. McCarthy immediately claimed and got radio time for a rebuttal, even though the President had not mentioned McCarthy by name. Similarly, when Secretary of Labor Maurice Tobin spoke in New York before the fifty-second annual encampment of the Veterans of Foreign Wars about "irresponsible slander from the privileged sanctuary of the Senate of the United States" his audience had no trouble guessing which Senator the Secretary had in mind. One of the veterans was on his feet in an instant, suggesting "that we invite Comrade Joe McCarthy here to give us the other side of the story," and McCarthy flew in from Boise the next day.

Before McCarthy arrived at the grand ballroom of the Hotel Astor, the veterans busied themselves with routine convention matters: presenting plaques to public officials who had helped veterans, listening to committee reports, affirming that they were "one hundred per cent behind this Indian boy, to see that he gets a decent burial," and voting to demand the removal of the Secretary of State.

The stage having thus been well set, McCarthy made his arrival at ten minutes after four, preceded down the aisle by an honor guard that protected him from veterans who pressed forward to shake his hand. McCarthy, wearing an overseas cap like the rest of the conventioners, blinked in the roar of applause and the glare of flashbulbs. He waved and smiled at all those who caught his eye.

"Give those Reds hell!" shouted someone from one of the balconies. "McCarthy for President!" was heard from the back of the hall. Still blinking, McCarthy smiled, swallowed several times, and waited for the ovation to subside. "A young man was on this stand, was it yesterday or the day before?" McCarthy began. "He had some

19

things to say about McCarthy, I understand. Let me say this: I hold no ill feelings whatsoever. I think he is a fine young gentleman. I think he is a fine young gentleman who was ordered to do a job and he did that job."

Having taken care of the Secretary of Labor, who is nearly nine years older than he is, McCarthy moved on to the heart of the matter. "I would, instead of indulging in general statements here today, I would like, if I may, I would like to give you a few of the issues we have discussed. The cases, if you please, that have been smeared by 'McCarthy' and 'McCarthyism,' these cases discussed on the Senate floor, after which the bleeding heart elements of press and radio have screamed to high heaven, 'McCarthy is doing this under the cloak of Congressional immunity.'" With the air of a magician pointing out that he has nothing up his sleeves, McCarthy said, "There is no immunity that surrounds this podium here today." There was considerable applause. The Senator—or rather, McCarthy, as he prefers to be called, even by himself—had a way of growling over important syllables that was effective with the veterans. They often chuckled at his inflection while applauding his sentiments.

Citing the McCarran committee as "the first good breath of clean fresh air we have seen in Washington in a long time," McCarthy went on to speak of the "sellout" of China: "There, my friends, there was signed the death warrant, the death warrant of every American boy who has died in Korea since the 26th of June. There was signed the death warrant of every American boy who will die tomorrow in Indo-China and on the sands of Arabia, and in the streets of Berlin and Paris on the day after that. So much for the general picture."

McCarthy next took up "the case of one of those whom I consider most dangerous to our country." Philip Jessup, who "belonged to—or I should say was affiliated with—not one, not two, not three, not four, but five Communist front organizations," exercised, according to McCarthy, "editorial control of the publication, officially named, not by McCarthy, but named by legislative committees as a front for a foreign power doing the work of the Communist party." From time to time one of McCarthy's assistants handed him books and papers which he held up to demonstrate the authenticity of his statements. Only once or twice did he actually read from

20

these documents; he preferred to give his own summaries of the contents.

"I have checks, my good friends, checks totalling thousands of dollars of Communist money used to support this publication. . . . You people don't mind if I take off my coat, do you?" There were cries of "no, no," which turned into laughter and enthusiastic applause when he rolled up his shirt sleeves. "Take off your shoes, Joe!" shouted a voice from the balcony. McCarthy smiled up at the balcony and said "Thank you." Clearly McCarthy was among friends.

Returning to Secretary Tobin's suggestion that if McCarthy really had any evidence he should take it to court, McCarthy admitted, "I personally don't know how to get Philip Jessup into a court." But he offered an alternative. "If the President's spokesmen have some way of getting Philip Jessup or Dean Acheson before a court," he said, tossing the ball back into the enemy's camp, "I will make them this offer. Let's place the stakes high. Let's place the stakes high. I'm taking them up on their offer. They made their threat: 'Let's throw it into cross-examination.' All right, let's do it. Let's get them before twelve men and twelve women in any jury room, if they are willing to submit either the Jessup or the Acheson case to a jury any place in this nation. And I will be glad to present the case against them and they can have as many lawyers as they want to defend them. We will let the jury decide. . . . If that jury, if that jury says, 'No, McCarthy, you are wrong. They are good Americans as they claim to be,' then I will do the thing that they were hoping they could accomplish for a long time. Then I will resign from the United States Senate— on condition that if the jury finds what I say is true and those people are bad for America, that then the whole motley crowd will resign!"

McCarthy had already spoken for about half an hour but he seemed to be just warming to his subject. "I'm sorry to take so much of your time," he said, "but I came a long way to see you." He asked if they wanted more, and they shouted back that they wanted more. "Give it all to us, Joe!" one man shouted. "McCarthy for President!" exclaimed another.

Next McCarthy proceeded to work over an individual

named Gustavo Duran, whom he described as "a man who was high in the State Department and then finally promoted to the United Nations, and upon the recommendation of the State Department." McCarthy spoke of an Army intelligence report showing "that Mr. Duran, while in Europe where he was born, was head of the S.I.M. That was a counterpart of the Russian secret police." It is perhaps natural that, in the tension of the moment, many listeners understood McCarthy to say that Duran was head of the Russian secret police. The New York *Daily News* account of the speech reported that "McCarthy held up a picture for his V.F.W. audience and said it was Duran in the uniform of the Russian secret police." The stenographer's notes indicate that McCarthy referred only to "the uniform of the secret police."

According to McCarthy, Duran went on from his post in an unidentified secret police to a job in the United Nations, where "his task was to screen displaced persons and decide which would make good loyal Americans."

Much of the remainder of the speech was devoted to quotations against McCarthy from the *Daily Worker* and other Communist publications. McCarthy indicated that he would not be intimidated by "the *Daily Worker*, the *Compass*, the New York *Post*, and other elements of the conservative press."

"As my mother once said," he remarked with a grin, "'Joe is too dumb to quit anything he starts.'"

In conclusion, McCarthy made it clear that his position was nonpartisan. He said that he was "much disturbed by the attitude of some of the members of my own party." He meant particularly "those who say, 'Let's conduct a safe campaign. Let's be little gentlemen,'" and he warned earnestly, "You can't fight this State Department crowd with a lace handkerchief." McCarthy feels that "loyal Democrats must defeat this Administration of which they have lost control." The Administration's momentum carries it onward, said McCarthy, and he quoted an appropriate passage from Shakespeare's *Macbeth* to show what he meant. "*I am in blood*," the Senator declaimed, "*stepp'd in so far, that, should I wade no more, returning were as tedious as go o'er.*"

A press conference was scheduled to take place a few

minutes after the speech in a screened-off area directly behind the platform. A large, bald man, whom everyone called "the admiral," seemed to be in charge. "He'll be right down," said the admiral. "He just went up to change his shirt and to take a small libation."

"Who paid McCarthy's freight for this junket?" one reporter asked.

"Oh, he paid his own way. We didn't pay a cent," said the admiral.

"I was going to say, if he charged you for that speech, you could get your money back," said the reporter laconically. The admiral looked at the reporter with something bordering on amazement. "Yes," he said, breaking into an uneasy smile, "yes, I guess you're right."

The admiral sat on the edge of a desk around which collapsible chairs were being arranged. "Yes," he said, "I guess it's like a friend of mine said the other day at the National Press Club in Washington. He said it's a case of fifty-fifty. He's about fifty per cent right and fifty per cent wrong, and he doesn't even slow down for the fifty per cent he's wrong about. I tell you, I don't think he has time. The people around him just keep feeding him on red meat. They feed him all this red meat, and he doesn't even have time to think. He has to keep on spouting it out." The admiral assured newcomers that McCarthy would be right down. "He went up to change his shirt and to take a small libation."

"What about a small libation for the working press?" one reporter asked.

The admiral laughed. "Yes," he said, "I guess that's right."

The honor guard still surrounded McCarthy when he arrived at the press conference. All of the reporters remained seated in their collapsible chairs while McCarthy walked through them and took his place behind the desk that had been prepared for him. A member of the honor guard in a sailor's uniform took a cigarette away from one reporter, snuffed it out in an ashtray, and carried the ashtray out of the screened-in area.

"What about this Duran, Senator?" one reporter began. "That's about the only new name you mentioned today, wasn't it?" McCarthy, who spoke very quietly to the reporters and smiled constantly even when their questions seemed to be a little pointed, admitted that he had mentioned Duran several times before. One member of the honor guard poured three little fruit glasses full of water and set them before the Senator, who drank sips from them alternately and moved them around the surface of the desk like the three shells under which a lucky guesser might hope to discover a pea.

"What is this S.I.M. he was in?" a reporter asked.

"That's the secret police in Spain," McCarthy said in a matter-of-fact tone.

"You mean he worked for Franco?"

"On the contrary," said McCarthy, smiling, "he was on the other side during the Spanish Civil war, in opposition to Franco."

"Now, Senator," said another reporter, "what kind of job has he got in the U.N. that makes him responsible for screening D.P.'s for American citizenship?"

"That was the IRO," replied McCarthy.

"What has the IRO got to do with deciding who's to become an American citizen?"

McCarthy shifted his weight in his chair. "I don't have the staff to go into it that far," he said.

A few days later a *Reporter* staff member was told by U.N. officials—in telephone calls taking up less than twenty minutes—that the IRO had no authority to pass on the political reliability of displaced persons, and that although he had once worked for the State Department, Duran, now an employee of the U.N. Secretariat, had never worked for the IRO anyway.

The reporters wanted to know more about McCarthy's way of answering Tobin's challenge. "They're asking you to charge them with a specific crime," a reporter remarked, "and now you're telling *them* to take it to court. How can *they* take it to court? What will the charge be?"

"No, no, no," McCarthy said, indicating that the reporter had missed the point entirely. "You can't charge them with a specific crime. What I'm saying is that they're good for Russia, bad for America."

"Well, if you've really got something, why don't you go to the nearest district attorney and file charges?"

McCarthy was firm on that point. "As long as the Attorney General is controlled by the Administration, I wouldn't have a chance."

A member of the honor guard reminded the Senator that he had a train to make.

In the hotel bar, the veterans were standing two and three deep, wearing uniforms that they had worn when they were younger. "Howsaboy?" one asked another. "Howsaboy?" was the answer.

"I say we never should have gotten mixed up in a political question in the first place," said one portly veteran. "But once that young fellow got into the subject of politics, we had to hear both sides. Hear both sides, that's what I say. Hear both sides, and then make up your own mind. Besides," he went on in a lower tone, "I think this fellow today must have something or he wouldn't keep at it the way he has. Take the case of that Russian who's in the State Department deciding which D.P.'s can become American citizens. Where there's smoke there's fire, I say. Where there's smoke there's fire."

A Day in the Country

BY DOUGLASS CATER

By ten o'clock Sunday morning, September 4, when I arrived in front of the United Office and Professional Workers' New York headquarters on 30th Street, a crowd, made up mostly of gaunt middle-aged men and their gray-haired wives, had begun to gather. A sharp-faced young woman passed back and forth shouting: "Get your tickets to Peekskill if you expect a seat on the bus. Two dollars for the round trip. There won't be any lunch there so you'd better buy some now before the bus leaves."

As she sold me a ticket she didn't ask whether I was a member of the union, nor why I wanted to go to the concert by Paul Robeson at Peekskill, New York, sponsored by the Civil Rights Congress. The previous week, its program had been broken up by combative anti-Communists. I was going along to report on this second try.

Soon after ten, younger people began to arrive, dressed mostly in picnic clothes, the girls wearing bright scarves. I got into conversation with a loquacious girl standing near me, and found out that her name was Marge.

"If the union says get here at ten, you can be sure the

buses won't leave for two hours," she said. "They've never started anything on time in their lives."

No buses had appeared, but a police patrol car was parked just down the street, and a couple of photographers were standing alongside it. Before long, the crowd had grown to nearly two hundred. There were more women than men, and a few had brought their children.

Marge introduced me to her companion, Rhoda, a dark, muscular girl, who was talking about Marshall Tito.

"A couple of my friends from Michigan, who used to be liberals, were trying to defend Tito the other night. They had to admit, though, that they couldn't get the real facts out there, when I showed them Starobin's article in the *Compass*."

By this time three buses had swung around the corner and drawn up alongside the union headquarters. A short, husky man in a T-shirt came out of the office and asked all the men to come inside for a minute. We filed in without saying anything.

In the meeting room the husky man asked everybody to sit down. Then he said, "I just want to divide you up so that there will be an equal number of men in all the buses. I'll count you off by three, and everybody be sure and remember his number."

He started to count, but there were a great many objections, because some of the men had come in groups and didn't want to split up. When this was settled, we all got up to go back out to the sidewalk.

Shortly after eleven the buses moved off, with the police car leading the way. Quite a few passengers were standing, or perched on seat-arms. When our bus, the third, turned the corner and started up Broadway, a large Negro woman named Winny, who was an organizer for the union, got up and announced that she and a fellow named Tom were in charge of the bus.

"If you have any questions, ask us. Don't bother the driver," said Winny.

"What's the driver going to do while we go to the concert and get our heads bashed in?" asked a friend of Marge's named Evvie.

"He's a nice guy," said Tom. "He can come listen to the concert, too."

Winny drew out a song sheet from her canvas bag.

"What about a few songs to work up our morale?" she called out loudly. "We'll start with 'We Shall Not Be Moved.'"

All the passengers sang the first stanza loudly, but began to falter on the following one. Winny stopped them.

"Here's a new stanza just for today. I'll read it to you and then we'll all sing it.

Robeson is our leader
He will be here today
Robeson is our leader
He will sing today

"Then the regular chorus:

Just like a tree planted by the water
We shall not be moved

Everyone sang the new stanza.

"That's the first time I ever heard *today* rhymed with *today*," said Marge.

"Best rhyme there is," Evvie answered.

By the time the bus passengers had finished off "Solidarity Forever," the bus had reached Columbus Circle.

Winny now got out a sheet of paper, and instructed everyone to sign it and put his local union number on it, together with how many hours he wanted to work in the American Labor Party primary. When the sheet had made the rounds there were only about fifteen names on it. Winny irately started it around again, saying that everyone was supposed to sign whether he wanted to work in the primary or not.

The New York police dropped out before we left Manhattan Island. We were unescorted till we got to Dobbs Ferry, where a motorcycle cop picked us up for a while. This caused general excitement. Ruth, a pretty little secretary in her early twenties, couldn't keep a quaver out of her voice.

"I just had to come, but I'm scared to death," she admitted.

"Were any of you up there last week?" asked Tom. No one answered.

"It's the same old story," he said. "We knew there was going to be trouble, but you can't get anybody aroused until after it's happened."

As we reached the outskirts of Peekskill, there were signs

27

that our arrival had been prepared for. An American flag was hung on almost every house. Here and there small identical signs were tacked up. At first none of the passengers could make out what they said, but after a while one of the men shouted excitedly.

"'Wake Up America—Peekskill Did.' Why, those fascist bastards! They're bragging about what they did last Sunday."

Further on, clusters of people had collected along the roadside staring at the procession. One bald-headed man peered belligerently at each passenger as the bus slowed down. Passengers and townsfolk watched each other, but no one said anything.

The bus came into open country again, and some disorganized singing started. Winny decided that it was time for a bit more leadership.

"Okay, you folks, let's show a little discipline. There won't be any more singing. If you have anything to say, keep it to yourself."

"Say, Winny, can't we even smile at these people?" someone called out.

"All right, all right, don't try to be funny," said Tom. "We aren't going to do anything provocative. They're just waiting for us to start some trouble."

The bus passed more and more policemen; local cops in blue uniforms, state highway patrolmen in motorcycle outfits, and state troopers in dark gray with large light gray ranger hats. They beckoned the buses along.

Soon the road began to grow more crowded. The bus was obliged to stop for long periods, and then to move haltingly. The passengers were restless. It was nearly two.

"Why don't we get out and walk?" said Evvie. "I don't know about the rest of you but I came out here to hear a concert."

No one made any effort to get out, however. At last the bus moved ahead rapidly, coming to a section where the road was solidly lined with people, six and seven deep on the embankment to each side. For almost two hundred yards the bus passed slowly between these ranks, with just a few feet clearance on either side. The people outside were shouting, screaming, and shaking their fists. Police stood at frequent intervals holding them back. Many of the boys were making obscene gestures. Pretty girls were by their sides, shouting, "Go back to Russia, you dirty Commies!"

The passengers in the bus didn't shout back; many of their faces were frozen into forced smiles. As we passed through the crowd, the woman ahead of me began talking to her four-year-old daughter, slowly, as if she were telling a fairy tale.

"See those people, Robin? They think because they're white that they are better than other people. Remember what I told you about those people who are trying to put those eleven men in jail? Well, these people are just like them. They are bad people. Also, most of them are not Jews so they think Jews are not equal to them."

Little Robin clutched her mother and stared out the window. It was hard to tell whether she was frightened.

Suddenly, the bus turned through a gateway and went down a slope. Young men wearing overseas caps with "Committee" buttons fastened to them waved us to a halt. As the passengers filed out, Ruth, the young secretary, was crying.

We hiked down the dusty road toward the bottom of the hollow in which the event was to be held. We saw the concert guards, strung out on the slope above, parallel to the avenue which skirted the grounds, and approximately two hundred feet back from it. Up on the avenue, separated by a fence from the grounds, the veterans' parade could be seen—a shiny helmeted band, Legionnaires in their caps and shirt sleeves, and groups of boys and young men in ordinary dress. They were marching back and forth, led by a motorcycle which backfired steadily, and, it was obvious, by design. Crowds lined the far side of the avenue, cheering the marchers.

The concert guards, wearing overseas caps, some in khaki shirts, some without shirts, stood three feet apart, hands on hips, silently facing the parade. Here and there small groups of reinforcements were stationed, waiting their turn at guard duty.

Down below, the huge crowd attending the concert was seated. Its members were sprawled about in the grass directly under the hot sun. There were at least fifteen thousand in all. Beneath a big oak tree was the speakers' platform, which consisted of the rear of a large open truck, with a grand piano on it.

The program had already begun. Howard Fast, the master of ceremonies, was introducing the guest of honor. At the mention of Paul Robeson's name, the crowd went into wild cheers, which were prolonged over several minutes. Up on the avenue, the paraders answered with boos, catcalls, and blasts of their band instruments, but the noise did not penetrate the depths of the basin. Now Robeson appeared.

After a few words of tribute to "that great American and fighter, Howard Fast," Robeson started to sing. His first number was the Negro spiritual, "Go Down, Moses." He stood braced against the piano, one hand to his ear so that he could hear his own voice above the roar of the state police helicopter overhead, the steady drum beat on the avenue some two hundred yards distant, and the regular blasts of motorcycle exhaust. The amplifier picked up his voice well, bouncing it against the summit of the slope.

Robeson said very little. Once when he was preparing to sing an aria from the Russian opera, *Boris Godunov*, he prefaced it by saying that "this opera shows the unity and strength of the people of that land, shown later in their effort to form and build a free world." There were cheers from the crowd.

The concert lasted only about forty-five minutes. Halfway through, Fast made an appeal for funds:

"Every dollar which you give today will fight for freedom and against the un-American filth walking up and down on the road up there."

Some of the men in the audience went up and joined the guards for a spell. The paraders had stopped marching by this time. Here and there boys gathered, shouting taunts at the guards. Policemen moved up and down the road, dispersing them, but they quickly reformed in different places. One large, well-built young man kept yelling:

"Come on up, any ten of you. I'll take you all on at once, you yellow-livered bastards."

From among the concert-goers a voice called out.

"Oh, dry up, will you?"

Quickly a half dozen guards turned around and cried: "Shut up, you hero!"

By a quarter of four the concert was over. A man on the platform directed the audience to return to their cars

30

and buses and await further directions. At his announcement, the disbanded marchers on the road above began to race toward the gateway that was the only exit from the grounds. A boy shouted as he ran: "First one out better have his insurance paid up!"

By five o'clock, a line of cars was strung out along the dirt road leading out of the grounds. State troopers and highway patrolmen were stationed just outside the exit, pushing the crowd back. Finally, the signal was given and the first car started to move out.

At once, a small bespectacled man dashed toward the car, arms flailing. As he came up to it, an arm shot out of the automobile window. Fist and chin met. The car drove off while the police picked the man up from the ground, and led him away.

Several cars made it through the crowds and disappeared down the road. A shower of bottles came sailing over the heads of the policemen and landed on some of them; those who had thrown them were quickly dispersed. As each car passed, one of the deputies gave it a resounding slap with his billy. Soon a steady stream of cars and buses was moving off the grounds.

Back in Bus Three, the passengers were growing restless. Our driver hadn't reappeared. A few passengers were all for getting out to look for him, but Winny exhorted them to stay in their places. After a long time, a committee member came over and announced that some of the bus drivers had gone into Peekskill for lunch and hadn't come back. He asked if anyone had a bus-driver's license. Walt, a social worker at a school for delinquent children, said he did.

"All right," shouted the committee man. "All men get off this bus except Walt. Only women, children and Negroes will go. We've got to get them out of here first."

A call went out to a couple of neighboring buses, which also no longer had licensed drivers to send over their women, children, and Negroes. Only a few appeared, so all of the original men passengers were able to crowd back on board. Just as our bus pulled out of the grounds, one of the girl passengers screamed and pointed to the car drawn up directly behind. A gray hatted state trooper had yanked its driver out and was beating him over the head and body with his billy. Other troopers were fanning out down the slope where the remaining cars were lined up. No one knew exactly

31

what provocation the driver behind us had given. Far down in the hollow the remaining guards were huddled together, waiting for transportation.

The girl kept screaming to Walt, the driver, to halt the bus. One of the men grabbed her and threw her to the floor to silence her.

"Go ahead," he shouted to Walt. "Let's get out of here."

The bus had slowed down. Now it picked up speed. About three hundred yards down the highway, a shower of stones smashed into the side, shattering four windows. More women screamed, and a baby who had been brought aboard by one of the new women passengers began to shriek. Everyone dropped down onto the floor, except the driver.

A little way down the road, the bus was stopped by a state trooper.

"Are you the authorized driver of this bus?" he asked Walt.

Walt replied that he was not, but that the driver had not returned, and he had a bus driver's license. All the passengers remained on the floor. After a few minutes, the patrolman motioned Walt to go on.

A mile or so further on, more stones were hurled at the bus. Three more windows were smashed. A shower of glass sprayed over me and the girl next to me.

Someone grabbed a newspaper to cover the broken window. It was the *Daily Worker*.

"Don't use that, for God's sakes!" shouted Marge. "Hasn't anyone got a copy of the *Herald Tribune*?"

The bus was careening along the highway. Walt, it turned out, had never driven a large bus before. Several times he swerved too far to the right and sideswiped guard rails along the narrow road. Once, passing a parked car, the bus scraped along its entire length. Walt started to halt the bus to look at the damage. The passengers shouted for him to keep going.

By now, it was totally dark, and the bus had got fairly well out of the Peekskill area. Most of the passengers had quieted down a little, and were back in their seats. No one attempted to open a window, even though the inside of the vehicle was sweltering. Men and women sat silently, staring out into the night. The baby had stopped crying. All along the road there were people on porches and lawns, watching the scarred buses pass.

Around eight-thirty, Bus Three lumbered into Harts-dale, and was once more stopped by highway patrol-men. Several other buses were already there, many of them even more severely battered than ours. One bus had three gaping holes in the windshield, directly ahead of the driver.

"We have a message that four buses were stolen," the officer said. "You'll have to wait here until we can check."

Some passengers suggested that everyone be allowed off the bus to buy Coca-Cola at a nearby shop. Winny refused to permit it.

"Come on," she pleaded, "let's show a little discipline. Wait right here in the bus and we'll get back safe."

"Damn it to hell!" a woman shouted, "if I hear that word discipline one more time, I'm going to scream."

"Why don't you just say 'Show a little inertia,' Winny? It's the same thing," suggested another.

After a half hour the patrolman returned to announce that Walt would not be booked for driving a stolen bus, but that we would have to leave the machine in Harts-dale. He said that there was a railroad station a half mile away.

The passengers of Bus Three filed out to join groups from the other buses. They were huddled around a young fellow wearing a committee cap.

"Now, if we just show a little discipline and good humor, we'll get back to the city in no time," he was saying.

The passengers began to drift in small groups down the street toward the railroad station. On the way they passed an elderly couple on the lawn in front of a house, watching.

"Look at the way those people walk," the man said.

Tom turned and spat.

"It's the old bastards like them who incite the younger ones," he said.

The local from White Plains came through Hartsdale at ten-thirty. Bus passengers got aboard and scattered through it, some wearily reclining on the seats, others still wide awake and talking noisily. A group sitting in the last car had a guitar and started to sing "Bandiera Rossa," the song of the Italian Communists.

In Bronxville, a portly middle-aged man wearing a sports jacket got on the train with his wife and daughter.

He glanced quizzically at the singers, who had started on "Solidarity Forever." Then he nodded to his wife. "Commies," he muttered.

After a while he started singing "The Star Spangled Banner" very loudly. His wife giggled. The other singers heard him and stopped. Then they joined in with him, soon drowning him out. One of them gave a signal, and they all stood up and removed their hats while they sang. The man in the sports jacket quit singing.

By the time the White Plains local pulled into 125th Street, the concert-goers had finished "The Star Spangled Banner." Most of them were lying back, trying to sleep. Some got off at 125th Street. The rest rode on into Grand Central. Before long they had all disappeared in the direction of the subway stations.

My Ninety Days in Washington

BY EDWARD CORSI

I served three years under President Hoover, two years under President Roosevelt, twelve years under Governor Dewey, and ninety days under John Foster Dulles. This last period of service—the shortest—was also the most educational.

I was thirty-four when President Hoover appointed me Commissioner of Immigration at Ellis Island. An immigration racket had been discovered, involving wholesale smuggling of aliens across the Canadian border and from Cuba. The then Commissioner of Immigration had resigned. It was in the midst of this nationwide scandal, indicating conditions in the service which called for immediate correction, that President Hoover asked me to take over. Possibly the work I had done with the foreign-born on New York's East Side and as director of Haarlem House attracted Mr. Hoover's attention.

I still remember what he told me: that he could think of no more dastardly thing than the exploitation of poor people's eagerness to come to America—people who then were exposed to deportation once they got here. Rigid restriction on the basis of preferential national quotas, then as now the policy of the United States, was not to my liking. But I was more concerned with providing a humane interpretation of the law than with changing it.

34

It may not be inappropriate to say here and now that during my years of service under Mr. Hoover's Administration, I developed a very high respect for him and that respect I have never lost. This much-maligned, misunderstood statesman stood and still stands for a kind of conservatism with which I do not always agree but which—as I have learned on more than one occasion—leaves room for dissent. Such a conservatism is based on principle, not on sloganeering. I am one of those who have not forgotten a time when Herbert Hoover was called—and rightly—"the great humanitarian." Certainly in my own personal experience as an official in his Administration, I came to realize that even when he was burdened with the Presidency the humanitarian in him was very much alive.

President Hoover and the high officials in his Administration who were connected with my work as Commissioner of Immigration knew about my liberal convictions and my faithful yet compassionate interpretation of the law. Their confidence never failed me. On the occasion of a dinner that friends gave me to celebrate my appointment by Secretary Dulles as his Special Assistant, Mr. Hoover sent the following telegram: MY ASSOCIATION WITH ED CORSI BEGAN SOME TWENTY-FIVE YEARS AGO. HE SERVED DURING MY ADMINISTRATION AS ONE OF THE BEST OFFICIALS IN OUR GOVERNMENT. HE HAS CONTINUED DISTINGUISHED SERVICE TO THE AMERICAN PEOPLE EVER SINCE. YOU WILL HEAR NO STATEMENT AS TO HIS ABILITIES, CHARACTER OR SERVICE THAT I WILL NOT ENDORSE.

It was an exacting, heart-rending job to be Commissioner of Immigration. I had good reason to be fascinated by the work, since I myself had come to this country as an immigrant from Italy. My mother brought me here when I was ten years old. My father was dead. He had been a prominent man in the old country, a Member of Parliament and undeviatingly a rebel. He thought that the House of Savoy was not good for Italy, and his devotion to the republican form of government earned him the confidence of his fellow citizens of Tuscany, who sent him to Parliament; it also earned him persecution at the hands of the royal police and forced him into exile in Switzerland for two years. Frequently when I had to decide immigration cases, I could not help thinking that if the 1924 law had been in effect at

35

the time my mother and I were immigrants, we might have had great difficulty in being admitted.

No position can more easily tempt a man to play God to other human beings than to be keeper of the gates to our country—a power that lately has been generously distributed to a large number of American officials all over the world. From my St. Peter-like position I think I derived a measure of humility and patience that has served me well during the last few months.

As Commissioner of Immigration, I had under my orders a force of several thousand officials for whose actions I was responsible. At the end of the Hoover Administration, President Roosevelt reappointed me—a Republican. I remained Commissioner of Immigration and Naturalization until 1934, when, in the dark hours of the depression, Mayor La Guardia appointed me Director of the Emergency Home Relief Bureau.

I thought I had seen enough human suffering on the East Side and at Ellis Island, yet I was staggered at the immensity of misery and despair to which I had to bring relief.

Those were the days when hundreds of thousands of unemployed were drifting through the streets of New York, and the city was called upon to house and feed 1.3 million men, women, and children at a cost of approximately $300 million a year. It was an appalling relief job, utterly unprecedented, for which the city was totally unprepared. Yet the job was done. As the director in charge, I had authority over a staff of eighteen thousand.

In 1943, I was appointed by Governor Dewey as head of New York State's Department of Labor. I was appointed for three four-year terms by Governor Dewey and confirmed on each occasion by the senate of the State of New York. To live up to my responsibilities I had to gain the respect of both management and labor. During that whole period, New York State held the national lead in peaceful labor-management relations and a minimum of time lost through industrial disputes. This fact was pointed out in Mr. Dewey's campaigns for reelection as governor and in his campaigns for the Presidency as one of the major achievements of his administration. The New York Labor Department has authority over unemployment insurance, workmen's compensation, the labor-management relations board, the mediation service, sickness and disability benefits, and so on. There again I was responsible for a large staff—more than fourteen thousand employees.

When in November last year the Democrats gained control of the Executive Branch of the government in New York State, I thought my career as a public servant had come to an end. I had worked for the city, the state, and the Federal government. I had given twenty-three years of my life to foster, to the best of my ability, the public interest. I had held positions of considerable authority and responsibility; twice I had run, unsuccessfully, for high public office—for U.S. Senator and for mayor of New York. Now the time had come, I thought, when I could take leave of public affairs and attend to my own.

I was considering various offers of private employment, particularly in the field of industrial relations. But I guess there is such a thing as the incorrigible public servant, the man always ready to give whatever administrative skill he has to the furtherance of the public interest. That tradition has been in my family for generations.

On December 1, while in Washington, I was notified that the White House was urgently trying to reach me. It was Maxwell Rabb, one of the President's assistants. He requested that I go over to see him immediately. I went to the White House that afternoon.

I have known Rabb for some time, and I have every reason to respect him. He is a serious, dedicated man, with a vigorous and forceful mind. I knew of his reputation as a trouble shooter for the President. The trouble he was shooting at in his conversation with me was very serious indeed. I knew the problem. The Refugee Relief Act of 1953 was not moving ahead as the President wanted it to. It was designed to bring in 209,000 people during its three-year life. Already more than one-third of its term had expired and less than eight per cent —not refugees as the President wished, but mostly relatives of people already here—had been admitted.

Would I consider, Rabb asked, working for the State Department to get the program really moving? He was sure that the Act eventually would work, and he thought I was the man who could do something to make it work.

37

I made it very clear to Rabb that I needed adequate powers to deal with the situation. I would not, I said, come down as an assistant to Scott McLeod, who had been administering the Refugee Act. Don't worry about McLeod, Rabb said. I insisted, for I knew what McLeod's reputation was among people familiar with immigration problems. I told Rabb that in the part of the country I came from McLeod's was a name used to frighten babies. Rabb replied that the Secretary said he would like me to have a position like the one he himself had held under Dean Acheson, reporting directly to the Secretary of State.

After a long discussion, I agreed to take Rabb's suggestion under consideration. Immediately, in my presence, he telephoned the State Department. Corsi might be interested, he said.

I returned to New York. The next morning I received this telegram:

I have long hoped to have you associated with me in the State Department working on matters for which you are uniquely qualified. I have hesitated up to now because of your heavy commitments in New York to approach you but I am hopeful that you might now be available. I am particularly interested in your coming in as a consultant to me with responsibilities in the refugee field under the present Refugee Relief Act. This law is administered by Scott McLeod and before we can make any final arrangement it would be necessary for you and him to have a meeting of the minds on that program. In addition to that program, however, there are a number of related matters in which you could be helpful to us. I would like to discuss these with you sometime in the next few weeks at your convenience and hope that you will at least keep the possibility open until we have had a chance to talk.

John Foster Dulles
Secretary of State

I delayed my answer for a few days. I had misgivings about re-entering public service. But I knew that the most important part of the assignment would be over with the expiration of the Act in December, 1956. And here was a possibility to serve in a field where the experience I had gained during my years of public service

38

could be of some use. I knew something about immigration and I knew something about finding jobs for people. A few days later, I wired Mr. Dulles my acceptance of his offer. The Secretary replied:

December 6, 1954

Dear Ed:

I was delighted to get your telegram accepting my plea that you come down here to work for us. As I told you, it will be necessary, before we finally firm up arrangements, for you and Scott McLeod to get together and work out some arrangement that you can recommend to me. I understand that he will not be back until just before Christmas and I hope we can both talk with you shortly after his return.

In the meantime, it is a source of great encouragement to me to know that you will be taking on this work by next month.

With warm personal regards.

Sincerely yours,

John Foster Dulles

Just before Christmas I went to Washington and, as suggested by the Secretary, had a conference with McLeod. Of course I knew that dealing with McLeod would be a tough game. But I counted on Rabb's assurance that I would be given the necessary power to carry out my work. At our first meeting McLeod was quite cordial. He wanted me to know that it was he who had suggested my name to the Secretary. We then discussed the program. He felt that he had been grossly misunderstood, that he really wanted the program to work, that there were certain people in this country who were making it difficult for him and the Administration. He felt I could be very helpful to him and to the program.

On December 30, a press conference was arranged in Washington at which the Secretary would announce my appointment. Just before this meeting, I had a short conference with the Secretary alone, followed by a meeting of three—the Secretary, McLeod, and myself—which was purely perfunctory and consisted of repeating that we were going to do something about the program and how I might be helpful.

Before going to the press conference at which the Secretary was going to announce my appointment, Mc-

Leod introduced me to A. P. Short, a public-relations man who commuted from Oregon to give McLeod the benefit of his advice. Short told me he hoped I understood that the public-relations line was to boost the program, to insist it was working. He said he hoped I might be helpful in boosting the program too.

At the press conference the Secretary introduced me as an assistant to him and as an assistant to McLeod in administering the Refugee Relief Act. He said he had known me for a long time—he didn't know just how long —and he knew how dedicated I was to the aims of the Act. He said it was a good Act, that he had made a good start in the administration of the Act, and that both he and McLeod felt the desirability of having the additional assistance of someone who was a specialist in this field. He added, "I think Mr. Corsi is better qualified than anyone else in the United States to take up this task." At the press conference McLeod pointed out that I had other duties—aside, of course, from the administration of the Act.

I was taking up my new stint of Federal duty in a blaze of glory.

Yet I felt I had better be reserved in my statements to the press. I limited my remarks to the single observation that in my opinion the President and Congress had intended to bring in the 209,000 refugees and that I would help bring them in. I could not in all honesty carry out the public-relations line Mr. Short had asked me to promote.

When I reported for work it was quite an anticlimax. It turned out that no office was assigned to me and no secretary. I was told that I would have to go to Europe in a couple of weeks. Meanwhile, I sat around McLeod's office using whatever empty desk was available. When McLeod was away I used his desk, but generally I used a little anteroom with safes in it: a tiny cell, insulated and soundproofed. It had two entrances, one from McLeod's office and the other from an anteroom in which a messenger sat at the entrance to the outside hall.

In my first talk with McLeod after reporting, he had indicated that nothing was more important for me than to go abroad. He had already arranged that I would be accompanied in Europe by John Rieger, a career service man who serves as general manager of the

Refugee Relief, and Roy Wade, McLeod's representative in Europe, who, I later learned, was a former Texas Ranger.

McLeod indicated that I might also take trips in due time to South America or the Far East or the Near East. I got the impression that he thought traveling was the best way to learn my job.

Three days after I actually reported for work the official appointment came, but it was as Assistant Administrator for the Refugee Relief Program—that is to say, assistant to McLeod—the very job I had told Rabb I did not want and would not take. The appointment of Assistant to the Secretary of State which Dulles had announced at the press conference had not been made. I felt that the best thing for me was to walk out.

I asked for an appointment with Rod O'Connor, Dulles's secretary, and made it clear that I would not have come down to Washington just to become McLeod's assistant. Only if I had been appointed Assistant to the Secretary could I have had authority and independence enough to collaborate with McLeod in the administration of the Act. O'Connor told me he would clarify this situation, and two or three days later the Secretary's announcement went out to the field that the position of Special Assistant to the Secretary for Refugee and Immigration Problems had been created and that Edward Corsi was designated for the position.

While waiting to leave for Europe I did not just sit around answering mail and congratulations and attending a few meetings with the staff of the Refugee Relief Program. I got right down to work. For a year, the various church and welfare agencies interested in bringing refugees to this country had been requesting a more reasonable interpretation of the Act. These voluntary agencies had to provide assurance of employment for each immigrant. According to the way the law was interpreted, only state employment agencies could certify these assurances. This meant forty-eight different interpretations of what assurance of employment meant.

I thought the only way out was for me to go straight to the Secretary of Labor, James P. Mitchell, and ask him that the State Department take over from Labor the responsibility of certifying the assurance of employment

41

that the voluntary agencies had secured. Secretary Mitchell said: "Ed, I'll do it if you get a letter from Mr. Dulles." Thanks to O'Connor, the Dulles letter went to Mitchell.

Though every refugee must have assurance of a job, I did not think this meant that a refugee must have a specific job kept ready for him while he was still in Europe. I felt, for instance, that if in a city a certain number of hospitals had available jobs for a certain number of refugees, this assurance should be enough to provide the prospective employee who was still in Europe with a job certificate.

I went to see Herman Phleger, Legal Adviser to the State Department, and together we worked out an interpretation of the law that greatly smoothed out the relations between the State Department and the voluntary agencies.

A feeling grew among the voluntary agencies that for the first time there was a willingness to interpret the law in such a way that its purposes could be achieved.

In my very frequent contacts with McLeod, I noticed a rather peculiar attitude on his part, a blend of whining and self-justification.

He complained of the difficulties of his position and the misunderstandings against which he had to struggle daily—of the fact that the inspection service had been taken out of his jurisdiction and that in general his responsibilities were being whittled down. Washington was a strange town, he said. Once you were appointed, your superiors left you entirely on your own. I suggested that some of his complaints ought to be taken up with higher authorities. He said that was not the way it was done in Washington. Higher authorities didn't really care to deal with other people's troubles. You had to fend for yourself.

It was difficult, he complained, to get the co-operation of other departments. The law itself was very difficult. He cautioned me about the need to go slow with the program because he didn't think that public opinion was in favor of the admission of immigrants to this country. As a matter of fact, he said that a public-opinion survey had been taken of sentiment on the Refugee Act and it had been found that six of every seven persons interviewed had expressed themselves as opposed to the further admission of any more people to this country. That was the feeling of Congress too, he said.

At times he commented on the concern of certain people on the Hill as to my liberal views. He had reassured them. I was a practical liberal, he said—in other words, a liberal with his feet on the ground. Once he asked me what Walter had against me (referring to Representative Francis E. Walter, D., Pennsylvania). I said I didn't know Mr. Walter, had never met him, and hadn't the slightest idea what he had against me. McLeod said that Walter had asked, You're not going to send that guy Corsi to the Intergovernmental Committee on European migration in Geneva, are you? McLeod explained there had been some speculation in the Washington press that I might be named to fill the post made vacant on that committee by the death of Ambassador Hugh Gibson. He then assured me that he had straightened me out with the Congressman. Actually he was always straightening me out with somebody. I had no idea there could be so many people in Washington who hated or mistrusted me.

McLeod said that he too was inclined to think that the McCarran-Walter Act's quota provisions were unworkable, that he himself had a plan for an entirely new system of immigration to the United States which he would discuss with me some other time.

In those days McLeod was so helpful that he nearly got me into real-estate troubles. He thought the thing for me to do was to buy a house in Washington. He recommended his real-estate agent, said he was a very fine man, not interested in money. This real-estate man got in touch with Mrs. Corsi and took her all around to see houses. Fortunately, Mrs. Corsi was too particular to settle on anything she saw.

McLeod was forever complaining to me about his problems. He had many of them, too many of them, and they were too big for him. He was trying to keep abreast of them, but it was getting too difficult. Nobody really understood him.

The day before I left for Europe McLeod phoned me in great agitation. A few days earlier, there had appeared in the Washington *Star* an article by Mary McGrory which caused a great deal of consternation in the Department. He said that his chief, Assistant Secretary

Carl McCardle, was greatly disturbed that I had granted an interview to the press without departmental clearance.

Although there seemed to be great commotion at my having defined myself as "a left-of-center Republican," I felt that the whole rumpus had been caused by Miss McGrory's implication that I held "complete authority and responsibility" over the Refugee Relief Act.

I flew to Europe on January 24. Both itinerary and purpose of the trip were established in my "Authorization of Official Travel."

ITINERARY: From Washington, D. C. on or about January 21, 1955, to New York, N. Y., Geneva, Rome, Athens, Naples, Salzburg, Vienna, Bonn, Frankfurt, Berlin, Paris and any other points in Europe or the Near East, etc. . . .

PURPOSE: To discuss visa and investigative procedures of the Refugee Relief Program with Foreign Governments and foreign service establishments in order to expedite the progress of the program according to P.L. 203.

Actually, whatever meetings I had on "visa and investigative procedures" were arranged, attended by, and reported back home by my two traveling companions, Messrs. Rieger and Wade. This was made unmistakably clear to me when two days after we reached Rome I received a cable from the State Department indicating concern at my failure to abide by Department protocol and requesting me to make all arrangements through the Embassy. The cable completely stupefied me, for I had made no appointments in France, none in Switzerland, and none in Rome except with one or two friends and relatives.

The President of the Italian Republic invited me to call on him as soon as I arrived in Rome. The initiative was his. I had previously met President Einaudi, just as I already had known quite a number of high government officials on earlier trips to Italy. When I arrived, some of these old acquaintances sought me out with the eager cordiality of men wanting to honor a native son who had made good.

But with the exception of the call on President Einaudi, all my appointments were made in accordance with Departmental rules through the Embassy, and I kept them in the presence of a third person as required by Departmental regulations. The third person was Cecil Gray, the American Consul General in Rome. Most of my appointments were with government officials, including some members of the Italian Cabinet, to discuss the program and the means of speeding it up. The rest were mere courtesy calls. Outside Italy, despite the stated purpose of my trip, I could not meet any foreign officials.

When I was in Bonn I discussed with the representative of the Intergovernmental Committee for migration the question of whether it was true that the people of Germany did not want to migrate to America. He denied this vehemently as one of the canards that enemies of Germany and immigration to the United States were trying to spread to keep Germans out. He suggested that I speak to the Minister of Refugees, a friend of his. I said I would like very much to meet him. It was to be arranged for me to call on him in Berlin. I never did meet this man. Behind my back my escort canceled the appointment.

If I met few foreign government officials, I certainly met plenty of U.S. officials abroad—and I heard plenty from many of them. The supervising Consul General in Bonn, whom I knew only casually, took me into a corner and asked me point-blank: What are you doing with those flatfeet? You're not really planning to waste your time on this project, are you? As for these characters and their boss back home, we're sick and tired of seeing them around here.

He referred to the frequent visits of McLeod and his staff to Europe as the Cohn and Schine act.

On a one-day visit to the operation center in Naples a high official shook hands at the door of his office and disappeared for the remainder of our visit. It was obvious to me that there was a bitter anti-McLeod, anti-security-gang resentment among the consular service officers in Europe. Some of them were wary of me, too, as if they thought I was part of the McLeod operation.

When I came back to Washington I felt that in spite of my two fellow travelers and in spite of all the petty bureaucratic troubles, the trip had been eminently worthwhile. I had gained some knowledge of the people who could make the Act work as well as of those

45

for whom it was designed to work. This knowledge on my part would make for new and far more cordial relations between the Department and such voluntary agencies as the Church World Service, the National Catholic Welfare Conference, the Tolstoy Foundation, the United Hebrew Immigrant Aid Society Service, and the Lutherans. I could already feel in dealing with representatives of these agencies that they were gaining increasing confidence in the Department's willingness to smooth out the operation of the Act.

In Italy I had succeeded in inducing the Italian government to organize immigration committees on the provincial level that would help the prospective immigrants to gather all the documents they needed to qualify for a visa. I had no doubt that the Act could be made to work. After all, I thought frequently, Max Rabb had been right. In this spirit of optimism, based on the specific knowledge of people and situations I had acquired, I started writing my report for the Secretary and McLeod.

Having been appointed Assistant to the Secretary, I had no reason to object to being at the same time Assistant to McLeod, a position, I was repeatedly assured, that I needed to get a line of authority.

But it was exactly my relation with McLeod and his outfit that made me feel that something had gone wrong since I had come back from Europe. I was able to see McLeod for only five minutes, but I thought this was understandable since he was about to enter a hospital. He asked me whether I had seen anything in Europe that should be done and that his office was not doing. I answered that since he had to go to the hospital we could talk the situation over when he got back. It turned out that I could not use the office of my predecessor, Tyler Thompson. Instead I was offered a bare little room, with a desk and two chairs. There was an enormous hole in the wall that no one had taken the trouble to repair.

I could not receive anybody in such a room. When Italy's new Ambassador, Dr. Manlio Brosio, arrived in Washington, he asked to pay an official call. The prospect made me uncomfortable and I managed to be invited for luncheon at the Italian Embassy. Finally I decided that enough was enough. Without asking any superior authority, I moved into Thompson's former office, which had been empty all the time. Probably this is what McLeod's friends had in mind when later they called me a "freewheeler."

After having made a study of the operation of the Act in Europe, I could now get to work at the Washington end. I soon came to know the staff man by man. Now I could find out how far I could rely on each of the top men—and for what. Incidentally, that staff of which I was deputy head was one of the smallest I ever had to work with: about sixty in all.

With things getting under way, I soon found out what made for some of the major problems at the Washington end. One of the most serious was that the prospective employers of immigrants—among them some leaders of American business—had come to the conclusion that there was no use waiting: The immigrants would never come. You could not blame them since the administrators of the Act had not bothered to make a census of the kind and number of skilled workers for whom there were jobs available. The result was that while the little Greek candy-store man who wanted his cousin to come over kept insisting to the Department that he was holding a job open in his store, the garment manufacturer got tired of reporting vacancies in his labor force.

It was not difficult to remedy this situation. In fact, it did not take me long to get in touch with potential employers and with trade-union leaders and learn from them the number of available jobs and reassure them as to the kind of workmanship they could count on. In this effort, the Amalgamated Clothing Workers and the International Ladies Garment Workers Union—thanks to the eager co-operation of Jacob Potofsky and Augusto Bellanca, Luigi Antonini and David Dubinsky—were of the greatest help. So were other unions such as the United Shoe Workers, CIO, and the culinary workers Local 89, AFL, and leading businessmen such as Spyros Skouras, president of Twentieth Century-Fox, and Fortune Pope, head of the Colonial Sand and Stone Company, who at my suggestion organized committees among citizens of their own national origins to promote the issuance of assurances. We now knew just how many shoe workers, bakers, cooks, etc., could find jobs in our country without displacing a single American.

47

All these negotiations did not require very great effort on my part, since I had acquired some experience in bringing together labor and management.

All that I had done at the American and European ends of the program, all that I thought had to be done next, went into my report to the Secretary of State. But of course I could not go ahead until the recommendations I made had been acted upon by superior authority. I was told that Secretary Dulles found the report excellent. I was also told I should discuss it with Livingston Merchant, Assistant Secretary for European Affairs, and with McLeod. Merchant was eminently available, McLeod eminently unavailable. For several days I kept insisting on a meeting. McLeod kept putting me off.

Finally, on March 16, he agreed to see me.

I assumed that McLeod would want to talk with me about the report to the Secretary. Instead he began by announcing that the security clearance on my appointment as Deputy Administrator had not come through. He said he would name me Acting Deputy Administrator.

He then regretted the attacks upon me by Congressman Walter and added that the only reason he was not replying to these attacks or offering any defense for me was that he had to be on friendly terms with the Congressman, who was in charge of the program's legislation and consequently an important figure in the administration of the program. He expatiated on how hard it is to argue with Congressmen. I discussed with him the nature of the Walter charges and assured him that there was absolutely no truth in them, nothing in my entire record that the Department might be concerned with. I added that I resented the Walter attacks deeply but that I would not let them interfere with my work—for at that time I was getting somewhere. McLeod smilingly said not to worry. Look at poor Frances Knight; they're trying to make a Nazi out of her. During the whole conversation McLeod was quite effusive, full of sympathy for me, Miss Knight, and himself.

I was about to leave when he asked me to hang around. Some boys were coming in. I found he was having a staff meeting to which I had not been invited. I stayed on for the meeting. McLeod announced that I would be the Acting Deputy Administrator and that they were to obey my orders.

I went back to work thinking that my troubles were on the way to settlement. I had my appointment as Assistant to the Secretary of State; while waiting for clearance, I had my appointment as Acting Deputy Director to McLeod; the staff had been told to obey my orders. The only thing that remained was to discuss my report with McLeod, and that would happen, I thought, in the next few days.

I never saw McLeod again or talked with him.

The first Walter attack had come at a meeting of the House Judiciary subcommittee to discuss refugee program legislation pending in Congress. At that meeting, Representative Emanuel Celler (D., New York) clashed with Walter, and Walter for the first time charged that I had been a member of the Lawyers Guild and the American Committee for the Protection of the Foreign Born. I promptly denied these charges.

Walter repeated the charges a few days later. At this point I had a meeting in the office of Assistant Secretary Carl McCardle (in charge of public relations) with O'Connor, Dulles's secretary, and Robinson McIlvaine, McCardle's deputy. I assured them that as far as I knew, the charges were meaningless. It was decided to issue a Departmental reply, which was delivered by Assistant Secretary Thruston B. Morton (in charge of Congressional relations).

At that time I received a memo from McLeod not to speak to the press unless I first cleared what I had to say with him or Al Short.

It was a queer order because it affected only that half of my official being which was subordinate to McLeod, and not the other half which was subordinate to the Secretary of State.

Dulles, however, lost no time in correcting this anomaly. On Tuesday, April 5, following the publication of Representative Walter's letter to Representative Peter W. Rodino, Jr. (D., New Jersey), again attacking me, the Secretary said in his press conference that he had no intention of getting into any controversy with Representative Walter, whom he regarded very highly, that the charges against me were being investigated, and that my appointment was a ninety-day one. This was the first

I ever heard from any quarter that my appointment was for only ninety days. Yet what hit me perhaps even harder was the fact that the Secretary had shown such Olympian impartiality between the accuser who had not proved his charges and the accused—a man whom he had called his friend—who could so easily prove that the charges were baseless.

I must add, however, that the Secretary's attitude was far from being unrepresentative of the Department. Very few people in it rallied to my defense when the Walter attacks began. In fact, it was very difficult to discuss them with anybody. Only two men gave me a feeling of friendship: O'Connor and Herman Phleger.

The evening of April 5, after the Secretary's press conference, I received a message that Loy W. Henderson, Deputy Under Secretary of State for Administration, wanted to see me the following morning at about 8:30 before I left for New York. In New York I was to have had a conference with the leaders of the Amalgamated Clothing Workers to make final arrangements for the admission of workers for whom they were prepared to guarantee employment.

I went to Henderson's office and found him a very charming man. He was sorry, he said, he had to make my acquaintance under such circumstances, but he had a message from the Secretary: Since my ninety-day appointment expired on the coming Sunday, the Secretary desired that I undertake a very important assignment to South America in connection with the resettlement of refugees on undeveloped land there.

When he got through, I said I didn't think I was interested and I didn't think I had been appointed for only ninety days. I couldn't understand the meaning of this decision by the Secretary. I felt that my accepting another assignment at this time under fire might expose me to the charge that I was running away. I was not interested in any other job with the State Department and I certainly had a reputation to protect. No, I didn't think I could go along with the offer.

Henderson made every effort to convince me with all the persuasiveness of an experienced diplomat. When he realized that I was not making any promises, he asked if I would think it over and come back on Thursday or Friday to talk the whole thing over with him again. I did not return to see Henderson. I realized fully what had happened to the two State Department jobs I had been given: The Assistant to McLeod was being shown the door, and the Assistant to Secretary Dulles was being sent off to South American pastures. I had to see the Secretary.

I met Dulles at four o'clock in the afternoon of Friday, April 8, in his own office in the presence of Rod O'Connor. The Secretary opened the conversation by saying that he very deeply regretted the unexpected turn of events. He wanted me to feel that he had my best interests at heart. He knew that this was embarrassing to me. It was embarrassing to him also. He sincerely hoped that I would accept the proffered appointment in South America.

I told him that I did not have any enthusiasm for continuing in the State Department. I thought a grave injustice was being done me, and my associations in the Department had not been pleasant. I could not continue in any capacity. I asked how I could be shifted from one Department assignment to another in the face of the Walter attacks, and what guarantee there was that Walter would not continue his attacks if I went to South America. O'Connor broke in to say that he felt pretty certain that Walter would not continue his attacks. I said that I was not particularly concerned about Walter's attacks, that I considered them to be the most shameful I had ever experienced in my public life. The attacks didn't frighten me. I had searched my soul to see if there was anything I would have to apologize for—anything that would impugn my loyalty to my country. I knew there was nothing.

The Secretary replied that some Congressmen were quite skillful in using the frailest evidence to smear people's reputations. Look what they tried to do to him in the Hiss case. He said, I've read your record, Corsi. It is a typical report of any one of us in public life. As far as I'm concerned, there is nothing in it that would in the slightest degree impeach your loyalty.

I said again that I didn't care what Walter had charged, I had nothing to apologize for. I considered this whole thing an injustice. He then said I must keep in mind that the project needed the support of Congress. It was essential that he maintain friendly rela-

51

tions with Congress in order to obtain the appropriations and legislation necessary for the Act. I said that I did want to let him know my bitter disappointment about the failure of the program which should have carried out the Act. I thought that the operations of the Act had been scandalous and that he would have to answer to the whole country for this failure. But I did not want to embarrass him; I only wanted to separate from the Department and call it finished. He asked that I not let my emotions get the better of my thinking. He did believe the South American assignment was a very important one.

We returned to the technicality of the ninety-day point. He was sorry. I said I would not have taken the job on this basis. He urged again that I take the new assignment and get away from it all for three or four months. Then we shall have a little talk, he said. I answered that I appreciated his kindness, but that I had no enthusiasm to work for him. He asked, Will you keep it open?

I shall keep it open, I said, and let you know. We shook hands. He smiled. I smiled. And I walked out.

It was a very queer thing, that interview. Mr. Dulles seemed so fatherly, so sympathetic, so understanding of my plight. There were moments when I felt he was begging for my sympathy. Four days later at a press conference he said that I was not qualified as an administrator.

On Monday morning I sent my letter to the Department telling them that I declined the offer. Then came the appointment with Republican National Chairman Leonard Hall. I had purposely sent my letter before seeing him because I didn't want to be asked by Hall to accept the job.

The lack of co-ordination or consultation between the White House and the State Department on this matter is indicated by the two telephone conversations I had on Thursday night with Jim Hagerty, the President's press secretary. I phoned him at that time and said, I think you ought to know that I think it's a lousy deal. He could hardly believe what I told him and asked, Where are you? Can I call back? I said yes. He phoned about 10:30. He wasn't able to reach the top persons but was sure I was wrong.

I never heard from Jim.

So my Washington career, which started with an urgent call from a White House assistant, ended with a call from the White House that never came.

I bear no grudge toward those people who, regardless of motive, were instrumental in providing me with an invaluable refresher course on immigration, labor, and Federal bureaucracy. It has been an unforgettable experience, and perhaps a salutary one—particularly since the unsought publicity that marked its ending has allowed the American public to share it with me.

True, during those ninety days I found myself involved with people and in situations not to my liking. But I was also privileged to work with religious groups, trade unions, big and little businessmen—people obviously concerned with their own creed, trade, business, or national origin, but above all concerned with the honor of our country.

It is their belief that this nation of immigrants, which by its own toil grew to be the leader of the free world, cannot be callous to the yearning of men and women to whom an American law has given the hope that they too may become Americans. Good Americans cannot tolerate that this law, inadequate as it is, should be made into a mockery.

I have been enriched by my recent experience, and I am proud that it has been brought to an end by some people's fear that in spite of all hindrances I might have been successful in making the Act work. Those in the State Department who invited me to Washington counting on my failure could not bear to be proved wrong. I am free now to share with the public the experience I have gained.

Unfit

BY SEC

Benjamin Franklin liked his wine,
Loved to talk, to flirt, to dine,
Toyed with lightning on a line—

Bad Security Risk

Thomas Jefferson worshiped art,
Loved people, though a man apart,
Was sensitive in mind and heart—

Bad Security Risk

Lucky us, that in their clime
Unorthodoxy was no crime;
They'd be out of luck this time—

Bad Security Risks

Senator McCarthy's Eggheads

BY RICHARD H. ROVERE

McCarthy and His Enemies, by William
F. Buckley, Jr., and L. Brent Bozell.
Regnery. $5.

Here are four hundred solemn and tedious but literate
and in several ways important pages in defense of Senator McCarthy. Like Boswell's sermonizing woman and
Dr. Johnson's dog that walked upright, they are remarkable for the simple fact of their existence. They constitute, for one thing, an affirmation of McCarthyism
bolder and more sweeping than any that other Mc-
Carthyites, the Senator himself most emphatically included, have made so far.

Buckley and Bozell will not settle for a merely prag-
matic verdict in McCarthy's favor, for concurrence in
the view that it takes a lot of noise to wake a sleeping
nation and that McCarthy is a noisemaker of unparal-
leled effectiveness. They work this and all the other
familiar metaphors now and again, but what they are
really soliciting is our assent to the extraordinary propo-
sition that "McCarthyism . . . is a movement around
which men of good will and stern morality may close
ranks." One can almost see McCarthy's formidable jaw
dropping as he comes on so startling a thought; it has
never, after all, occurred to him to bring good will and
stern morality into the argument.

Reading this sort of thing, McCarthy may be led to
reflect on the advantages of having eggheads of one's
own. But if his intuitions are as sound as some of us believe them to be, he may be led to other reflections.
For while it would seem reasonable, almost inescapable,

54

to assume that so exalted a view of McCarthyism must rest on a boundless admiration for McCarthy, this does not seem to be the case at all.

These young authors (Mr. Buckley may be remembered for his book of a couple of years ago saying that God and country no longer enjoy an intimate association with Yale, and Mr. Bozell is a New Haven contemporary) labor mightily to read reason and truth and consistency into McCarthy's humbug, but they give not the slightest indication of admiring McCarthy himself. They have produced a devotional essay that contains not a word of devotion, true or simulated. Nowhere in this defense of McCarthy is there a single warm or friendly phrase about the man himself. The most that can be said of Buckley's and Bozell's attitude is that it hovers somewhere between ambivalence and repugnance.

The evidence of this is not to be found in their repeated admission that McCarthy butchers truth. (According to Leo Cherne, a professional statistician, there are sixty-three such concessions, or about one to every six pages.) Buckley and Bozell may be disturbed by this habit of McCarthy's, but their argument is never seriously discommoded by it; their position throughout seems to be that some things are more important than truth. What does appear to upset them, though, is McCarthy's personality. They are unable to bring themselves even to the point of discussing it.

This work, which appears to be a biography of a fascinating and truly protean figure, is actually nothing more than an examination, close but never close enough, of only one side of McCarthy's many-sided life; it deals only with the record of McCarthy's public discussions, if they can be called that, of Communist infiltration of the Federal government. The study is framed in time by McCarthy's discovery of the Communist issue in early 1950 and by his speech on Adlai Stevenson just before the election of 1952. Almost everything else is left out. No one would guess from anything that Buckley and Bozell have to say that McCarthy is a politician; that he has had certain transactions with other politicians of his time; that there have been some interesting speculations about his past and about his aspirations for the future; that he comes from a state named Wisconsin, which has a political climate of its own; that, like any other human being, he has traits which distinguish him from other human beings; that he has had, even in the period covered by the book, a good many concerns besides Communism—that he is, in short, a person.

The subtitle of the book is "The Record and Its Meaning," but the record is so narrowly construed as to rule out everything but the speeches and testimony in which McCarthy has ascribed various degrees of political guilt to others. For the authors, he exists only as a machine of denunciation. They are, of course, much too intelligent to fail to see the interrelatedness of elements in a career; they are, in fact, at pains to point them out and explore them in the lives of men of whom, along with McCarthy, they take a poor view. But every time the question of McCarthy's personality appears to be germane, they rear back and then move along to something else. At one point they tell us that they regard a discussion of McCarthy's motives as a "parlor game" they don't wish to play.

What goes on here? How does it happen that volunteers in a movement for men of stern morality beg off from all discussions of the morality of the movement's leader? How it happens is not of much importance, it seems to me, alongside the fact that it *does* happen. Buckley and Bozell are hardly the first young intellectuals to handle the problem of faith in a leader this way. The Communist intellectuals of twenty years ago had no very high opinion of the Communist leaders either in Russia or the United States. They regarded them as intellectual and moral inferiors, and they neither liked nor admired them. But they followed and defended them, triumphing over all misgivings and even somehow strengthened in their faith by admitting the shortcomings of the leadership. In a sense, indeed, the shortcomings revealed the true strength and greatness of the leaders, for it is characteristic of the intellectual to regard the man of action as being both worse and better than himself.

I daresay it was *de rigueur* among young Nazis, too, to speak, among themselves, rather disparagingly of the mind and morality of Hitler and his associates and at the same time to point to the weaknesses of the Führer and the Gauleiters as being among the sources of their strength as leaders. Thought, the intellectuals know, inhibits action, and plainly, therefore, action must inhibit thought.

In any event, what is instructive about this book is not its revelation of the way the politically bewitched mind works, but its revelation that McCarthy and McCarthyism have achieved the power to bewitch. If, as I am inclined to believe, Buckley and Bozell are representatives of at least a significant portion of their generation, their book will stir memories and a sinking, here-we-go-again feeling in members of my own generation, which is now crowding middle age and enduring the contempt of the young Buckleys and Bozells. One had hoped that McCarthyism, which is essentially nihilistic and has an even more remote connection with justice, liberty, and human fellowship than the Stalinism of the 1930's, would lack the power to stimulate such responses in young men, but evidently it doesn't. Buckley and Bozell don't admire McCarthy and probably don't even like him, but McCarthy's thrashing about persuades them that he is a man of action, a doer, and they are for him.

Cheerfully finessing morality, or at least declaring it irrelevant to the higher righteousness, they set about defending McCarthy with a refinement of McCarthy's own techniques of debate. By this I do not mean anything so simple or gauche as the "smearing of innocent people"—one of the complaints against their man that the authors discuss with a great air of patience and forbearance—but rather that, like McCarthy, they have liberated themselves from the fetters of any particular discipline of debate and are free, therefore, to select from the arsenal of polemics any weapon, any idea, any dodge or pitch or gimmick that suits their passing needs. One moment finds them wrestling Greco-Roman, the next jujitsu, the next West Country, or Devon, style.

Consistency is to be found only in the lacquer of reasonableness and serious intellectual purpose that glistens on the surface of their argument—there and in the oppressive, thoroughly bogus air of scholarship and research they create. These writers may be accused of taking facts lightly, but they cannot be accused of taking them for granted. They overlook facts by the carload, but once they decide to deal with one they give it the full treatment. Citations abound. So do footnotes. The appendices are long and numerous, manifestly the prod-

57

uct of much labor. The presumption created by such an approach is that, whatever else may be said of it, it is not frivolous.

The presumption, of course, is false. The book is breath-takingly frivolous, just as its hero is. I have often thought that the cream of the jest for McCarthy must lie in the success he has enjoyed in turning the devices of scholarship against scholars. This superb faker has long known what triumphs of fakery can be won by the man who "documents" everything he says, who carries about a great wad of papers and books and photostats, who appears before audiences with the dust of the archives still clinging to him. The bulging briefcase is to McCarthy what snapping red galluses were to old Gene Talmadge. The suckers gape in wonderment, the true believers twitch in ecstasy when McCarthy holds aloft a scrap of paper—hot, he says, from the filing cabinet. The man positively flaunts the stigmata of the pedant; in the 101 pages of his own book, *McCarthyism: The Fight for America*, there are 314 meticulously numbered citations. Anyone who employed them to run down sources would see for himself how McCarthy butchers truth. But McCarthy knows a secret: He knows that people won't run down sources but that they will be mightily impressed by being given the opportunity to do so.

This is the way Buckley and Bozell work. Bookish by nature and only recently discharged from the sacred groves, they display an academic *savoir-faire* that makes McCarthy, by contrast, look a bit of a rube. But the purpose and effect are the same. Take as an example their treatment of McCarthy's very first speech on Communism, the one delivered in Wheeling, West Virginia, on February 9, 1950. For page after tiresome page, Buckley and Bozell debate with themselves over whether McCarthy on that memorable occasion said that he had the names of 205 Communists in the State Department or whether the figure he gave was 57, as he later claimed. They finally resolve the problem in favor of 57, but not before they have scrupulously examined every last scrap of evidence in favor of 205. They appraise the credentials of contenders on both sides, subject their competing claims to a rigorous scrutiny, devote themselves to a ponderous textual examina-

58

tion of the two versions of the speech. They worry the problem with all the zeal of a Jean Champollion working over the Rosetta Stone. It is a trying but impressive performance, and it is almost certain to leave the reader who has no independent knowledge of the controversy feeling that Buckley and Bozell don't prejudge questions of fact but get their answers the hard, fair way.

Their answers to what? To absolutely nothing, for this particular question is no question at all. It doesn't matter the least bit whether McCarthy in his maiden speech on Communism used the figure 205 or 57 or 81 or 9,000. Any figure would have been a fraudulent one because McCarthy didn't have *any* names. Moreover, the very sentence in which he used whichever figure he used contained several demonstrable untruths to which Buckley and Bozell pay no attention at all. What McCarthy was reported to have said was this: "I have here in my hand a list of 205—a list of names that were made known to the Secretary of State as being members of the Communist Party and who nevertheless are still working and shaping policy in the State Department."

McCarthy later beefed about the figure, but this, like his friends' discussion of it, was only a cover-up for the simple fact that he had nothing. What he held in his hand was not a list but a letter James Byrnes had written to the late Representative Adolph Sabath on the State Department loyalty program. From certain statistics in the letter, the figure 205 emerged as one that applied to people who had been investigated but not discharged. There were no names in the list. The letter was more than three years old. The list could not have been submitted to Dean Acheson because he wasn't Secretary of State at that time. The people the letter referred to but did not name were not all in the State Department when McCarthy spoke. Some had died, some had quit, some had been dismissed for other reasons. Only one or two had been accused of Communism. Only one or two at the most had anything to do with policy. A couple of hundred pages after Bozell and Buckley have settled on the figure 57 as the accurate one, in their bland and plausible that-settles-*that* manner, they tell us that McCarthy "has publicly accused, as of questionable loyalty or reliability, a total of forty-six persons." A lengthy footnote, positively reeking of judiciousness, warns us that this computation may possibly be in error but that it "is as close a figure as diligent research will bear out."

Of their diligence there can be no doubt. It takes great application to spin out the irrelevant for pages at a time, and this book is indisputably a masterpiece of irrelevance. On the hastily constructed theory that McCarthy's real contribution is in "bringing to the loyalty-security problem a kind of skepticism with which it had not been approached before," they carry us off into a long, carefully worked-up disquisition on procedures in the field.

The notion that McCarthyism may be forcing an undesirable spirit of conformity on the Republic leads them into an essay on the philosophy of comformity in which they are able to disgorge huge chunks of reference-room knowledge and to indulge in the kind of casuistry and logic-chopping that never fails to delight young men of their sort. None of it has very much to do with McCarthy or McCarthyism, but the brilliance of this book lies in the authors' ability to make the utterly irrelevant seem urgently relevant. This is also, of course, one of the basic gifts of the man they don't like to talk much about but are nevertheless intent on celebrating.

It is all, to be sure, strictly for the birds, but that is no consolation, for we know from McCarthy's success how full the woods are of birds, and we know from this book that its bright young authors, too, are feathered.

Lives and Deaths
of Whittaker Chambers

BY MAX ASCOLI

In writing *Witness*, Whittaker Chambers has opened the
second round of what he calls "the Case." This may turn
out to be a service to the nation if—and it is a very large
if, in no way dependent on Chambers—"the Case" is
thoroughly and fearlessly debated, if his testimony is
examined and cross-examined, as that of any witness
must be. So far, there has not been much evidence of
this.

Yet this time we are not taken by surprise, buffeted
by headlines, stirred up by revelations or lurid gossip.
This time we have a huge book in front of us to read
and to ponder. The adventures of Alger Hiss, as told
by Whittaker Chambers, are meant to corroborate the
indictment to which Mr. Chambers, in his own terminology, bears witness. This indictment is against the prevailing values of our democracy and against the leaders
who guided our nation through the New Deal and the
war.

These men stand accused of having worked for the
victory of our deadly enemy, Communism, although
only a fraction of them did so knowingly. "Thus men
who sincerely abhorred the word Communism, in the
pursuit of common ends found that they were unable to
distinguish Communists from themselves, except that it
was just the Communists who were likely to be most
forthright and most dedicated in the common cause.
This political color-blindness was all the more dogged
because it was completely honest. For men who could
not see that what they firmly believed was liberalism
added up to socialism could scarcely be expected to see
what added up to Communism."

The author brings forth his indictment not in a bill
of particulars but through a detailed description of what
he himself has done and seen throughout the whole
range of his life. What happened to him is made to
carry a message of universal and of immediate importance. The basic themes of his message are reiterated

rather than explained, for the author, like other religious writers, relies on the habit-forming persuasiveness of reiteration.

Mr. Chambers's book must stand or fall on the validity of his indictment. It is not up to him to decide whether the religious message of his book has canonical virtue or is apocryphal. *Witness* cannot just be considered as a piece of literature or a contribution to the history of our times. We cannot put the book on the shelf, after having given the author an "A" as a storyteller, a "C" as a philosopher of contemporary history, and a "D" as a theologian. To do this is to exhibit at its weakest that facile liberalism which Chambers scorns.

The book is all of one piece. With artful and deliberate lack of discretion, the dismal, at times nightmarish life of this human being is exhibited to millions of Americans by the man who has had the hard luck to live it. For all its emphasis on religion, *Witness* is a political book and a major event in present-day American politics.

Chambers's is no isolated voice. For years it has been first whispered, then said, then yelled into all the microphones of the nation that an unspecified number of our national leaders have knowingly or unknowingly connived with the enemy. In creating these fears and apprehensions, no influence was greater than that of "the Case"—first round. Now all those who are prone to believe in the undefined, unspecified guilt of an Administration or of a generation will be heartened, for "the Case"—second round—has found the Book.

In giving us the tale of his life, the author has set himself a number of different goals. He wants to denounce the Communist danger at home, to confess what his own role has been in the Communist conspiracy, to explain the queer halting course of his denunciation of Alger Hiss. He manages to give a justification for every instance where his behavior has been odd, as on the various occasions when he perjured himself. He wants to make of his past testimony in courts and in Congressional committees the evidence of his right to be a witness for his God.

Above all, he wants to get even with his enemies, as many another author of a religiously inspired book has done before him—Dante first of all, who, even from the height of the *Paradiso,* never stopped lashing out at those who had wronged him.

Scarcely anything that has been said against Chambers is left unchallenged or unanswered in this book. To those who questioned his sanity and searched for the peculiarities of his family background, he offers a clinical, detailed, sometimes lurid description of the traits that he inherited and the environment that shaped his youth. He stretches himself on the couch, and tells the analysts —whom he hates en masse—all the things that they want to hear from him, and that fall into their set categories. Thus he reports how horrible he felt when, as a boy, he had to kill a chicken: "I tied the chicken's legs and hung it, head down, from a nail, and as quickly and as mercifully as I could, severed its head. The knife fell as if gravity had jerked it from my hand. Then I hid." He knows that some psychoanalysts will detect here the pattern of his behavior in later life. He dares them to.

Then he proceeds: "All right. As a man, I will kill. But I will kill always under duress, by an act of will, in knowing violation of myself, and always in rebellion against that necessity which I do not understand or agree to. Let me never kill unless I suffer that agony, for if I do not suffer it, I will be merely a murderer." This passage is characteristic of the whole book; the author lifts himself to the pulpit by the bootstraps of his public self-analysis.

It was in his childhood, he says, that he developed "a deep distrust of the human race." "I never had any real friends." "By degrees I told myself: I am an outcast. My family is outcast. We have no friends, no social ties, no church, no organization that we claim and that claims us, no community. We could scarcely be more foreign in China than in our alienation from the life around us."

There is a ring of unquestionable truth in this description of his squalid childhood. For Chambers, schooling—the process of formal learning—never became an education. According to his own record, he never acquired that modesty, that patience in comparing his ideas and feelings with those of other men before him and around him, which is education. All his life he has remained somewhat unrelated and lonely. For him the only way of communicating and perhaps of grasping

63

ideas is by inflating to enormous proportions the accidents of his life.

In his youth he was an omnivorous reader. But of all the books he read the only one that made a dent on him was *Les Misérables* by Victor Hugo, that writer who created gigantic figures—all reeking of ham.

There are pages of *Witness* that cannot be read without a sense of horror, pages describing things that happened to the author which the reader wishes he had never read, for such things should not happen to any human being. This is the case, for instance, in that scene where, in Chambers's house one night, his father beat and nearly killed his brother, until Chambers grappled with his father. Toward the end of the book, his description of his last attempt at suicide—when the Hiss case was reaching its climax—does not spare us any detail: Chambers lying in bed, breathing the poisonous fumes, the pictures of his children, one in each hand, and the letters on the table to be read after he is dead. But he has to tell the reader about the contents of these letters.

There seems to be no reason why millions of Americans should be made privy to such wretchedness—unless it be that although reading Chambers is no pleasure, being Chambers must be incomparably worse. The author knows this, and uses it to the hilt.

Invariably, society is made responsible for all the gruesome things that happened—such as the suicide of the author's brother. With the crude precision of a case history, all the details are given of this unfortunate man's drift toward death—for no force could stop him. Yet when at last he frees himself from what little life is left in him, the author says, "Such fortitude and such finality are like a smile before a firing squad."

In all his leaps from the episodic to the universal, from occurrences to ideas, Chambers seems to have a rather personal and peculiar notion of ideas that is unrelated to their socially established meaning.

Such is the case with his concept of history, which he obviously borrows from Marxism. The words "history" and "historical" appear with extraordinary frequency in the book, often several times on one page. Invariably "history" means necessity—a superhuman power that makes men act, and on which human will cannot exert much of an influence. To Chambers, history is not some-

64

thing that men make and for which they have a share of responsibility. The "logic of history" told Chambers that Communism was the only way out for the twentieth century. The man who leaves Communism finds "himself facing the crisis of history." The party has a "historical purpose," is manned by that "modern secular secret order which has dedicated its life and its death to initiating a new phase of history for mankind." It is, of course, the party that has to "solve the immensely complicated problems of revolutionary struggle posed by history in our age." "The motive forces of history conspire unknowably." The first paragraph of the same page starts, "History was moving torrentially," and he adds three lines later, "the historic crisis . . . reached a new crest." He means that the Second World War was starting.

History, according to Chambers, moves in one direction: toward Communism. Communism "is the central experience of the first half of the 20th century." It gives men "a reason to live and a reason to die."

This insistence on men dying for their faith runs through the book. There seems to be no higher criterion for either a man or a faith. Twice he quotes his assertion, made on a broadcast, that he still shares with Alger Hiss "the conviction that life is not worth living for which a man is not prepared to dare all and die at any moment." According to Chambers, a well-spent life seems to be a form of staggered suicide.

This is a peculiar attitude, since there has seldom been an absurd cause for which men have not been ready to die. Among those who are at all times ready to die can be found many whose lives aren't worth living. For the hard business of living is ordinarily one of paying for what we do with a different coin from that of our life—coins called work or success. Chambers has remained a frustrated Kamikaze—first in the cause of Communism, then in that of anti-Communism.

Even what Chambers calls Communism bears little resemblance to what is generally known by this name. Communism, he says repeatedly, is based on faith in Man. Communism as previously known is based on faith neither in Man nor in Men, but in a total subjection to a merciless, undeviating history. Indeed, it is the mystical, irrevocable character of this subjection that has made many people reject their Communist allegiance.

Actually, Chambers, who is obsessed with the idea of Communism, underestimates its danger, for he sees it acting primarily as an underground conspiracy. But the tragedy of our time is that there are millions of men who embrace Communism to free themselves from some of the ills that torture them—and thus are enslaved. Not the spy or the secret agent, but the professional agitator, skillful in finding his work wherever there is human suffering, and in creating human suffering, represents the major threat to our society.

Chambers talks of God. Indeed, he has dedicated his life to God. God has spoken to him at least once. It was one day when he was coming down the stairs in his Mount Royal Terrace house in Baltimore. "As I stepped down into the dark hall, I found myself stopped, not by a constraint, but by a hush of my whole being. In this organic hush, a voice said with perfect distinctness: 'If you will fight for freedom, all will be well with you.'"

This sounds like one of those compacts which the first Patriarchs entered. But it is difficult to see how Chambers's god can keep his part of the compact, for he is a horribly weakened god, abandoned by large masses of men who have gone to the other side—the side which Chambers maintains is winning. There is not much hope to be found in this book that the trend may be reversed and that the attempt to stop Communism can be anything but a suicidal foray on the advancing conquerors. Yet, through Chambers, this god asks for the tribute of men ready to die. This mortally wounded Moloch is not the God of the Judeo-Christian faith.

In the whole book, Christ is hardly if ever mentioned, although the verbiage of Christian ethics and Christian charity is largely used. But the person as well as the meaning of Christ are not to be found anywhere—the respect for the human person that the Christian faiths consider sacred because Christ accepted human shape.

For it is true that the struggle of our time is a religious one: a struggle where various Molochs (called Communism or nationalism) stand against men's will to rule themselves and to maintain their communion with God through many churches or through no church—as Christ told the Samaritan woman. This faith in the human person, always meshed into politics yet somehow independent of it, has become the faith of our civilization, East and West, and is shared by hundreds of millions of baptized and unbaptized people.

It is faith in freedom. This unfortunate man Chambers has extremely vague notions of freedom. He says, "freedom is a need of the soul, and nothing else." He does not know how freedom is organized and released, or what a system of law is, or how laws exert their checks on men's instincts. Indeed, not only the democracy of the New Deal but the idea of political freedom is alien to him.

One night, when he was about to leave the Communist Party, he says, ". . . I faced the fact that, if Communism were evil, I could no longer serve it, and that that was true regardless of the fact that there might be nothing else to serve, that the alternative was a void." It was not just on that one night that he faced the void which his education had not filled and which Communism could not cover up. What that void means is no values; no purpose, no design, no faith in life. The Russians have a word for it: nihilism.

There is so little hope left in Whittaker Chambers that whatever happens in his favor seems to him a freakish reprieve from doom. Chambers has no qualms about aligning himself with whatever institution or interests Communism fights. And why should he? Whatever Communism attacks is not destined to live long.

Nihilism, in his case and in that of some other former Communists, is what remains of the Marxist conception of history in the minds of men who still adhere to it but no longer want to be its agents. Since he refuses to be the tool of the inevitable, the nihilist enjoys a vacation from history. He can get a free ride on any forlorn counterattack against the inevitable.

Yet this unfortunate, lonely man is now offering millions of Americans the opportunity to relive, through his book, his own life. Thanks to his profession and his native gift, he has acquired a remarkable power of communication. But what he can communicate is, above all, his nihilism, the lonely experience of his own self, of a man never entirely identified with anything, either Communism or God, and forced to replace all these accepted standards of value with his own homemade substitutes. He communicates to his fellow citizens universal distrust of their leaders, not a promise of salvation. But he does impart to them that thorough despair for which only the iron discipline of Communism can be a cure.

Other former Communists had already advanced the

Rasputin-like theory that to fight Communism, which is the evil of our times, one must have been a practitioner of evil. But no one had ever gone as far as Whittaker Chambers. He still boasts of his attachment to some of the most typical Communist values. He even makes a plea for his onetime profession, spying: "Like the soldier, the spy stakes his freedom or his life on the chances of action."

Constantly he exhibits, flagellates, ultimately extols himself. Constantly he makes it quite clear that whatever he has done to others, it is he who has suffered the most. His whole story is construed as a slow, tortured ascent, Chambers's immolation to what he is the witness for. This becomes particularly striking where he describes what he underwent while denouncing Hiss.

In answer to the question that a journalist put to him at the time, "What do you think you are doing?" he replies, "I am a man who, reluctantly, grudgingly, step by step, is destroying himself that this country and the faith by which it lives may continue to exist." When he decides not to destroy the microfilms, he says, "I knew, too, that whatever else I destroyed, I could do what I had to do only if I was first of all willing to destroy myself." Later, when he considers suicide, he says, "Whether I lived and bore a witness of justice, or killed myself and bore a witness of mercy, I would in either case destroy myself."

Once, in answering Mr. Nixon, who had asked him about his motives in accusing Alger Hiss of Communism, he said, "There are in general two kinds of men. One kind of man believes that God is a God of Justice. The other kind of man believes that God is a God of Mercy. I am so constituted that in any question I will always range myself upon the side of mercy." He must have forgotten at that moment that there are also the Communists in this world, who do not believe in God—either of Justice or of Mercy.

His last attempt at suicide, at the time he was testifying before the New York Grand Jury, he describes as having been at least partly successful. "Still, no one who has been through such an experience can be expected to be quite the same man again. He is both freer and stronger, because he is, ever after, less implicated in the
68

world. For he has been, in his own mind at least, almost to the end of everything, and knows its worth."

In a chapter entitled "Tomorrow and Tomorrow and Tomorrow," the author makes it clear that there is not much of a tomorrow left for him. After the trials, there is not much energy left, either—aside from whatever energy might have been required for the writing of these 799 pages. At the end, the book has the inexorable accent of the *Consummatum Est*.

Just because this book is no ordinary piece of literature, but a very important political fact, it is imperative that it be answered and not just reviewed. The episodes it reports may be all true. But the frame of reference and the perspective are, to say the least, arbitrary.

From the sense of doom, of inevitable Communist victory, only the enemy can benefit. Moreover, this pessimism is utterly unjustified, for in fact we are fighting against Communism and we certainly will win if we do not let nihilism becloud our vision and sap our strength.

It is not possible to derive from this book any other sentiment than a profound pity for Whittaker Chambers. But all the accidents, the quirks, the oddities of his life cannot be considered representative and exemplary, even if his desperate loneliness is endowed with the power of communication—amplified by the *Saturday Evening Post* and the Book-of-the-Month Club. We do need to revise our recent history, for we can no longer rely on the happy improvisations that allowed Roosevelt's America to emerge from the depression and from the war. But these blanket indictments of all who have led us during the last twenty years, and of the democratic tenets our nation lives by, cannot remain unchallenged. Only too frequently of late the sewers have been overflowing into Main Street. Behind Chambers, anguished in his search for God, come Lait and Mortimer—and the rest.

Perhaps we ought to have less shyness and self-consciousness in asserting our religious beliefs. Our times are so serious, the fight against Communism so demanding, that we must call on all the support we can get from the faith that has made our civilization. We all have our share of guilt for the life that is described in this book, and we can never pity its author enough.

But we will not trade Christ for Chambers.

The Way the Evening Was

BY ANDY LEWIS

I was sitting on the steps with Frank when my brother Gil came around the corner in this car. He just stopped there, and sat and smiled at me.

"For the love of God," said Frank, "where did you get a car?"

"I made it," said Gil. He doesn't like Frank. "Pile in," he said to me. "Take you for a ride."

"Where did you ever get a car?" said Frank.

"Come on, Buddy," said Gil, "let's go ride."

"You want to come?" I asked Frank.

"If your brother's crazy, do you have to be crazy too?" he said. "Where do you think he got it?"

"I guess he took it," I said, and I got in with Gil. It was almost a new car, big and black, and it smelled nice. Gil started slow, and Frank ran alongside with one hand on the window frame. He couldn't decide whether to come or not. Gil stopped for him, and he got in and rode for a while, but after we'd gone a couple of blocks, he made us let him out again. "You're both crazy," he said. "You don't get me to go with you."

Neither of us said anything. Then we went along down the hill, onto the avenue. The avenue is wide, and it was a nice warm evening. Gil turned the headlights on, and we kept on along to the parkway. The parkway is even broader than the avenue, with green grass on both sides. It slopes down to little ponds. Once in a while ducks with blue heads come there—the most beautiful blue you ever saw. There are fountains there too, and summer nights sometimes we used to come over in a bunch and lie around. And there's a ball park. When the police were having a big campaign, we used to use it. "The Buckleys" we called ourselves, because that was the name of the councilman who gave us equipment. But we lost a lot of games in a row, and he didn't buy us any more equipment, and the campaign for boys' clubs ended. Only pick-up teams play there now. They keep it worn down along the base paths, but the rest is scrubby.

70

Gil was still driving slow and over close to the curb. I rolled all the windows down, front and rear, and we let the wind blow on our faces. Then I got the radio turned on and found some music. I think it was the biggest car I ever was in. It was wonderful. We'd stop for lights, and other people would drive up alongside. We could look over into their cars. Some had little kids in the back seat standing up on the upholstery or wrestling around with the lap robes. A girl looked over at us once, and then away, and then smiled.

"Look," I said to Gil. "Look, did you see that?"

"What do you expect?" he said. "I'm a very handsome man."

"Turn down this next street. I want to drive."

"Can you drive?" Gil is two years older than me.

"I can if you can," I said. I made him stop, and climbed over him and under the wheel. I was excited and I pressed the starter with the motor already going and it made a whirring noise. Gil was all for climbing back, only I wouldn't let him. I was too happy. I didn't want to drive fast anyway on a night like that. I went out into the parkway again. The parkway is city, all right, not country—apartment houses on one side and stores on the other. But right in the middle of the parkway it's better than the country would ever be. The city's right there and all—you can smell it—but there's all the trees and grass you could ever use. I think it must be better than just the plain country.

Gil leaned back when he saw I wasn't going to run into anything, and I drove up by the Garibaldi fountain. Garibaldi was an Italian general. There's a big pool underneath, so that the water comes spraying down in a circle and makes a cool noise all the time. There's an Italian named "Begeeno"—that's what he's called, but I don't know what his real name is—who sells candy and novelties there.

"Stop," said Gil. "We'll get some popcorn."

Begeeno came trotting over bowlegged when he saw the big car. And then he saw it was the two of us. "For the love of God," he said.

"Hello, Begeeno," said Gil, grinning at him. "Two boxes, okay?"

"How do you like our car?" I said.

He didn't say anything but went and got the two

71

boxes, looking at us over his shoulder. He came and handed them in to us. Gil gave him a quarter.

"Look," said Begeeno. "You don't keep. You take back."

"Take what back?"

"Car," said Begeeno. "You take car back, you two."

"It's a nice car," said Gil. "Listen to the engine, Begeeno."

Begeeno had been waving the quarter at us. Now he held it back in the window. "Please," he said. "Anyway, you take money back. Cops ask you, you don't stop here, you don't see me. Give me back popcorn, huh?" He looked as if he wanted to reach in and take it away from us. His forehead was all twisted up.

"They wouldn't do anything to you, Begeeno," said Gil. "Just for selling us popcorn, they wouldn't do anything to you."

"You go away now," said Begeeno. "Please." He dropped the quarter inside, on Gil's lap, and it rolled down between the cushions. "I don't see you." He went bowlegged back to the wagon and stood looking away from us hard.

"Pull up to the other side, Buddy," said Gil. "There'll be somebody lying around."

I did, and there was, all right. Two little bunches—one boys and the other girls, each sitting a little way apart, propped up on their elbows, making cracks at each other and looking across, and waiting for just one to cross over. "I see Nutsy," said Gil. "I see Doris."

"Which one is Doris?"

"The thin one with all the black hair."

"She isn't thin," I said.

They all saw us at once and jumped up and came around. They stood in a half circle around the window or walked back and forth rapping on the fenders and jiggling the license plate. "Frank said you had a car," said Nutsy. "The way he talks everybody'll know. He hates you."

"Frank is smart," said Gil, as if he didn't care much. "Come for a ride."

"Thanks, but no thanks," said Nutsy. "You ought to get this away somewhere, honest. Kiley's brother has a garage. But you got to get it out of sight."

72

"Listen to the engine," said Gil. "You want some pop-corn?"

He leaned forward to offer the popcorn to Nutsy, and I got a chance to look at Doris. All I could see before was the edge of her hair, but now I could watch her face. She looked in at the cushions in the back seat and then at the dashboard and then past Gil at me. "Hello, Doris," I said.

"Hello," she said. Nothing shy about her. "Are you Gil's brother?"

"This is Buddy," said Gil. "Buddy, this is Doris. Doris, this is Buddy. I'm *his* brother."

"Come ride with us, Doris," I said.

"Oh no you don't," said one of the other girls right away. She was a thick-faced one, and spotted. "You don't get in that car, Doris. You hear what I'm saying?"

"Who are you?" I asked her, but Gil put his hand on my arm. He was looking out past Nutsy and the others. There was a man standing about ten feet away watching us. He was young. I thought for a moment he was a plainclothes man, but he wore a bright jacket. Tan, I guess it was, almost golden, and plainclothes men don't dress that neat. He was watching the whole gang of us. I wondered how long.

"Shut up a little," Gil said to the others, and he went out to where the man was standing.

"Is it your car?" Gil asked him.

He smiled and shook his head.

"No, not mine."

"You know whose it is?"

"No, I guess I don't." Still smiling.

"And were you going to tell some cop?" Gil wasn't threatening. He was just asking.

"I thought about it," said the man. "I couldn't decide about you."

"But you aren't going to tell a cop," said Gil.

"I wasn't sure," said the man. "You think I ought to?"

"I guess so," said Gil. "But you aren't, are you?"

"No, I guess not. Don't worry."

"Oh, I wouldn't worry," said Gil. "Only I thought *you* would. You want to come ride with us?"

He shook his head and smiled at Gil and then around at everyone else. Then he went off past the fountain.

Gil came back to the car. "He's a nice fella."

73

"Do you know him?"

"I've seen him around," said Gil. "I can't place him."

"I've seen him too," I said, "I wish I had a jacket like that."

"Maybe you will," said Gil. "You're a young boy yet."

"Listen how quiet it is." It was, too. No talking from anyone for a minute, no sound from cars, only the fountain spraying.

Then all the others started talking again. "You don't get in that car, Doris," said the thick-faced one, right where she'd left off before. "Come on."

She tried to walk Doris away. "Those two are crazy."

"This is too public here," said Nutsy. "We better move out. You too."

"I like it here," said Gil.

"Leave her alone," I said to the thick-faced one. "Come along with us, Doris."

"I'll come," she said. "Do you want to come too, Marg?"

"Doris!" said the thick-faced one. "You don't know where they'll take you. What am I supposed to tell your folks?"

"I don't know," said Doris. Gil got out and held the door open for her, and she fitted in between us. I felt her leg against mine, and I went and pushed the starter again by mistake. It whirred, and Nutsy jumped.

"Doris, what am I going to tell your folks if you don't get back?" We drove along a little. When I looked in the mirror, the thick-faced girl was still leaning over the curb and shouting at us, and the others were still looking after us. But later on, I knew, they'd walk back on the grass by the fountain and lie down in one bunch. And still later when it got darker, if it was still warm, they'd go off by twos. I hoped for his sake Nutsy didn't get the thick-faced one.

We drove around for a little while more. The overpasses on the parkway are paved with some kind of metal, and when we went over one there was a singing noise with the tires. It smelled sweet in the car. I thought it was coming from outside, but it wasn't. It was inside with us. Then I thought it was perfume, but it wasn't. It was just Doris. She smelled good, and I was going to tell her so.

"Say," said Gil, "let's go back and get Mom. We could give her a ride around. She'd love it."

"What will we tell her about the car?"

"Say we borrowed it. Say we borrowed it from Kiley's brother. He's a big shot."

"Have you ever seen him?"

"No," said Gil, "but he's a big shot."

"I've seen him," said Doris. "He's not much of a big shot." She was laughing, and the wind coming in the car blew her hair across her mouth.

"Well, let's go get Mom anyway. It's a good idea. And anyway I didn't have any supper."

I drove back across the park to our end, and up through the streets. I had to go slow so as not to hit kids. When we stopped in front of our place, five or six of them came and stood around and stared. Gil gave them what was left of the popcorn and told them to go away. He and Doris and I went to get Mom.

We didn't see Frank inside anywhere, but when we went past the third floor we could hear his folks arguing. Everybody in the place had got used to the noise, so that we hardly ever noticed it except late at night. They never threw things or hit each other—just talked.

Up on the next floor we didn't think anyone was inside at first because there was no light showing under the door. But Mom was there all right—sitting in the dark, leaning out on the window sill, and looking at the lights all the way across the city to the river. She sat up, wiping her hand on her dress and smiling at Doris.

"This is Mom," Gil said to Doris. "Shake hands with her, but she can't speak English." Doris shook hands, and Gil told Mom her name, very slow, twice, until she could say it.

Gil told her we hadn't eaten. She found some bread for us, and there were two meatballs in a frying pan on the stove. She heated them up, and we ate them. Doris said she had already had supper. Gil and Mom talked, and I translated for Doris until we were through eating. Then Gil told Mom about the surprise, about how she could come riding with us. She didn't ask any questions, just put on a coat and came down with us, slippers and all. She didn't say anything when she saw the car either, but she drew in her breath. Gil was going to have her sit in front, but she went in back instead, very careful of the upholstery.

"We better get some gas." Gil drove up four streets to the garage. It's a big place, but all it sells is gas. The

75

garage part is closed. There were big green oil drums standing in a line in front of the service door. There was one little door set into the service door, and while we were getting the gas a man came out through it, wearing a white shirt but wiping grease off his hands.

"That's Kiley's brother right there," said Doris. "This is his place."

He stood under the sign wiping his hands until he saw Doris. Then he came over. He had a big smile for her, but partly he was looking at the car too. "What do you know, Dotty?"

"Hello," she said.

He stuck his head and shoulders in the window, still smiling big for her. The brim of his hat got in my way, so I took it off and handed it to him. He looked at me for a second, not knowing whether to get tough or not. Then back to her, "I like that dress," he said. "I like what's inside."

"I know you do," said Doris.

"You better not ride around in this deal," he told her. He looked at Gil. Then he looked in back and saw Mom. That startled him. "What's the story with her?"

"She doesn't talk English," said Gil.

"Well listen then," said Kiley's brother. "A deal like this, new, it's bad to keep around. And I got three cars in the shop now. It isn't worth much to me."

"I've got news for you," said Gil. "We don't want to sell it."

"I tell you what. I'll keep it in the shop, we'll do all the work on it, and I'll get rid of it for you, and only keep a little piece. You won't get rid of it otherwise."

"Never mind," said Gil. "Never mind."

"Well, what do you have in mind then? Listen, I was trying to do you a favor . . ."

"We're just going for a ride," said Doris.

Kiley's brother put the hat back on his head, and mashed it down. "Haven't you done enough advertising already? They tell me you been riding around in it all evening. Listen, Dotty—" He pushed still more of himself inside the car. "You better get out of this. Let these jokers do what they want."

"No."

"Come on inside." He put on the big smile again. "I got something to show you."

"I've seen it," said Doris.

"Listen, I've got a crate in there that makes this look like a pushcart. You want to go riding, for Christ sakes, I'll take you riding."

"No," she said. "I want to go in this car." She wrapped her fingers over my wrist. I nodded to Gil, and he started up. Kiley's brother had to jump back or we would have taken his head and shoulders with us. He knocked his hat off on the window frame, and I handed it back to him. He stood there while we went off, beginning to get mad. Mom smiled back at him.

We drove for a long time then, all through the city, and then across the bridge and out towards the country. We went along the turnpike, past the chicken farms and roadhouses. It was real dark by then, but still warm and sweet-smelling. Doris leaned against my shoulder, and Gil turned the radio on again. He got a variety show. We'd hear the voices, all fuzzy, and the clapping like hailstones. It would go and come. Then he got music, and that was better. I wish I could remember some of the music they played. When I looked at Doris, she had her head tipped back, and any time I turned around there'd be Mom in the darkness in the back seat, smiling.

It's a strange place, out on the borders of the city, but I liked it. We drove through and up into the foothills, and I liked that even better. The road is winding there, and there are cable fences where the hills go down into valleys. There were poplar trees all along, and their leaves would shine when they caught the moonlight. I wish I could remember more about it. But we drove all over the hills, and then back to the city.

Gil turned left off the bridge, and we went down to the center. It's full of one-way streets that go by the sides of department stores. We went up one and down the other, looking in every window. In some there were people rolling rugs or undressing dummies or arranging luggage. They never looked at the people outside on the sidewalks, but you could see that they knew about them and were feeling important, even if all they were doing was taking the skirt off some cardboard lady.

The one-way streets all go up to meet the main drag. Gil pulled up at the head of one of them. There was a no-parking sign there but he kept the engine running, and there weren't any other cars. We just sat and looked

77

out into the big avenue at the crowds coming from the theaters. They'd hop down off one curb and cross over our little street and hop up the other curb. Up over their heads there was a sign that was supposed to blow smoke rings for a cigarette company. But there must not have been any smoke in the machine because all there was was the man looking surprised, with a big round empty hole for a mouth.

It got late, and the crowds got a little thinner. The wind started up and blew their clothes around them and picked up newspapers and blew them in their faces so that they turned their backs to it sometimes. And then the next thing when I looked out, there was the man in the tan jacket again, standing on the corner. He came over.

"There you are," he said.

"Here we are, all right," said Gil. "Were you looking?"

"Well, I wondered if I'd see you again."

"Come on in," said Gil. "Take a load off. This is Doris, and that's Mom in back. She only talks the old language."

"I'd like to," he said. "But thanks."

Gil was going to try to persuade him, but then Mom started crying. It's hard to tell when she starts crying, because she always starts low. But she began crying louder, and talking to us, and looking around in her dress for a handkerchief.

Doris took her own handkerchief and used it on Mom's cheeks, and pushed it into her hand. "What is she saying?"

"She says she knows we took the car," I said. "She says she didn't care before because it was so nice. She says we've got to give it back."

"Well, I'm sorry," said the man. "I didn't mean to upset her."

"It's all right," said Gil. "I guess she's right. We can't keep it, I guess. I don't know what we'd do with it." He reached back and patted Mom's shoulder and told her not to cry. Mom wanted to get out, but Gil grabbed her and told her not to cry.

"I tell you what," the man said. "Why don't you just go off and leave it? And then I'll tell them there's a car here, and they'll take care of it."

"I guess that's fine," said Gil. So we got out, the four

78

of us, and said good-by to the man and went off to the subway.

"I wish I knew how come he was there," I said.

"Don't worry about it," said Gil. "He just was."

"All the way over in the park. And then here in the center. You saw him too?" I asked Doris.

"Sure I did."

"How are we going to pay for the subway now?" said Gil.

But then he found some money in his pocket and Doris found some too so we could buy the ride home.

"You or me better marry her," said Gil.

It was fine, with the yellow lights in the green cars, and everybody sleepy, hanging onto the straps and leaning back and forth together. Mom was happy again, and she went to sleep with her head leaned on a fat woman's shoulder.

Gil patted her awake when we came to our stop, and we walked home in the middle of the street. Almost everybody had gone to bed. There was only a light here and there in the windows. And everything was quiet. When we got to our place and stood outside, there was the noise, thin and high up, of Frank's parents arguing with each other, but that was all.

Gil and Mom went inside then, and I walked on with Doris two more blocks to her place.

"Do you have to go in?" I said.

"I don't want to worry my folks," she said.

"You go in then," I said. "But when they're asleep and know you're all safe," I said, "then will you come back down?"

"I will," she said. "You wait for me. Sure I will."

So I waited, and she did come back. It was a good evening, a good night—different, the way a dream is.

The "Night of Horror" in Brooklyn

BY MARYA MANNES

During last November and December a trial was going on in Brooklyn. There was another trial going on at the same time in Cleveland, and that one was big news. It seemed to matter much more whether an osteopath had murdered his pregnant wife than whether four teen-

79

agers had, without reason, beaten and tortured a man until he staggered into the East River and drowned.

Yet it mattered last August 18, when people first read of it: "Four Brooklyn youths were charged yesterday with a series of crimes that included beating and kicking a man to death, horsewhipping young women and burning the soles of a vagrant's feet, beating him, and throwing him into the river. . . .

" 'I can't understand what would make boys do such terrible things,' Edward S. Silver, Kings County District Attorney, said after hearing their confessions. 'They apparently had no reason except the thrill they got,' he added."—the New York *Times*.

People read excerpts from some of the alleged confessions made by the boys to detectives. "Last night," Koslow was reported as saying when he told of the Negro's drowning, "was the supreme adventure for me. . . . park bums are no use to society and are better off dead." Mittman, the second boy, was quoted as saying that he used the victims as punching bags "to see how hard I could punch."

For a few days then, horrors hung in the air, and good citizens shook their heads. The boys were put in prison until their trial, and the talk about them subsided. It was too hideous to be sustained, too close for comfort.

For those who saw the trial the horror revived. For here were the boys themselves, ten feet away; not headlines, not files, not cases, but young living beings who had caused death; and for hour after hour one was impelled to examine their features with the same passionate, inquiring intensity with which one listened to the evidence of one terrible night in August.

It was no effort to see evil in Jack Koslow, the oldest defendant. So manifest was his sickness of soul that he could have posed as one of the tormenting demons that populate Hieronymus Bosch's visions of hell. His skin has been described as "sallow," but that gives no hint of its dead green-whiteness, in eerie and surprising conjunction with thick hair that is dark red and wholly without shine, receding from his forehead in a high crest. His features are delicately ugly: a long thin curved nose with a sharply articulated ridge; a thin, downturned, and usually derisive mouth, lips colorless, the upper extending slightly above the lower; a weak but bony chin; a white, undeveloped neck. His eyes are strangest of all. They are dark brown and seem pupilless, and their look is hooded as if by a transparent extra lid. When Koslow walked in and out each day manacled to his guard, you could see how tall and thin he is, and how his narrow head hangs forward from his body like a condor's.

Melvin Mittman, seventeen, is physically his antithesis. His body is barrel-thick and strong, his shoulders wide, his head square, his features blunt. He has an upturned, broad-based nose, small thick-lashed eyes under glasses, dense hair growing low on his brow, and a strong round chin. Throughout the trial until the verdict, when he wept and buried his face in his hands, he was expressionless. You would not have picked him out of a group, as you would Koslow, as having something "wrong" with him; he seemed just stolid and enclosed. Yet where Koslow's hands were white and thin and smooth as a girl's, lacing and interlacing during the trial and drumming little dances, Mittman's hands, abnormally short and thick, with hair on the fingers, made one inevitably imagine them pounding flesh.

The third boy, Jerome Lieberman, also seventeen, was another matter. Here was a diffident, tremulous kid with blinking eyes, a soft mouth, a defenseless neck; the only one of the three defendants to look miserable. Indeed, he was a defendant for only half the trial. He was dismissed for lack of evidence of any direct involvement in this particular case.

The fourth and youngest boy, Robert Trachtenberg, fifteen at the time of the crime, was separated from this trial and appeared only as state's evidence. Tall, darkly handsome, of aristocratic bearing, his speech distinct and mannerly, Trachtenberg inspired one chiefly with incredulity as to the innate viciousness attributed to him —if not in connection with this particular crime, then in involvement in other crimes for which he has yet to stand trial. As one woman reporter said, "He looks like the kind of boy any mother would be proud of." He looked, more than any of the other three, like the kind of boy who could be salvaged.

Here were the four, then, and this is the story of what they did on the night of August 16, pieced together by their own words, clinched by an absent but tangible exhibit: the body of Willard Menter dredged from the

81

East River on August 19 and identified by them as the victim of their acts.

The four boys had met by prearrangement this warm summer night. First Trachtenberg picked up Lieberman, his special friend, at the latter's home around eight; then the two met Koslow at the Marcy Avenue subway station; then the three picked up Mittman at his home and off they went.

They discussed what to do. Mittman suggested going to New York and picking up girls. Koslow said no, let's go bum-hunting. It is pertinent to note that in none of the testimony did any of the other three ask what bum-hunting was or argue against it. Koslow has been charged with beating up a man of sixty named Kostyra earlier that same evening; the other boys have been charged with wantonly beating to death on August 6 a middle-aged vagrant called Rheinhold Ulrickson.

The four wandered about rather aimlessly for quite a while until they converged on a place called Triangular Park. "Park" is a euphemism: The triangle is a patch of dusty grass and concrete bordered on three sides by benches and a railing; an island cut off, as it were, from casual access by three intersecting flows of traffic.

The boys stood at the gate of the park. It was about nine o'clock. On a bench at the near side of the triangle two men were sitting, playing chess. On a bench at the far side a man was sleeping, a Negro.

(*"How would you categorize this method," Koslow was asked by Detective Duggan after his arrest, "in which you went out looking for bums?"*

A. *"Just hit or miss. I'd find one. If he was particularly distasteful to either myself or the other boys, the person who he affected most would do what he pleased with him. . . . Sometimes I see a drunken bum, very soused. He looks at you out of one eye. It's disgusting. It incites me to hit him."*)

In Triangular Park the four boys walked over to the sleeping Negro and formed a screen. Koslow was facing his feet, which were bare.

Koslow struck a match and approached a flame to the man's soles, but he did not wake up. Then Koslow lit a cigarette and touched that to the bare brown feet.

(*"What made you use a lit cigarette on this Negro's feet before you took him down to that pier?"*

A. "Big gag.")

At the trial, then, Assistant D.A. DeMeo asked Trachtenberg what the Negro did or said. Trachtenberg said that he raised himself half up from the bench, suddenly. "What did he say then?" Trachtenberg, the quiet, subdued, handsome boy, then let out a scream that splintered the courtroom air and was followed by shuddering silence.

So the Negro screamed, he said, and Koslow urged the boys to hit him. The two youngest, he said, himself and Lieberman, demurred. Whether Mittman beat Menter then is not clear. What is clear is that Koslow told the Negro: "Put on your shoes and get up and come with us." And the Negro, scared of this menacing wall of youths and the tone of Koslow's command, put on his shoes and stood up. Koslow and Mittman then flanked him and the three proceeded toward the river, the Negro weaving and staggering, the boys steadying and propelling him on their five-block walk to the pier in the shadow of Williamsburg Bridge.

The two younger boys had asked the older ones at the park where they were going, and when they were told it was the waterfront ("*So we could bang him around in private*") they hung back, apprehensive. According to Trachtenberg, they split up then for a while until curiosity got the better of them and they went to the pier.

Koslow has told what happened on that soft night, with the water slapping under the barges and at the sides of the rotting pier.

"*He [Mittman] hit him with either a right or a left . . . The bum put his arm up to his face, doubled over and laid sideways over the board that separated the pier from the water. I bent over to punch him. I brought that punch up from the floor. As I was about to land the punch he was in the water, either he slipped or fell. By that I mean he was ducking the punch . . . just as he hit the water, he put his hands forward like this. He didn't just crash into it. Then I saw him in midstream.*"

"I saw him come up twice and go down again," said Mittman.

Trachtenberg and Lieberman were then standing at a barricade about fifty or a hundred feet back of the pier. ("*They did not have the hatred we did,*" said Koslow.) Then Trachtenberg heard Mittman's voice calling "Hey,

83

Bob! Come over here!" and then again, "Hey, Bob, you know what Koslow did? He pushed a man in the water!"

Then, according to Trachtenberg, Koslow came up again and said, "Man's in the water, boys." And young Lieberman said, "Why did you do it?" and then Koslow said, "Now we're all murderers!" and told them to keep quiet. Otherwise, he said, I will get the chair, you [Mittman] will get life, and you two [Trachtenberg and Lieberman] will get five years apiece.

After this they were very quiet and stopped talking about it as they walked home, the younger ones separating from the other two and getting home shortly before midnight. "The river," . . . said Lieberman, "I couldn't sleep all night."

At about five that morning the police came to both. Koslow, arraigned on charges of beating up Kostyra earlier that night, had told of this later event. Mittman was picked up with Koslow.

The parents sat in the courtroom and listened to this day after day, although not all of them every day. On two different occasions Mr. Mittman and Mrs. Koslow collapsed and were taken away. But usually Mr. and Mrs. Koslow sat together, apart from the other parents, and Mrs. Mittman sat next to Mr. and Mrs. Lieberman.

Mrs. Koslow is small with bleached hair. Her face is tight and rather empty, and she wears glasses. She bears no resemblance to her son. But Koslow's father's face is the aging matrix of his son's: the same shape of head and bones, but crushed and sagging with grief.

Mr. and Mrs. Mittman might be the couple who run the cleaning shop or the stationer's next door. They are short, well dressed, self-respecting in manner. They seem like good people, and such is their reputation. The mother has given the son her features, but while they are pleasing in her they are only coarse and immature in him. Mrs. Mittman's face was controlled in court, but blurred by nightly tears.

Mr. and Mrs. Lieberman, too, look like good people, quiet and middle-class. Mrs. Lieberman is a strong woman, broad-boned and east European in feature, while her husband, bald and myopic, seems mild and complaisant.

Again and again at the trial one looked at these parents and asked—as they ask themselves—what had they done to produce such issue as these? What had they failed to do?

Koslow's attorney, State Senator Fred G. Moritt, was unusual in his role of lawyer and seeker after justice. Dressed like a song writer (he is a successful one and a member of A.S.C.A.P.), theatrical in his many objections and interpolations, he seemed a little out of place in a court otherwise imbued by Judge Hyman Barshay's uncompromising dignity.

Basing his defense of Koslow on "mischief," Moritt struck an odd note as he wound up his summation by reading to the jury a verse of his own contriving (based on "Ten Little Indians"):

Four little bad boys off on a spree,
One turned state's evidence, and then there were three.
Three little bad boys, what did one do?
The Judge said, "No proof" and then there were two.
Two little bad boys, in court they must sit
And pray to the Jury, "Please, please acquit."

No one in the courtroom smiled except Moritt and Koslow.

Before this, Moritt had deplored the death of Menter, vagrant though he was, by intoning the words of another poet, John Donne: "Any man's death diminishes me . . ."

It was implied during the trial that the death of Willard Menter did not diminish society. Menter ran a blower in a secondhand burlap-bag factory, surely a lowly pursuit; and his only happiness seemed to consist in occasional binges that he would sleep off on park benches. The best that was said of him was spoken by his brother: "Willie, he'd drink a little bit, but he didn't start no fights." His life was without much sense and his death was without any sense. But it is precisely the senselessness of his death that makes this crime both terrible and important, throwing into blinding focus the one great question not only of the trial but of the time: WHY DID THEY DO IT?

It was the law's concern to establish whether they did it and how they did it, not why. And when it had been shown to the jury's satisfaction that Jack Koslow and Melvin Mittman had caused the death of Willard Menter, the law had done its part. At the end of the

85

trial nothing was known of these boys because nothing was asked.

Outside the courtroom, though, one man in particular did ask questions. He was Dr. Frederic Wertham, who was senior psychiatrist for the Department of Hospitals in New York City from 1932 to 1952, directing the mental-hygiene clinics at Bellevue Hospital and Queens Hospital Center. Dr. Wertham, who has published two books on juvenile delinquency, *The Show of Violence* and *Seduction of the Innocent* (the influence of comic books on today's youth), was called in by the court to determine whether Jack Koslow could plead legal insanity. After examination of Koslow, Wertham's findings on this point were negative: The boy knew what he had done and was aware of right and wrong—for others, at least. Neither the court nor Koslow's counsel, Moritt, went further. Legal insanity was out, and that was that.

But Wertham went further. He got permission from Judge Barshay to examine Koslow as much as he wished before the trial, and the psychiatrist spent many hours with the boy, gaining his confidence. Since he believes that the violation of this confidence is not only permissible in such special circumstances, but might be helpful in the interests of truth, Wertham has told this writer the essence of these interviews. What follows is a paraphrase of Wertham's notes and comments on Koslow.

Koslow is a very intelligent boy: well read, well spoken, with a glibness that is enormously persuasive. ("His intelligence is like a knife without a handle. . . .") By his own admission, he has been able to talk anybody into anything.

He is the only son of a middle-class family intent, as most Americans are, on improving their place in the world. The Koslows lived first on the lower East Side of Manhattan, then moved to the Williamsburg section of Brooklyn and finally to Flatbush, where Koslow's father is an industrious and skilled auto mechanic. Their son has never suffered privation, but he has always hated his father and oriented himself toward his doting mother. He claims that his father has beaten him often, and it is Wertham's impression that this may well be true, the older Koslow goaded beyond endurance by his abnormal and unrewarding son.

The first overt sign of this abnormality came at seven, when Koslow was referred to the Bureau of Child Guidance as being too difficult to handle, both at school and at home. Dr. Harry Gilbert, the supervisor of psychiatrists for this board, said that he was found to be "aggressive and subject to fantasies about killings." He had also a vociferous love of the Nazis, expressed partly by crying "Heil Hitler!" in class. This was in 1942, when the Nazis were at their crest; and Koslow told Wertham that his love of fascism and force, of irresistible brutality, of a supreme "elite," started then.

He was examined by Dr. Abram Blau, among others, at the Bureau. Dr. Blau, a psychiatrist of the highest reputation, reported that the child had been disturbed from early childhood and strongly recommended treatment.

According to Gilbert, Koslow was given four treatments, and his parents were interviewed by the Bureau. But then Mrs. Koslow became ill and took the boy out of school for a month, and when he returned she told the Bureau not to continue the treatments.

Koslow remembers Blau well. He told Wertham he wished his father had been like Blau.

The boy was physically very under par: He had all the childhood diseases and at nine trouble with his legs —a systemic swelling and weakness that, he says, handicapped and depressed him.

In all his contacts, at school or at home, Koslow was argumentative, domineering, discontented. He could get on with others only if he could influence them; and as he found it difficult to influence his teachers he was constantly at loggerheads with them in spite of his high I.Q. (at nine, 135) and his genuine scholastic abilities. Because of these he was put in a class for "gifted children" in high school, but instead of being gratified by this distinction he resented keenly what he referred to as being "put apart"—isolated even more from his fellows.

Koslow got through high school in three years, graduating at sixteen. During this time he had also managed to teach himself German, the language of his idols.

In 1952 he went to New York University to take a dental course at the urging of his mother, but he was so obviously intractable that the university authorities sent him to the Testing and Advisement Center, one of the best clinics in the country, for psychiatric examination. There another eminent man, Dr. Wallace Gobetz, reported that Koslow was either psychotic or on the verge of psychosis, and sent him to Dr. J. Allison Montagu, who made a diagnosis of "incipient schizophrenia," recommending intensive treatment.

The youth's parents, dismayed and angry that their son was virtually suspended from the university because of his alleged condition, took him instead to a private psychiatrist who signed a report testifying that there was nothing wrong with Koslow and that he should be accepted at N.Y.U. for further courses. In February, 1953, the youth spent another very brief period at the university and got along so badly that he left of his own accord. "I was a failure," he said.

Subsequently he went to work, holding about six different jobs for brief periods. There was always something wrong with the job, he said. He found fault with every thing and everyone. And from June, 1954, onward, Koslow was one of the unemployed, sleeping much of the day, roaming much of the night, hunting for bums.

"I'm a fascist," Koslow told Wertham simply. "I always have been. I'm a fascist and a white supremacist. Everybody is, really. That's all the talk you hear around anyway. . . . Violence? It's everywhere. All I'm interested in is violence—destruction—death." These were his actual words.

He told Wertham (whose identity he was not told) that he was an addict of horror comics. "There's some guy," he said, "a psychiatrist—who keeps saying they have a bad effect on kids. I read about it in the *Reader's Digest*. Listen—I could tell that guy something!"

Wertham told Koslow he was "that guy" and the boy seemed amused. On one of his visits Wertham brought him a paper-covered set of "Nights of Horror," in fourteen thin volumes. "Is this the sort of thing you read?" he asked. Koslow leafed through them and nodded. "That's it. Only I have a better edition."

For the benefit of those who have not seen the publications, they constitute what Wertham calls "the pornography of violence." The illustrations are chiefly concerned with voluptuous women in a minimum of suggestive underwear being tortured in a variety of ways: bull-whipped, burned with cigarettes, strangled

88

with wire, and so forth. They in turn inflict certain elaborate punishments on men, of a clearly sexual nature. The text is cigar-store Spillane, more explicit in its sadism, more viciously saccharine in its "romantic" passages.

"Nights of Horror" might leave the mature adult with no other reaction but disgust. What it might do to the immature—even the "normal" immature—is anybody's guess. In any case, it is a fact that Koslow and his companions have tried most of the refinements in the series. He even told Wertham that they had made one of their beating victims kiss their feet in between blows and kicks, a scene clearly illustrated in "Nights of Horror." "It is hardly something," said Wertham, "that a boy would do spontaneously—that is, without getting the idea from somewhere."

"Nights of Horror" has now been banned, but thousands of copies are still circulating, under counters and in private collections.

Koslow had in his room a collection of bull whips. One of them, for which he paid $3.75, he ordered through an advertisement in a comic book, either "Uncanny Tales" or "Journey into Mystery." He also carried a switch-blade knife which he got from a schoolmate who bought it through a comic book. Under the new comic-book code, such advertisements are banned, although this does not mean that the supply houses no longer exist.

Koslow owned a "costume" consisting of black pants, black boots, black shirt, black jacket, and black gloves in which he acted his role of "vampire" at night. Sometimes he wore them all; on the night of the Menter killing, he wore the black pants. The vampire suit is an old standby in horror comics, merely a more sinister version of the tight over-all ritualistic uniform of the superman, good or evil.

In Koslow's statement to Detective Duggan when he was taken to the pier to identify Menter's body, he said (of the moment after Menter was in the water): *"I just saw the belly float—float."* (In a comic book, a thug who has just watched a victim drown says, "Makes a pretty bubble, doesn't it?")

Koslow and Mittman were ostensibly a loyal and devoted pair. When they heard the jury's verdict of first-degree murder with recommendation of life imprisonment, and Koslow groaned and Mittman wept, Koslow put his arm around the other boy. The two seemed to function as mind and body, Koslow doing the planning and direction, Mittman—usually shy and quiet—the rough stuff. Koslow himself did virtually none of the fighting.

"*He* likes crime comics," said Koslow with amused contempt of his partner. "You know, 'Superman' and all that." Crime-comic addiction was clearly of a lower order than horror addiction—kid stuff.

Although several psychiatrists who have never seen the boys announced respectively at the time of their arrests that they were either rapists or homosexuals or both, Wertham finds no evidence to support either claim. He says Koslow is sexually underdeveloped and misdeveloped, that none of the boys were really concerned with sex even when they talked of girls. What bound the four together was a compulsion to watch other people in agony.

They also needed to assert superiority, to "Be Somebody." Mittman said he punched bums because it made him "feel big and strong." Koslow said, "I had to do it to preserve my individuality."

According to Wertham, Koslow is primarily a masochist, both perpetrator and victim in an equation too complex for discussion here. Yet Wertham believes he could have been "saved" and his energies and talents channeled into constructive outlets had he availed himself of the advice and treatment offered him from the age of six onward. He might never have been a "success" or a whole man or an attractive human being. But he need never have been a threat to society, Wertham thinks.

The other three boys—Mittman, Lieberman, and Trachtenberg—appear to have no psychiatric history at all. Yet no one knows how many girls they have horse-whipped or how many "bums" besides the ones publicized they have kicked and beaten. Both Lieberman and Trachtenberg face trial in the death of Ulrickson.

In the files of the police department and in the memories of seasoned police officers, crimes such as theirs were virtually unknown before the Second World War. Exceptions like the Leopold and Loeb case only proved the rule. Boys under eighteen may have killed out of sudden rage or performed acts of violence, but boys under eighteen from "good homes" did not torture and kill for pleasure. This is something new. And it is something that exists on a greater scale than we dream of: The partners Youth and Brutality have pushed the delinquency rate in this country to an all-time high.

No informed and responsible person will say that the roots of this epidemic of violence are horror comics or crime comics or gangster movies or crime plays on television or the crime-laden tabloids. But a number of informed and responsible people say that their cumulative effect on young minds may be an important factor. Certainly a hundred boys could read "Nights of Horror" or "Uncanny Tales" and commit no acts of violence. But who is there to say that the hundred and first, as sick as Koslow, as weak as Lieberman, might not? If there is indeed a virus of violence abroad (and the evidence is enormous), then should it not be located and controlled like any disease, for the protection of the susceptible—and of society itself?

Who is there to say, further, that constant exposure to violence and brutality does not in the end weaken the immunity of the "immune," so that violence becomes familiar and therefore acceptable? The police will tell you that to many delinquents nowhere nearly as sick as Koslow, violence is the natural order of things. "It's all around . . ."

It is not up to the courts to solve the why of this particular Brooklyn murder or of others destined to be committed by the young. It is up to society.

We must find ways to prevent the stupidity or ignorance or fear of parents who, seeing the danger signals flown, do not heed them.

We must find the causes of this susceptibility in the young, this vacuum that can be filled with violence, this boredom than can be relieved by the suffering of others. What is it that they miss and do not have? Why is action equated with destruction, adventure with death?

Koslow and Mittman, they say, went to the Synagogue. Trachtenberg and Lieberman liked books and music. But where did ethics come in, or a simple regard for life?

We must find out if the backwash of the last great war has left this wrack; whether killing for cause is a prelude to or preparation for killing without cause.

These are some of the questions we must ask ourselves, so that before there is much more time for this horror, we can act on the answers.

Elizam—A Reminiscence of Childhood in Ceylon

BY T. TAMBIMUTTU

Elizam had no choice in the matter. Her wishes, her own decision to dispose of her future as she wanted, if she had thought about it at all, had not been given a moment's thought by anybody. I was only a child, but people were always asking me what I wanted to be when I grew up, and they seemed to be very much interested when I replied "a doctor" or "an engineer." I had that freedom of choice, but Elizam had not, and it made me furious.

Although she was ten years older than I was, I felt that I understood her, and I was sure that Elizam did not wish to leave us. But the fate that had seemingly blessed her two elder sisters had now overtaken her, and she looked miserable on the morning she was married. Her big eyes, framed by long lashes, had lost their usual brilliance.

She was dressed as I had never seen her before. A gay wedding sari had replaced the simple bodice and sarong she had worn ever since I could remember. Rubies set in gold hung from her ears. Gold bangles tinkled at her wrists. Around her neck she wore the traditional gold ornaments—a choker with pendant, a triple gold chain, and the *thali* or wedding necklace. The jewelry had been given as a dowry by my mother. Elizam would have been given more if she had been married off in our village like her sisters. They had received cottages on Grandfather-with-the-Beard's estate for as long as it belonged to our family, as well as the right to farm a bit of the land.

For Elizam Mother provided only clothes and jewelry. It was sufficient that Mother had found her a husband who could support her and her children. Elizam's chocolate complexion was not popular in the marriage market, so that even a poor farmer was a "catch" on which Mother congratulated herself. But Elizam did not seem grateful.

I hated the bridegroom as soon as I set eyes on him. He

was a *chuvvalai*, or fair-complexioned man, not much taller than Elizam, who was big for a Ceylonese girl. He arrived in his bullock cart from his farm at Kantalai, about twenty miles from Trincomalee, to have a look at Elizam before giving his consent. I could tell from the way Elizam hid in the kitchen and refused to come out that she didn't want to get married.

Mother called to the girl several times as if she had some household task for her, but Elizam knew there was a suitor around the place and wouldn't emerge. Then Mother asked me to call her, but Elizam knew that I had been put up to it.

When it was time for tea, it was her cousin Sita who served it. Elizam still hid in the kitchen, and no amount of threats from Mother could make her come out. But Mother was not really angry. She was hugely amused at Elizam's shyness, a natural and proper attribute of a bride-to-be. But Elizam was not just being coy. She didn't want to get married at all. She had been with us most of her life—in Atchuvely, in Singapore, and in Malaya—and she wanted to stay on.

The farmer could have peeped into the kitchen, but that would have been undignified. It is not really necessary to see a bride before marriage. If she is seen at all, it is only by accident—at most an accident that had been staged by one of the parties. The farmer waited patiently, however, chewing his betel leaf and tobacco as if he belonged to the house.

I can't remember what eventually brought Elizam out. It may have been the arrival of the vegetable or oil seller. Anyway the farmer saw her full, strapping figure by the kitchen door—the kitchen was a separate building—and he went away well content, having given his promise. He may not even have noticed the beautiful molding of her oval face.

When Elizam got married she was saying good-by to her childhood. Like her sisters and cousins, she must have joined us when she was two or three. Her parents and the parents of her cousins lived in cottages on Grandfather-with-the-Beard's estate in Atchuvely village. Their children were sent into the service of my grandfather or that of his children up in Trincomalee. If they received any pay at all, it was sent to their parents, but they had a comfortable home and as soon as they reached the age of seventeen or eighteen were married off with a small dowry. That was one duty we had toward them.

Elizam called us by our own names, which was forbidden our other servants. Though she did not attend school, as we did, it was she who dressed us for school. She saw to it that we got there safe and was always there by the school gates at four to see us home again. In the mornings, between classes, she or her cousin Sita brought our glasses of milk.

She rubbed our bodies with sesame oil on Saturdays and then bathed us after we had run about under the morning sun for an hour or two. Earlier in the day she had boiled limes, *cheekakai* pods, and bassia meal. She shampooed our hair with the mixture and then rubbed in the limes. The rinses left our hair softer and glossier than any patent shampoo could have done. It was she who arranged our visits to the harbor and the various beaches of Trincomalee. Once a year when we camped in the jungle at Madhu or Paalai Oothu, it was she who slept with us beside the campfire. When the wild boar was brought in, it was Elizam who broiled the first pieces, though she was not the regular cook, and she always gave me the largest piece. She packed parcels of the meat to send to relatives and dried the rest under the sun. When we brought back birds from our shoots she cooked them for us, or when we brought green mangoes that we had stoned down from a nearby grove she secretly dressed them with salt and chili for a relish which we loved dearly but which was forbidden by Mother.

She was always preparing surprises for us. As we dug into our dinner of rice and several curries, with her fond voice coaxing us on, we would come across all kinds of delicacies hidden under the rice—eggs, chicken legs, fried shrimps, cuttlefish or roe, soft-shelled crabs, stuffed bitter gourd, fried wild boar, fish baked in ashes, meat wrapped in leaves, or a quail so tiny that you could eat its wafer-thin bones.

Elizam was the household expert on the preparation of that king of soups we called *kool*, whose only occidental equivalent I can think of is Provençal bouillabaisse. This main-dish soup is a north Ceylon specialty, and Elizam knew all its village mysteries.

On our family's *kool* day, a day to which we looked forward because there were no tiresome solid chunks of meat and vegetable to eat, Elizam superintended all the stages of its preparation, from the buying of fish to its eating. It was her special day in the kitchen. The matrix of the soup was made of a flour ground from the plumules of palmyra seeds. In it floated grains of rice and bright red stars of chili. Into the pot went tiny dried and fresh fish, medium pink fish and medium blue fish, small crabs, large crabs quartered, fillets of more fish along with their heads, the chestnuts of the jack fruit, the crisp fleshly jacket of jack seeds, tiny immature jack fruit cut into wedges, large "double shrimps," and the leaves of a certain creeper with red fruit that had a special rough texture which was delightful to chew.

In Trincomalee we always ate the soup out of bowls, but the way Elizam served it back in Atchuvely village was out of individual cups made of the glaucous jack leaf. Elizam herself took charge of the pot, ladling it out with her long shapely arm, her blue-black hair done into a very large bun at the back. Even Mother, who often superintended our dinners, left the *kool* ceremony to Elizam.

Another village ritual perpetuated by Elizam in our urban surroundings was eating the pulp off the large palmyra seeds after they had been dipped in a weak solution of tamarind. It is a messy but delightful business. For the poor of the village it was sufficient dinner. When we went on hikes with the Boy Scouts she gave us parcels of *kattu choru*. Cooked eggs, meats, fish, vegetables, and rice were wrapped and pinned with a palm sliver in banana leaf and placed in a palm-leaf basket. The banana leaf, which cooked in the slow heat of the food inside it, flavored everything delicately. We also loved her *palanchoru*, which is cooked rice left overnight in water and made into balls filled with delicacies like shrimp or turtle meat. The proper way to eat it is off a small banana leaf held in the right hand.

Then there were Elizam's *pattchadis*. Between her cousin Sita and herself, all the *pattchadis* of Atchuvely were made available for our table. *Pattchadi* of bananas, *pattchadi* of eggplants, *pattchadi* of dried fish or

95

shrimps, all baked in ashes, *pattchadis* of green ginger, neem flowers, lotus roots, banana inflorescences and their purple spathes, hibiscus blooms, heart of banana stem, portulacas, edible leaves of weeds, and tender stems of *pirandaithandu* creepers.

All this was now about to end. Elizam's younger sister Innesu, who had been brought up in Grandfather-with-the-Beard's household, had come up to take her place, but things would never be the same again without Elizam. Her father, who had come up from the village, was hilarious with the many guests. He was tipsy on arrack. But her mother was crying quietly, and I could see that Elizam would cry too before long. She was a wife now, this was her going-away party, but she looked very upset.

As is usual in Ceylonese weddings, the men were in the drawing room and the women in another part of the house. Being only eight, I was allowed to wander from one part of the house to the other. The men who liked a drink took trips to the small bar almost hidden away in a corner. That is also a tradition—to do the drinking away from the general company so as not to give offense.

The whole house was reeking with the pungent odor of black Jaffna cheroots. Many of the guests were hardened smokers from the north, including Elizam's mother, who smoked her own home-grown in a clay pipe. The teetotalers dug into the plates of tidbits and slaked their thirst with quantities of lime juice and carbonated water.

The time was drawing near for Elizam's departure. The *koorai*, or special wedding sari (which would become an heirloom), was carried in on a brass tray by my mother and offered to each guest in turn, who touched it with the right hand for good luck.

After I touched Elizam's sari I went to the study room and opened my desk. I wrote in Tamil on a sheet of paper: "Dear Elizam, Come back to see us soon. Thurairajah." I went to my mother's room and saw the *koorai* sari on the brass tray on the side table. I took a pin out of the sewing box and pinned my note on one of the inside folds. Elizam was bound to find it the first time she wore the sari.

The bridegroom had now drawn up his cart and two bullocks in front of the house. Accompanied by the women, Elizam came out and got into the front seat. There were tears in her eyes.

The bridegroom cracked his stick and the bullock cart creaked up the rose-pink gravel road on which the sun lay like golden coins. My brothers and I and our neighbors the Wambeek boys ran behind the rattling cart as far as the first crossroads. Through the thatch roof of the cart we saw Elizam turn around to have a last look at us. She did not wave.

I can't even remember whether we lit Chinese fire-crackers at Elizam's wedding. Maybe we did.

I think I may have gone to bed with a book and no lunch that afternoon, as I usually did when I wished to protest against anything. That was a last resort to have my own way, and somehow it usually improved matters. If I did do this on Elizam's wedding day, I feel sure that I did it with no other motive than to mark the occasion with personal regret, as on the day our dog Luxmi died.

On the following Sunday, the second day after Elizam's wedding, there was the rumble of cartwheels outside our house at lunch time. When I went to the front door to see who it could be, Elizam rushed up and folded me in her arms and kissed me, a thing I can never remember her doing before. Her husband was standing by the cart smiling sheepishly.

There was tremendous excitement in the house at Elizam's return, with all of us tumbling around her and her sister Innesu full of smiles. Mother looked puzzled and she asked Elizam's husband what the matter was.

Apparently Elizam had found my note when she was dressing in her *koorai* sari to pay her first visit to the local church. She had burst into tears, and nothing would console her. She wanted to return to Trincomalee at once. Her husband had no choice but to drive her down at once the twenty miles in his bullock cart. That was how we happened to see Elizam in her *koorai* sari. She looked wonderful.

Elizam spent that day with us and promised to return to see us, which she did often. We were even taken one day to see her at her home in Kantalai near the famous irrigation tank built by King Aggabodhi II in A.D. 601. It was full of crocodiles. All the birds of creation seemed to be at Kantalai—teals, cormorants, Indian darters, and flights of terns, snipe, flycatchers, flamingoes, wild duck, waterfowl, minivets, peacocks, gay-colored jungle fowl, the solitary pelican, sunbirds, tailorbirds, golden orioles, bluejays, jungle crows, coucals, hawks of all sizes, bee-eaters, *buttagoias*, and all the kingfishers—river, giant, pied, and stork-billed. Truly it was a beautiful place to live in.

That day Elizam cooked for us her famous *kool* in her tidy thatched cottage, with jack fruit from her own tree, palmyra shoots from her own beds, and rice from her own fields, but we did not know then it would be our last. She died soon after in childbirth.

Elizam's sister, who looked very much like her, grew more dear to us as the years passed. Today we are as fond of her as we were of Elizam. She too was married off at the age of eighteen. But at that time we were much older and better able to appreciate the festivity of the occasion.

I distinctly remember that we did light Chinese fire-crackers at Innesu's wedding.

NOT SO FAR AHEAD

The Age of the Thinking Robot,
and What It Will Mean to Us

BY ROBERT BENDINER

Probably not since Dr. Freud reached the crest of his
popularity has the public been treated to a flow of
synthetic words as glittering and bewildering as those
now being poured out by the prophets of the new industrial technology. Literature on the subject, which is
piling up by the ton, is often rounded out with a glossary
for the layman, and one enterprising firm has actually
issued a little dictionary of the jargon, from "automation," the sacred key word, through "cybernetics" to
"servomechanism" and beyond.

It is perhaps too much to expect precision in this new
argot when the concepts, especially of automation itself,
are still so varied and the inferences drawn from them
are so dazzlingly at odds with each other. Take automation—at the broadest of its dozen definitions—to mean
the operation of a productive system without human operators or hardly any, and you will discover from a bewildering day's reading that "The automatic factory and
even the automatic office are coming nearer to reality
[but] as in the past, these changes will of course be
gradual. . . ."—Haldon A. Leedy, Illinois Institute of
Technology. Then again, "Automation will mushroom
. . . we want it to mushroom . . . we couldn't stop it
even if we wanted to. It will bring great change to all
of us."—Gordon S. Brown, Massachusetts Institute of
Technology. Or, more to your taste if you are in a hurry,
"The automatic factory is not merely coming. It is already here."—National Association of Manufacturers.
But, strangely, "There are no such factories and no such
machines, nor will there ever be. . . ."—Benjamin F.
Fairless, United States Steel Corporation.

You will learn from John Diebold, editor of *Automatic
Control,* that automation is "a pattern that will have
more meaning for our individual lives and for our collective future than the double-mushroom shape of atomic
explosions." You will learn from this same Mr. Diebold,
who is something of a high priest in the movement, that

99

its "probable impact upon the economy has been greatly exaggerated." To the United States Chamber of Commerce, the whole thing is just a "bogeyman conjured up by the collectivists to replace an unpromising bogey named 'Economic Collapse.'"

In such swampy terrain it behooves the observer to move with caution, but on the basis of what has already occurred, it takes no unusual rashness to report that major changes are in fact taking place in American manufacturing, processing, and office work. They are changes of such scope and nature that, as we shall see, it is fatuous to regard them merely as extensions of the technological progress we have known for a century. Add to them the imminent introduction of atomic power into private industry, and it becomes startlingly probable that, war or no war, the United States of 1970 will no more resemble our present society than it resembles Andrew Jackson's.

What is there in automation that takes it out of the normal stream of mechanical progress and gives it an entirely new dimension? Unlike individual machines that have revolutionized only their own industries, automation calls for a basic change along the whole productive front. It is comparable, not to the linotype in printing or the Bessemer process in steel, but to such historic concepts as mass production itself, concepts that revolutionized whole economies and made sweeping changes in the social structure.

Where the first Industrial Revolution substituted machinery on a vast scale for human and animal muscle, the second promises on a comparable scale to substitute machinery for the human brain—not at top levels, of course, but in the normal run of the productive process. Since James Watt put steam to work, men have labored at their separate machines, feeding them, guiding them, correcting them, timing their operations, and in general controlling their work at every stage of the procedure. Today automated equipment, given advance instructions by punch cards or recording tape, can process raw materials, assemble the parts, correct its own errors, reject or rework parts that do not measure up to specifications, and even inspect the finished product, the linked chain of machines operating as an integrated whole and controlled by a central electronic brain.

Considering the enormous possibilities in automation, both industry and labor are approaching with a caution that borders on the jitters what an N.A.M. booklet archly calls "the fairyland of the world to come." Captains of industry who fear that the very word "automation" will prompt organized labor to painful demands tend at times to belittle the whole development, while at other times they revel in its promise of low-cost abundance. In the same way, trade-union chiefs have one eye hopefully trained on the coming era of plenty and the other cautiously fixed on the more imminent possibility of technological unemployment.

Mr. Fairless and countless other preachers on the subject never tire of pointing out that, far from being new or strange, automation goes back at least to the flour mill that one Oliver Evans operated near Philadelphia in 1784—a system of conveyors run by water power in which the grain was picked up, carried through several grinding operations, and delivered as finished flour. Punch cards? No newer, they point out, than the player piano and Jacquard's loom.

True enough, these were remarkable devices in their day, but they no more rob of significance this second Industrial Revolution now upon us than the wheel and the lever can be said to have taken the edge off the first. For automation at its fullest is not merely the existence of separate machines, however automatic, but the controlled operation of an entire factory or process in which the machines, as linked units, automatically perform their manipulations in specified sequences, with electronic judgment substituted for the perception of the machinist or foreman. With complete automation, operators disappear from the scene, leaving huge and highly productive plants to be manned only by a maintenance crew and a few engineers to set the equipment and check the dials for trouble signals.

Only a few factories are completely or nearly automated, but even a cursory survey will reveal the deep inroads that have already been made.

Naturally enough, it is in the production of dangerous war materials that automation has had its most complete workout. In Bedford, Ohio, a chemical company turns out a monthly quota of 650,000 pounds of napalm, the jellied gasoline used in incendiary bombs. On any

101

given shift the entire plant, ten thousand square feet in area, is operated by four men and a supervisor, whose jobs consist mostly of maintenance. Automatic-control panels regulate the flow of ingredients, and a sequential interlocking of motors and conveyors does the rest. Production costs are fifty-nine per cent lower than with the conventional method.

Similarly, 155-mm. shells are turned out for the government by United States Industries, Inc., in an automatic factory at Rockford, Illinois. "It is impressive," says the corporation's president, "to watch this tremendous plant operating and to listen to the sounds of the metal being worked in so many ways at such a rapid pace, to see the whole operation being conducted through stations throughout the plant, full of blinking lights and clicking relays, attended by one or two men at each station."

Automation has made most headway in industries most readily reduced to a continuous-flow process—such as oil refining, flour milling, and chemical production.

"A man may work for months on a pipeline or in a refinery or even in the production fields," says an official of the Oil Workers Union, "and never see nor touch oil." To be sure, refineries have been highly automatic for many years, ever since the laborious method of distilling oil in batches was abandoned. But automatic production is not the same as automation, and it might be well at this point to state the most essential difference.

In a word the difference is *feedback*. Not to make a mystery of it, feedback is a technique for self-correction. An outfielder chasing a fly ball constantly corrects his speed and direction as his mind estimates and re-estimates the location at which the ball will descend. That is feedback with a human mind giving the orders. When a ship is set to steer a certain course, the steering mechanism will automatically swing to starboard if the ship veers too far to port, and vice versa. That is feedback with an automatic compass giving the orders. In automated equipment an electronic brain constantly compares variables in the work being done—temperature, speed, thickness, or whatever—with a set of given specifications, continuously correcting the machinery to which it is linked until precisely the prescribed conditions are met, down to the finest tolerances.

102

It is this tremendous advance that is at the heart of true automation, making it possible in refineries for a few skilled workers to sit at a master-control panel and watch the equipment itself guide crude oil through various intricate steps until it emerges as gasoline or some other petroleum product. An industry spokesman says that a refinery that employs eight hundred people without modern instrumentation could do the same job with twelve people if instrumentation were utilized to the fullest possible extent.

Solids are harder to handle, but some of the most complex problems were solved by the time the Ford Motor Company opened its much-publicized engine plant near Cleveland three years ago. Here six-cylinder engine blocks are turned out by the union of an electronic brain, fed by twenty-seven miles of wire, and forty-two mechanical hands in the form of automatic machine units. Through this giant complex, 1,545 feet long, rough castings are pushed, pulled, turned in every direction, conveyed, and subjected to cutting, drilling, honing, milling, boring, and broaching in more than five hundred manless operations, each one checked and inspected only by the "brain" itself for performance and accuracy. Thoroughly instructed in advance, it decides when a block is ready for the grinder, how fine it is to be ground, and where it is to move when it is done. A block that once took nine hours to complete is now sped through in fifteen minutes.

Where it once took thirty-nine men working twenty-nine machines just to drill the necessary oil holes in a crankshaft, only nine men are needed for that job at the new Ford plant. Most of the small crew lost in the acre of machinery stand by and watch, and replace worn tools whenever a "toolmeter" panel flashes the signal that some particular instrument is approaching the end of its usefulness. "Ours is the only foundry in the world," says the manager proudly, "where the molding sand used to make castings is never touched by human hands except maybe out of curiosity."

Perhaps laboring the obvious, a Ford spokesman is quoted by Walter Reuther as saying, "Automation reduces labor tremendously. Our experience has shown that we can count on a reduction of twenty-five to thirty per cent in what we call 'direct' labor." No men were laid off as a result of this stride in automation simply because it was an addition to existing plant, established in a period of expanding production.

Most automation men agree that the electronic displacement of humans will go farthest and fastest in the office. There, according to a leading accountant, "computers are . . . going to be like bulldozers in the construction industry." It took only a short time to realize that electronic brains which could do a year's astronomical computations in a few minutes or speed an anti-aircraft shell to its moving target could be turned from science and war to the requirements of business. Instead of storing its magnetic "memory" with data on velocities, voltages, temperatures, and the like, one had only to feed it information on payroll rates, income-tax data, overtime, Social Security, etc. The result, as scores of users of I.B.M. and Remington Rand computers can already attest, is that these machines now make up the most complex payroll, perform the necessary accounting operations, and, with their own high-speed printers, run off the pay register and make out the checks.

Insurance companies are particularly ripe for this sort of automation. Three of the largest have already gone electronic, with machines like Univac and I.B.M.'s "701" hired to bill customers for premiums, calculate agents' commissions, figure dividends, and work out all the necessary actuarial data. Prudential is counting on its electronic computer to replace sixty to seventy-five other machines along with their operators—two hundred in one department alone.

What the Ford engine plant represents in the way of robot industry, General Electric represents in the field of office automation. In its Major Appliance Division at Louisville, Univac has been assigned to far more than turning out the payroll. Its chief contribution will be in the highly complex work of inventory control. According to W. W. Smith, who serves as Univac's superior, "If the decision is made to increase the production of appliances from one thousand to two thousand per day, Univac within a matter of hours will be able to show the effect on every item of inventory. . . . To do the same job on a manual basis as one part of total manufacturing planning often requires up to three weeks or longer."

To mention all the types of robots already holding down jobs in American industry and business would tax the reader's patience, but the following items will at least suggest the variety of machine talents to be had on the market today:

Baking: You can "tape" cake or bread now by merely inserting the necessary instructions in a machine.

Radios: Thanks to a system for eliminating wire circuits, which require soldering at all contact points, radios can be and are being turned out automatically. Motorola is reported to have a machine that can spit out complete sets once the components are fed into it. Raytheon Manufacturing Company has a chassis-assembly line, geared to a thousand radios a day, that is operated by two employees where standard methods of production would require two hundred. Admiral, working through a gadget called Robot I, can assemble half a television receiver chassis in a matter of seconds.

Tanning: Automatic controls in a big Milwaukee tannery now mix the acids and oils and regulate the drying temperature while conveyors put the hides through various processing machines. One-third of the men do the work formerly required and turn out a better product in less time.

Electric Power: A conventional plant of the Cleveland Electric Illuminating Company employs a hundred men for 290,000 kilowatt-hours of production, but the company's new push-button plant employs twenty-eight men for 420,000 kwh. This is typical for the industry, which turns out five times the electric power it did twenty years ago with only fifteen per cent more personnel. But what has utility workers far more agitated is the prospect of atom-produced electric power in less than ten years. A pilot plant going up right now is expected to need only six men to furnish electricity for the entire City of Pittsburgh.

Telephones: Even in this industry, where electronic automation is as old as the dial system, the innovations are astonishing. Through Direct Distance Dialing, now available to some subscribers, a caller may by fingering a few digits get the services of an electronic long-distance operator. In fifteen seconds the robot will have located the shortest telephone path from, say, New York to Los Angeles, made the connection, and recorded the call for your bill.

While most of the country still regards such reports as good reading of the "ain't-science-wonderful" variety, the blossoming of these marvels has alerted intelligent industrialists, labor leaders, and sociologists to the prospect of great change, with or without a prolonged struggle.

At this stage, it might be said that a strained air of reasonableness prevails, with a good deal of nervous anxiety showing through on both sides. In the National Association of Manufacturers booklet "An Introduction to the Automatic Machine Age," the future is painted in rosy hues, but there will be responsibilities too, "including the responsibilities of industry for . . . the reallocation of man-power to dry up temporary pools of unemployment."

J. Douglas Elliott, a high official of the Detroit Edison Company, concedes with others that "These new brains are going to replace workers—a lot of workers," though in the long run they will create more jobs, shorten working hours, and increase our standard of living. But in spite of these ultimately fair prospects, he adds, "Management men are somewhat ill at ease, too. . . . They are apprehensive about labor problems resulting from mass layoffs and the problems of hiring and training highly skilled technicians to keep their operations going."

At the same time, sterner voices are being raised on the industrial side of the fence. John I. Snyder, Jr., president of United States Industries, Inc., puts it bluntly: "It often has been thought that automation in its ultimate sense in any industrial plant is a desirable goal because it will reduce labor costs. . . . But reduction of labor costs is only a part of the point. Another highly desirable feature of automation in relation to labor is the fact that machines are easier to control than people (and this is a blessing in our democratic society). The more machines the fewer people, and therefore the easier the control problem." Even assuming that Mr. Snyder is talking strictly about mechanical controls, his point remains that the main trouble with labor today is people.

The same general sentiment was voiced at one of *Fortune* magazine's round tables by Dr. J. J. Brown of Aluminium, Ltd.: "Now men by definition are difficult and tricky things to play around with. You have employee-relations men, time-study men; you have training and educational directors; you have personnel men, washroom men, cafeteria men. That all costs money. My point is this: that if we could take some of the money that we are spending in trying to ease the pain of our assembly-line personnel, and apply that money for some research to get the men out of there entirely, we would be far better off in the long run." A sociological note in another issue of the same journal, by the way, reveals that so many of the employees to be supplanted are young women, at least in offices, that engineers have taken to estimating the new machines in terms of "G.P.'s or girl-power displaced."

But probably it is J. J. Jaeger, a Pratt and Whitney official, who has expounded the hardheaded view most candidly: "I don't think we are consciously trying to ease the burden of our workers nor consciously trying to improve their standard of living. These things take care of themselves. They have a feedback of their own that closes the loop automatically. I don't think it is the part, nor can it be the part, of industry to try to plan the social aspects of this thing."

It is precisely this supposition—that some natural law, some self-regulatory process, will automatically take care of any surplus labor—that rouses the fears and suspicions of trade-union leaders. In the long run, society will no doubt adjust itself to the change, just as it did some generations after the beginning of the first Industrial Revolution. But labor is not willing to buy an eventual boost in living standards for all at the cost of any such prolonged suffering as followed Watt's tinkering with a teakettle. "The long run," in Reuther's view, ". . . is not the consideration, for, as Lord Keynes once said, in the long run we are all dead."

Nevertheless, and in spite of what Fairless professes to see as "a great propaganda campaign which is clearly calculated to discourage and retard technological progress," there is absolutely no sign that labor plans to throw *sabots* into the servomechanisms or even to emulate the vain and foolhardy war against canned music in the 1930's. What most trade-union leaders want, and feel strong enough to demand, is a planned transition, with shock absorbers to soften the bumps on the way to the New Abundance.

So far, automation has been marked by no mass layoffs, and indeed the temperate attitude of leading users of advanced equipment has given the industrialists at least a debater's advantage. They point out that while fifty thousand telephone operators have been replaced by the dial system, net employment in the industry has steadily gone up; that General Motors has about doubled its employment since 1940 in spite of increasing use of automatic machinery. According to *Business Week*, Pontiac executives, knowing that "the saving of manpower is a ticklish subject with labor," kept its working force intact, using its new equipment to increase production by twenty-five per cent.

Those industrialists who uneasily concede the possibility of "displacements" quickly fall back on other defense positions. Where mechanization created hazardous and spirit-deadening tasks, making man a degraded servant of the machine, they say that automation will eliminate these jobs, put a premium on technical skill, and upgrade the labor force all along the line.

What's more, they argue, automation will be limited to the very big manufacturers, processors, and offices that can afford the expensive equipment. And finally, like all technological change in the past, it will create new industries and make additional jobs. The automobile gradually retired the blacksmith and the stableman, but look how many jobs it opened up to mechanics, garagemen, rubber workers, motel-keepers, and road-builders!

Obviously there is much that is solid in these arguments, but there is also much that is dangerously hazy and speculative. These weaknesses, which we will consider next, are not lost on those who want to get industry committed now to sharing the blessings of the new technology.

A fifty-seven-year-old hide stripper in a packing house has been relieved of his job, one of the most highly skilled in the business, by a machine that neatly peels off an animal's skin once a semi-skilled workman has made a single incision in the carcass. The veteran employee is not fired. He is simply allowed to work out the few remaining years before his retirement at an inferior job, though his pay may remain the same. Yet the old job classification, with its high rate of pay, is gone from the
108

contract at the next bargaining session with the union, never to reappear. In this year's negotiations with a leading packer, more rates were "bargained out" as a result of new machinery than in the last fifteen years put together. In other industries, too, the individual's chances of being imminently downgraded are greater by far than the reverse prospect, and his eye, reasonably enough, is on the year ahead; not, like that of the sociologist, on the far horizon.

A telephone operator is replaced by a new dial system. She does not show up in the company's statistics as dropped, simply because it had the foresight to hire her as a temporary worker. "For about two years in advance of a particular dial conversion," I was told by Joseph A. Beirne, president of the CIO Communications Workers, "the company will hire new operators only on a so-called 'temporary' basis. They are told they have employment only until the dial cutover is completed." If the operator does have permanent status, the company may offer her a job elsewhere, but, Beirne explains, often this is at a location far removed. "Many take their termination pay, or their pension, and drop out of the labor market or get other jobs" rather than be uprooted.

It is this hidden, creeping type of unemployment that is becoming a source of concern. As one executive candidly concedes, "The person most seriously affected at the moment is the 'employee' not hired."

Just how "seriously affected" is already being indicated in Census Bureau figures. Certainly nation-wide *employment,* in terms of the number who hold down jobs, is rising, but the productivity of our factories and offices is rising so much faster, thanks to technological advance, that the yearly additions to the labor market are not being absorbed, and so *unemployment* too is on the rise. *Life* is led to reflect: "With a total of 2.7 million *not* working, we have been able to turn out *and consume* virtually as much goods as at the record heights of the boom. What this indicates is that the U.S. may be able to produce and consume at boom-time levels yet still have a 'permanent reserve' of unemployment, which may increase."

Will the N.A.M.'s "temporary pools of unemployment" be dried up simply by the increased need for technicians and distributors? Or by newly created industries? Ultimately, no doubt, but the evidence is that without countermeasures they will deepen before they evaporate. For a displaced baker who has no chance of becoming an electronic technician, "ultimately" can be a painfully long time.

There is little reason to believe that electronic equipment will long remain exclusively in the hands of the top corporations. On the contrary, competition is expected to force the smaller outfits to adopt modern methods on pain of either going out of business or merging with the giants. Medium and small computers are already being turned out and sold to moderate-size concerns on the theory that they can take the place of big staffs that such employers never could afford. I.B.M.'s "650" rents for as little as $3,750 a month and does far more than could be done by the equivalent ten clerks whose salaries would come to that amount. When the market for computers is thoroughly exploited and displacements mount in geometric rather than arithmetical proportions, will employers still find spots for supplanted workers, even at reduced pay?

As for jobs in those new industries, labor has its fingers crossed. Electronics manufacturing itself, the fountainhead of automation, should be a haven right now, but the fact is that as far as jobs go, it is already contracting as sharply as the industries it serves, and for the same reason. The Bureau of Labor Statistics testifies that in this field also "employment has not kept pace with production during the past seven years. Electronics output in 1952 was 275 per cent higher than in 1947 but was produced by only 40 per cent more workers." At International Business Machines, which with Remington Rand is the chief source of computers, output per employee has more than doubled in a decade.

Until automation actually forces a far greater leisure for Americans, thereby fostering new businesses and services to cater to that leisure, it is not likely to inspire any tremendous wave of secondary investment. Professors Walter S. Buckingham and Sherman F. Dallas, in a paper on the subject presented to the Southern Economic Association, flatly predict that by its very nature automation "will not make the far-reaching investment impression that the introduction and later improvements in automobiles, railroads, and canals, for example, created."

Granted then that there is at least some reason for apprehension, at least in the short run, what can anyone reasonably expect industry to do about a trend as inevitable as taxes? Far from preparing to ram their heads into a stone wall, labor leaders are set to go along with the big shift—but they want a hand in the proceedings. As long ago as 1948, UAW contracts gave the automobile companies a free hand in introducing technological changes. Reuther is, if anything, more lyrical than the NAM itself when he eyes the prospect of "abundance in terms undreamed of before" and of "vast improvements in the living conditions of the American people." And in the AFL George Meany simply renounces the tradition. "The trade union movement does not oppose technological change." What the AFL wants is severance pay for people displaced by machines, the retraining by management of employees so that they can man the new machines, and, sooner or later, a reduction in hours—a thirty-hour week for all by 1980.

The CIO, especially Reuther's Auto Workers, has spelled out the program of demands in more specific detail. Its argument is pitched to the need for keeping purchasing power high enough to buy the ever-increasing volume of goods that the improved technology can provide. This means higher pay for automated jobs, even though the work is less onerous, and it means the guaranteed annual wage.

Actually it did not take automation to give rise to the notion of the guaranteed annual wage, but the demand for it clearly has been stimulated by the new threat to labor's position. It will not only help stabilize purchasing power, the argument runs, but will also "serve as a regulator of the process of technological change, tending to minimize its disruptive consequences. It will affect management's decisions concerning both the timing and the placement of new automation installations."

And, not least, it will tide over the victimized individual, sometimes lost sight of in a mound of statistics, until he either finds a spot at the work he knows or has trained himself for something else.

Not that the unions think this retraining process should be left wholly to the employee. On the contrary, they are in voluble agreement that management has an obligation to retrain its veteran employees wherever possible rather than turn them out in favor of young technicians fresh from school.

Unquestionably this "upgrading" of the labor force will present one of the great headaches of the next decade. Take it straight from the National Manpower Council:

"Many of today's electricians will have to learn electronics if they are to retain their skilled status. Pipefitters may have to learn hydraulics. A skilled worker who formerly measured with calipers and now uses a micrometer will soon have to learn to work with tolerances measured with light waves . . . there may be almost no place left for the unskilled industrial worker."

The semi-skilled are in every bit as bad a way, according to the industrial-relations editor of *Factory Management and Maintenance*. "The jobs that are 'duck soup' for elimination by automatic production," he says, "are mainly the semi-skilled ones, such as machine operating and materials handling. Some observers believe the factory of the future will go so far as to wipe out this great 'middle class' of industry."

Some will be fortunate enough to acquire these higher skills and avoid supplanting by trained technicians. All major industrial plants have training programs now and will almost certainly expand them. "The factory of the future," one executive says, "may not be a college, but it's going to look more like one than you might think." For those who make the grade it should be a safe, quiet, white-collar haven where, one engineer told a recent convention of steelworkers, he "would not think it facetious if the workmen wore tuxedos on the job." With somewhat less abandon, a workman in a new Ford plant recently made the same point to a newspaper interviewer. He used to go home every evening jittery with exhaustion, he said, but now "I run a whole battery of machines by pushing buttons and reading dials and go home feeling like talking to my family and reading."

Unfortunately, however, the number who will be needed and trained for button pushing and dial reading will be a small fraction of the total force. The rest will have to pin their hopes on the gradualness of the shift to automation, or preferential hiring at plants slowest to make the change, on pensions or unemployment insurance, and ultimately on drastic reduction of the work week.

In the last analysis it is this steady increase of leisure that will have to be relied on to solve the problem of the technologically displaced. And leisure, of course, means paid leisure—something very different from the happy notion of the oil-equipment executive who recently announced that, thanks to automation, "We hope to be able to eliminate the overtime pay we're saddled with." For the six-hour day or the four-day week—ultimately perhaps both—will make a great difference in the way we live and the services we need.

As the number of workers in the productive industries shrinks, the new leisure should require a steady rise in the number engaged in facilitating travel, in offering entertainment, in adult education and cultural activities, in the rebuilding of roads, and in numerous other activities called for by a people who will have twice as much free time on their hands as their grandparents.

Not all the burden for the readjustment, of course, will fall on industry. A drastic overhauling of our educational institutions will be needed to reduce the unskilled to a minimum, if necessary by new teaching techniques; to provide the technicians for the new day; to train the servants of the new leisure; and, not least, to enhance a nation's capacity for leisure, as distinguished from idleness.

Even while the N.A.M. calls for readjustments in curricula to "put greater emphasis on the electrical, mathematical and mechanical sciences," it suggests that "practical education" is no longer adequate. It would be a fatal error "if Americans were transformed into highly specialized cavemen, woefully deficient in the arts and letters." The concept appears to be gaining among industrial and business leaders that as our complexities deepen, technology is not enough. Executives must understand human relations, economics, psychology, and therefore, at last, philosophy, with all that it entails. Witness Bell Telephone's experiment of sending a batch of its top young executives to the University of Pennsylvania for ten months' exposure to the humanities—from Bhagavad Gita to Ezra Pound.

Some sociologists feel that the fear of more leisure is acting as a brake on technological change. In a society rooted in Calvinist doctrine many Americans, David Riesman observes, look upon increased leisure as "a threat, a problem, a burden, or hazard." Diebold thinks the gradualness of the change will permit adjustment on this front, as on others, but he concedes that, barring an all-out war, sooner or later we will have to face the question, "Are we capable of developing a culture that does not depend upon work to give meaning to our lives?"

Depending, again, on the speed of change, government will have to bear a degree, probably a high degree, of responsibility for salvaging those unskilled workers who turn out to be a drug in the labor market. As anti-boondoggle an organ as *Life*, foreseeing trouble, proposes that government "draw a line—perhaps the present line of 2.7 million—above which unemployment will not be allowed to go" before public works now in blueprint are put into concrete. "Fortunately," the magazine points out, "nearly all such measures can be made in capital improvements—new highways, schools, better housing, etc.—which will eventually pay for themselves by what they add to the income and brainpower of the economy."

To this catalogue might be added airports sorely in need of expansion, city redevelopment, and parks, not to mention the need of government aid to prevent the creation of ghost towns by shifting industries.

How fast is automation moving? Some observers think it is moving at a slower rate of speed than the limitations of either technology or economics dictate. But it is coming swiftly enough for all that. The U.S. Chamber of Commerce, which is far from trying to arouse public concern in the matter, solemnly cites predictions of the three-day weekend within the next decade, as against Meany's ultracautious target of 1980.

According to the Stanford Research Institute, factory sales of data-processing equipment, a good index of the advance of automation, rose from zero in 1940 to $25 million in 1953 and are expected to reach $500 million by 1960. Similarly, instruments for industrial control leaped from $3 million in sales in 1940 to $65 million

114

in 1953 and are expected to hit $150 million in five years.

Want ads plead constantly for engineers and technicians, and investment houses publicly exhort customers to put their money in the booming stocks of automation-equipment makers. Where Ford stamped out four of its car parts automatically in 1947, it now does thirty parts almost without manpower. But perhaps the most striking evidence of the advance comes from the Federal Reserve Board. Its index figure for the manufacturing and mining industries in November, 1953, was 129. In November, 1954, with almost a million fewer people in those industries, the figure was still 129.

No one can say how far the expected "dislocation" may go, how many humans may lose their jobs to Univac, Eniac, and Multra; to Armatrol, Serva, and O-Man; or how many jobs these genies may in turn provide for those they have displaced. Certainly no one with the least sense of history would either want to expect to arrest a trend that will increase the world's wealth and reduce human drudgery. Where the first Industrial Revolution degraded men to the level of a machine part, the second should liberate him from the machine completely.

But if it frees some only to leave as many others stranded, dazed, and for years without the wherewithal to buy what the machines produce, it will hardly have paid its way—at least for a generation that already has all it can stand in the way of large-scale hazards. A measure of coherent planning, a sustained sense of responsibility in industry, labor, government, and education—these are the least we will need to ease us into the second machine age more smoothly than our luckless forebears went into the first.

AND STILL THE ORIENT

Formosa—The Test

BY ALBERT RAVENHOLT

The struggle in Korea has distracted American attention from the alarming possibility that our actions on Formosa may involve the United States in a general Asian war. It has also encouraged us to ignore the possibility that the American Navy and Air Force may not be able to frighten off or halt a Chinese Communist attack on that island. If the Chinese Red forces should capture Formosa *despite* United States opposition, it would be a major disaster, even if the fighting did not precipitate a world conflict. And yet these are the prospects, unless the United States acts with great speed and realism.

Earlier hopes that the leaders of the Central People's Government in Peking would call off the invasion of Formosa simply because an American fleet had moved in have now been exploded by recent reports from the mainland. All along the China coast the Communists are continuing their preparations. Some reports suggest they are making special arrangements to deal with the U.S. Navy. Meanwhile, the People's Liberation Armies in Manchuria are being reinforced with almost a quarter of a million veteran Communist troops from west and south China. These forces could go into action in the Manchuria-Korea area at about the same time as the Formosa invasion.

Chinese Communist forces that are available for the attack on Formosa include units of about eighteen armies numbering roughly five hundred thousand men. Most of these troops are concentrated around Shanghai and Hangchow Bay, and in Chekiang and Fukien Provinces. It is believed that seven armies are slated for the initial assault. The remaining armies, together with special troops, supposedly will follow later. So far the operational commander has been General Su Yu, the principal organizer of the massive Communist offensive south across the Yangtze River in April and May, 1949. That offensive broke Nationalist mainland resistance and won Shanghai, Nanking, and the industrialized areas of the lower Yangtze Valley.

During the past eight months these forces have prepared for what the Communists describe as "the greatest offensive in modern Chinese history"—the assault on Formosa. Farmers from many areas of east China have been conscripted to build roads and airfields and to transport supplies. Large shipyards in the Yangtze Valley have been building or altering invasion vessels. Other craft are reported to have been shipped by rail from north China and Manchuria to the Yangtze.

The Nationalists estimate that, in addition to their larger and more modern ships, the Communists are collecting about five thousand wooden junks. Many of these are heavily armed and carry fifty men each. Together with regular invasion barges, LST's, and ex-Nationalist naval vessels, these junks are believed adequate for transporting the forces considered necessary for the assault. The Communists have also trained in Shanghai a special cadre of political workers fully informed on conditions in Formosa.

It is difficult to predict how much Nationalist resistance these Communist forces might encounter on Formosa. The island's beaches are dotted with hundreds of concrete pillboxes. Miles of barbed wire have been strung along the coast. The Nationalist Navy and Air Force have been "streamlined." Many of the sailors and airmen are willing to fight the Communists, and their units will probably remain loyal so long as they have hopes of winning. An armored force commanded by Chiang Kaishek's second son, General Chiang Wei-kuo, is equipped with more than one thousand light and medium tanks and about as many trucks. But Formosa has high mountains and many fast rivers, and engineers fear that the destruction of a few key bridges could immobilize most of the tanks not already waiting for repairs.

There are good reasons for doubting the ability and willingness of the ordinary Nationalist soldier to defend Formosa. A private soldier is paid the equivalent of seventy-five U.S. cents per month, is given his rice from a food allowance equivalent to two U.S. dollars per month, and must buy fuel, salt, vegetables, cooking oil, and, if possible, meat. Eggs cost the equivalent of ninety cents a dozen, and other prices are on the same level, so it's not surprising that many soldiers are underfed. Medicines in warehouses often are not distributed, and soldiers have died from malaria because they lacked atabrine. Enormous quantities of supplies were lost to the Communists on the mainland last year, and the Nationalist ground forces now are critically short of several kinds of ammunition. These conditions exist despite the struggle of many junior officers to overcome the difficulties that have shackled the Nationalist armies for the last ten years.

The greatest military weakness of Formosa is the Nationalist high command. Generalissimo Chiang Kai-shek still promotes and demotes officers without telling their superior commanders. Several notoriously unsuccessful and corrupt generals have recently come back into favor. Other Chinese generals who might have helped to clean up the Nationalist establishment are kept busy wooing senior officials of SCAP in Tokyo. Since President Truman's announcement of U.S. naval intervention, important elements in the Nationalist Ministry of Defense have adopted an attitude of, "Let the Americans do it." Able young officers are haunted by the prospect that when an invasion comes, Chiang Kai-shek will continue his old practice of haphazard interference with established defense plans by giving direct orders to regimental commanders. If that happens it will wreck all chances of using the roughly 250,000 more or less well-trained combat troops on the island most effectively.

Last spring there was evidence of considerable good will toward the government among important elements of the Formosan population. The Nationalist officials on Formosa include some of China's ablest financiers, engineers, scientists, and administrators. With the help of ECA and American agricultural and industrial specialists they have made noticeable improvements. Land rents have been reduced to 37.5 per cent of the main crop. Rice production this year should reach 1,400,000 tons, which is equal to the peak achieved under the Japanese. Such reforms have been partly responsible for the Communist failure to win the allegiance of Formosan revolutionary groups. The Formosans also are influenced by their fear of mainland ties that would reduce their standard of living to the level of the great majority of Chinese.

Since early June this "friendship" for the government has been largely replaced by widespread and growing resentment against the Nationalists' open and secret police methods. Chiang Kai-shek and some of his most influential advisers apparently are convinced that they lost the mainland partly because their police control was not sufficiently thorough. The recently increased police activity has resulted in the execution of an unknown number of alleged Communist agents—most of them officials of Nationalist military organizations.

Police control has also been extended to the schools. The Generalissimo's elder son, the Russian-educated General Chiang Ching-kuo, commands an organization that has placed "professional students" in most classrooms to report on teachers and students. Fear and hatred are generated by these methods.

As they prepared to capitalize on the situation, the Chinese Communist planners originally failed to indicate how they planned to eliminate opposition from the Nationalist Air Force, with its more than 150 fighter planes. Now, however, it is known that the Reds have a vigorous and fast-growing air force. At last count Communist combat aircraft in central, south, and east China numbered about four hundred. These include Japanese wartime models, Russian-built conventional and jet-type planes, and fighter-bombers purchased from eastern Europe. It is not possible to estimate how many planes there are in northwest China and Manchuria, where the Communists are running an extensive pilot-training program. With Russian assistance, they have rapidly expanded their air-warning and anti-aircraft establishments. Dozens of American and Japanese wartime airfields have been reconditioned. By using these airfields the Communists can base their planes in the remote interior beyond the reach of the Formosa-based fighters, and "stage" to the coast for quick strikes.

Any realistic appraisal of American chances on Formosa must also take account of possible direct Russian assistance to the Chinese Communists. The Sino-Soviet Treaty of Friendship, Alliance and Mutual Aid was signed on February 14, 1950. It provides that if Japan or any power associated with Japan attacks China, Russia will "immediately render military or other aid with all means at its disposal."

The Chinese Communists have charged that use of the U.S. Navy to block their invasion of Formosa constitutes aggression. They have not yet claimed that

Japan is involved. But to do so would require little more than another phrase in their propaganda. They have emphasized that the American action was taken without United Nations sanction. Their statements quoted at length from President Truman's January announcement that the United States would not interfere in China's internal affairs.

The original Chinese Communist plan is believed to have set September, 1950, as the invasion date for Formosa. However, the Communist leaders in Peking have rarely attempted a major task until they were confident of success. Their timetable may now depend upon when they receive additional aircraft, and possibly submarines, to cope with U.S. naval units. If the attack does not start before late October, rough weather may force a delay of months.

Those who assume that our Navy and Air Force can easily halt such an invasion are probably not aware that the Nationalists have found the wooden junk one of the hardest of all vessels to sink. When their junks were hit by 40-mm. shells, Communist soldiers dived into the water and plugged the holes with canvas. American-built destroyer escorts that tried to ram the junks loosened their own plates and failed to damage the wooden vessels. When ten to fifteen heavily armed junks closed around a destroyer escort, the larger vessel sometimes was captured or put out of action.

The experience of American soldiers with Communist mass attacks in Korea gives us an inkling of what the U.S. Navy and Air Force will be up against in trying to halt an invasion by thousands of Chinese Communist vessels. The Chinese craft will furthermore be protected by a powerful air force of their own. Once the vessels that are not sunk reach Formosa, there will be very little that our Navy and Air Force can do about the assault. And with even a small number of Chinese Communist troops ashore, many things could happen; the struggle might turn into a free-for-all wherein the Formosans would seek to get rid of their mainland rulers and the Communists, too. In any event the outcome would be largely out of our control.

Capture of Formosa by the Chinese Communists despite American military opposition would have profound political and military consequences throughout Asia. In
120

Asian eyes the United States already has been humbled by events in Korea. If our intervention on Formosa ends in disaster, many Asians' confidence in the United States will be completely shaken.

The possibility cannot be ruled out that once their reinforcements are in position in Manchuria, the Chinese Communists may follow the example of the United States and link the issue of Formosa with the war in Korea.

In view of these prospects, it is necessary to consider the alternative policies available to the United States. Our security demands that we not only choose a sound line of action, but act.

The most obvious alternative is for the United States to withdraw its fleet and planes and permit the Chinese Communists to take Formosa. Apart from American domestic political considerations, such action would have serious consequences in Asia. It would hand the Chinese Communists a major propaganda point and confirm them in their belief that the United States is a "paper tiger." Many of the Chinese who still look to America for leadership would probably turn against us. It would also put the Communists on the island and further embitter many Formosans who feel that the United States wronged them once by giving their country to Chiang Kai-shek and his appointees after V-J Day. But such action could be made simple and quick and it would leave our forces free for use elsewhere. We would also retain some of our reputation in Asia for not seizing territory.

A second course of action would be for the United States to eliminate Chiang Kai-shek and his group as a government and encourage the Chinese Communists to accept at least interim American or United Nations control over Formosa. Substantial information indicates that to accomplish this it would be necessary to assure the leaders in Peking of representation in the United Nations after the Korean issue has been settled. The Chinese Communists have argued they must have Formosa because it is Chinese territory. But a much more important reason is the presence on the island of the Nationalist régime blocking Peking's recognition in the world as the Chinese government. Once the Chinese Communists were assured of this "face-saving" gain, other factors might come into play in China that would encourage them to leave Formosa alone. The greatest of these is the enormous cost of the invasion. The recent disastrous floods in central China, foreboding another terrible famine next winter, should make this consideration even more important.

A third alternative would be for America to prepare for general war in Asia. If the United States continues to use its forces to protect the Kuomintang leaders on Formosa, there is ample evidence that Peking, at the opportune moment, will act as if we had declared war. Should the United States become involved in a "Korea-like war" with the Chinese Communists while the Soviet Union remained officially aloof, it would be difficult to estimate the consequences.

Chinese Communist reinforcements recently sent to Manchuria or en route there total about 250,000 men. In addition an "elite force" numbering about 500,000 is supposed to be training in Manchuria, with the Russians providing specialized instruction and unknown quantities of equipment. The armies moved north include the most veteran units of the Chinese Red Armies—many of the troops that have been hardened by twelve years of constant fighting. It is reasonable to assume their combat efficiency will be at least equal to that of the North Koreans.

Meanwhile, the Communists have kept about 260,000 front-line troops in south China. Most of them could be made available to help Ho Chi Minh "liberate" Vietnam, where they would outnumber French troops about two to one.

For the second or third alternative, the early movement of American ground forces to Formosa appears necessary. Information from the mainland indicates such action would at least delay the Communist invasion; it would force the Chinese Red generals who are contemptuous of the Nationalist military to remake their plans. Troops might also be useful in making the reforms necessary on Formosa if the threat of internal revolt is to be overcome. The Formosans are eager to participate in the defense of their island themselves. Some of them were conscripted into and trained in the Japanese Army. A new administration might find them useful.

Once genuinely within the western orbit, Formosa

could be made to serve more important purposes than as a piece of Pacific real estate with military possibilities. More than any other area of equal size in Asia it offers an opportunity for creating at an early date a high standard of living for the average person. The island has great natural resources already partly developed. It has a literate population that is willing and able to work hard, and a high concentration of scientific and managerial talent, particularly among the mainlanders who have settled there. If the relatively small number of men on top who have blocked positive efforts departed, it is likely that great creative energies would be released. The United States then could help build the kind of show place in Asia that would be a powerful argument for what Americans want to offer.

The New Great Debate

BY MAX ASCOLI

Senator Knowland was unquestionably right when, last November 15, he asked for a full Congressional inquiry into the foreign and defense policies of our nation. At least on this point, there should be no partisan quarrel: Even a new Great Debate, with all its histrionics, is not too high a price to pay for the badly overdue reorientation of our foreign policy. The debate had better start right away, for, as Senator Knowland said, time is running out. Next April, the Asian-African Conference will be convened in Bandung, Indonesia.

Our country cannot scoff at continentalism or bicontinentalism: Eisenhower's America finds itself committed by President Monroe's doctrine. Together with continentalism, anti-colonialism has been for the United States a time-hallowed standard of rhetoric, supported by a fairly consistent record of performance.

Yet in spite of this record the United States is now a power that most of the countries of Asia and Africa either mistrust or fear. The Asia-for-the-Asians drive may end with the Asians all being gobbled up by the biggest and most voracious fish in Asia—Red China. Actually, Red China is bent on playing in Asia the role which according to the Communists has been ours in the

Western Hemisphere. The Communist claim is an unmitigated lie, but Red China's will to impose on the whole of Asia its imperial power is a horribly real fact.

The American inclination has been to answer the threat of Communist imperialism in Asia as well as in Europe with a sort of a global Monroe Doctrine. This is perhaps one of the basic assumptions of our foreign policy that most urgently needs to be questioned. For the global Monroe Doctrine—at least in Asia—has not worked.

While the nations of the West have become alerted in various degrees to the threat of Communist imperialism, those of the East have still too vivid a memory of the old uncamouflaged type of colonialism to recognize the threat of the new one.

The NATO structure has served the West well—evidence being the constantly growing Communist outcry against it. But perhaps our greatest mistake is the assumption that the chain of alliances which has proved effective in the West can serve equally in the East. The sham Eastern NATO is very much like a dental set resting on a few cavity-ridden shaky teeth. This kind of denture may be good for grinning, but not for hard biting.

Neutralism has not made, so far, substantial headway in the West, but it is sweeping the non-Communist East. In the coming Asian-African Conference, it may organize itself on a bicontinental basis. Or the conference may pave the way to Mao's triumph.

What ought to be debated now, in Congress and out of Congress, is whether we should not revise our attitude toward the neutralism of the non-Communist nations of the East, understand it, and help to make it real. Perhaps the interest of our country and of the West would best be served by assisting the eastern powers to make their neutralities at the same time armed, collective, and positive. We should not worry if these neutral nations are collectively armed, since we know that in our time aggression can only come from one quarter. We should help these nations make their neutrality positive, so that their national sovereignty may become rooted in national solvency and in the peoples' well-being.

We ourselves can be somewhat neutral or detached when it comes to judging the domestic order of the eastern nations. We can help the Pakistani people reach a decent measure of welfare, even if their democracy is of a rather unconventional character. We can establish some solid understanding with that truly remarkable man Nehru without necessarily cussing or swooning whenever we mention him.

Mao's Government will be present at the Asian-African Conference, as well as Ho Chi Minh's. These men are masters at intrigue and blackmail. Should we play their game vicariously through the few allies we shall have at the conference? Or should we urge these allies to shun the conference and give Mao and Ho the chance to have their way?

We must face the Asian-African Conference with the patience and discretion that become the strong. As the nation that set the pattern both for neutralism and for continentalism, we can show the way to the peoples of Asia and Africa. For without becoming a militaristic or imperialistic power, without loosening the ties with the other republics of our hemisphere, we have finally found in the United Nations the way to outgrow both continentalism and neutralism. We can also show by deeds—our own and those of the United Nations—how assistance can be given to hard-pressed peoples struggling against old and new colonialisms.

In South Vietnam, for instance—and right now.

Chou En-lai
at the Asian-African Meeting

BY JAMES CAMERON

Bandung

There should be some way of summing up a meeting of twenty-nine nations in an obscure hill town of west Java to determine the future behavior and political attitude of the greater part of humanity. There should be some succinct definition of the pattern they devised to involve every living soul with the technical distinction of a colored skin. There should be, but there isn't.

If the Asian-African Conference succeeded in its objectives it is because it had no objectives. If it justified its theme, it was because its theme was the biggest in the world. Even if Chou En-lai (suave as a soapstone

Buddha, suggesting Metternich in a boiler suit) had not chosen Bandung for his sudden experiment in conciliation, the show would have been unique. Even if Jawaharlal Nehru had not so effectively lost patience with his too Oriental fellow Asians, it would have been salutary. Even if Bandung had not soon crystallized itself as the forum of the uncommitted, the first seriously radical challenge to the principle of power, it would still have been a phenomenon because it defied all its inherent contradictions and, in fact, produced results.

Perhaps not many, and largely on the negative side. The thing was so immense and diverse it could aim only at the stars, as something large and lofty enough to escape argument. To reach accord on such a basis was easy and meaningless enough; actually the Asians and Africans did rather more than that.

"An event such as has never taken place since God created the Universe . . . The waves shall breathe it to the beaches of the world . . ." Thus the local Indonesian paper, with the kind of overcharged political lyricism that filled the stifling air. In committee the poetry dwindled and petulance crept in, sternly controlled by the handful of powerful men who were going to have harmony if they had to beat it into each other's skulls. The newly varnished doors opened and the politicians emerged, their faces wreathed in practiced smiles. "Mr. Prime Minister . . . Your Highness . . . Excellency . . . If you please, Comrade Minister. . . ." Sahibs and Effendis and Bungs and Sirs. Promptly at sundown every day the tremendous rain came down like a torrent of lukewarm tea.

In the elegant Colonial Club the representatives deplored colonialism, invoking peace behind a screen of ferocious-looking little Amboinese soldiers with machine guns. The town dedicated itself to the rejection of the West by crowding the air with the technological howl of loudspeakers summoning the delegates' Plymouths and Dodges, and the sirens of motorcycle outriders in white steel helmets like those of American M.P.'s.

Down with imperialism, said everyone, in the only official common language, that of imperialist Britain. President Sukarno arose, keynoting the opening session with a quotation not from the Buddha or the Prophet or the Vedas, but from Longfellow's poem about Paul Revere.

There they were, sweating it out under the gently smoldering volcano: twenty-nine states from Japan around the globe to the Gold Coast, as diverse and incompatible a miscellany, one felt, as could have been rounded up. Nevertheless it *did* represent 1.4 billion human beings, by any count a great deal more than half the population of the world.

At the beginning, the Conference indeed seemed somewhat obsessed by its own multiplicity; few speakers could resist making a litany out of their own catalogue— Buddhists, Hindus, Moslems, Christians, Jains, Sikhs, Confucians, Shintoists, Zoroastrians; the phrases rolled on, suggesting some kind of implicit virtue in variety. One found oneself, in the soporific heat, making a sort of game: Democracy, Theocracy, Monarchy, and Socialism, Capitalism, Communism, and all the permutations in between. I found a Democratic-Marxist-Theocrat today; what did you find? Only a Methodist Sikh. They say there's a party tonight for the oppressed Mormon minority in eastern Cambodia. The color bar downstairs is very strict now; it seems they won't serve white people. What *will* the Turkish delegation do? It was all pretty silly at the beginning.

Then suddenly the Conference began in earnest and things fell into place; it began to make sense in a way that was not only moving and dramatic but somehow intensely logical. These *were* the people of whom President Sukarno was talking—into a badly adjusted microphone, while an imprisoned bird wheeled and darted frantically across the high roof of the auditorium: "For many generations our people were the voiceless ones in the world, disregarded and living in poverty and humiliation. Then our nations demanded—nay fought for— independence, and with that independence came responsibility. But we do not regret that."

Down below, the place throbbed with color and self-conscious eccentricity, with every sort of robe and veil and tunic, shalwar and lungi, dhoti and burnoose, tarboosh and kaffiyeh, and the simple sharkskin splendor of the Beirut business suit; something terribly serious halfway between a political convention and a costume ball.

There was not a lot that could be said; clearly the early agenda had to be couched in terms broad and high-minded enough to ensure general approval, without presenting much initial danger of controversy—human rights, dependent peoples, the relaxation of tension, all expressed over and over in terms of indistinguishable piety; resounding declarations of common purpose. But what, one wondered, could that common purpose be? What could possibly be in common between China, say, and Yemen? What was the political link between Liberia and Nepal?

Color itself could hardly be enough to make blood brothers of the impassive Chou En-lai and the dapper little ex-King of Cambodia. It had certainly never resolved the trouble between India and Pakistan. The two Vietnams sat side by side on the far flank, but only by the hazards of alphabetical arrangement, and how much divided them besides an arbitrary and dubious frontier! Sukarno invoked the "moral voice of nations," not for nonwar but for peace as an absolute, a concept rather well understood in Asia. It was that simple, naïve goal which united the delegates.

Everyone had said again and again that this Asian-African encounter was to be an anti-imperialist conference, which was inevitable, and an anti-American conference, which it by no means turned out to be. This, we were told, was the East's first, maybe last, chance to define the doctrine of noninvolvement. It was not going to be easy in the presence of states so deeply committed as China on the one hand and Thailand, Turkey, and the Philippines on the other. Even on the second day the honeyed words were cut into by a sizzling anti-Communist attack from Dr. el Jamali of Iraq. It was received with rather rueful courtesy by those who might have agreed but who had obeyed the ground rules of expressed unity. There was much more of it to come.

Not, oddly enough, from Carlos Romulo of the Philippines, who had been cast from the start as the Washington spokesman. He said: "I think that over the generations the deepest source of our own confidence in ourselves had to come from the deeply rooted knowledge that the white man was *wrong*, that in proclaiming the superiority of his race, *qua* race, he stamped himself with his own weakness. . . . I ask you to remember that just as western political thought has given us all so many of our basic ideas of political freedom, justice, and
128

equity, it is western science which in this generation has exploded the mythology of race."

After this unexpected argument of reverse-screen liberalism, most of the following polemics were rather flat. Prince Wan of Thailand had to justify SEATO by an enormous quotation from the Buddha. Japan joined in the anti-imperialist chorus with the slightly uneasy air of a man who knows himself to be the only ex-imperialist in the hall, whose previous associations with this part of the world had been very much at the end of the gun. (A few eyebrows had been raised anyhow by the presence as chief delegates of Tatsunosoke Takasaki, who had personally run the heavy industry of the puppet Manchukuo, and of Masayuki Tani, whose function had been to promote the celebrated Co-Prosperity Sphere.) Mr. Takasaki took the rostrum with a certain diffidence. "In the war," he said, "I regret to say that Japan inflicted damage on her neighbors. She ended, however, by ruining herself." He said he was very sorry, and indeed he looked it.

Nobody cared very much about Mr. Takasaki, who as everyone knew was only in Bandung to do some business. (He emerged finally, after a week of intricately organized unobtrusiveness, with seven new international contracts for Japan.) But then nobody was interested in anything much, those early days, except in Chou En-lai.

The performance of the Premier of China throughout must be set down as one of the deftest and most persuasive pieces of political virtuosity ever produced by that accomplished and impressive man. From his first-act entrance—standing immobile on the dais, yelping a few phrases in his surprisingly shrill falsetto voice and leaving the rest to the interpreter—to his skillfully timed offer to the Americans at the end, he had all his potential opponents groping against the steady tide of sweetness and light. There was nothing to counter; it was what everyone wanted to hear.

Chou flummoxed everyone from the start by issuing an advance script of his speech and then delivering one completely different. "To begin with," said Chou, "we are here to seek unity and not to quarrel. We Communists do not hide the fact that we are Communists, because we think it is a good system. But we haven't come here to look for divergence but for common ground. We could," he said, "have submitted the Taiwan [Formosa] question to the meeting. Or we could have brought up the matter of our entry into the United Nations. We didn't, because that would have dragged the Conference into disputes without finding solutions."

He continued on this unexceptionable line for some time, pointing out that there are, after all, many more non-Communist Asians than there are Communist Asians, and that he was making no complaint about that. "We Communists are also atheists," said he, "but we respect those who have the religious faith we don't have. Tolerance is the thing," he said, bowed, and stepped down to reload for the committee stages.

Slowly the committees moved through their work. Chou scored another success by signing with Indonesia the agreement on the overseas Chinese who have presented problems for years, not only to Indonesia with its two million, but to all the other states of Southeast Asia, where some eight million more live and carry on most of the business. Chinese law has always held them, whatever their birth, to be Chinese nationals. Chou agreed at last to a year's period in which they may choose their nationality: that of Communist China or of their domicile. But not of Nationalist China.

It had seemed sometimes that the delegates, awed by the vast possibilities for divergence among themselves, would steer clear of all detail and agree only on the eternal verities. But by and by the points of agreement emerged, and with each it became clear that someone had made a sacrifice of some sort of principle for the sake of presenting to the world a united front. There was unanimous agreement on taking the case of the Arabs against that of Israel in the Palestine problem—although of all the Middle Eastern states Israel is the only one that has recognized China, China cast its vote against Israel. There was unanimous agreement on Indonesia's claim for West Irian (Netherlands New Guinea) against the Dutch—and Turkey, although aligned both emotionally and militarily more closely to Holland than to Indonesia, voted against its fellow NATO member. It was obvious that concessions could be made.

Meanwhile, Bandung was certainly having the time of its life. It is a dull little town in the highlands of

Preangen, a plateau of breathtaking beauty, ringed with green mountains and buried, in this rainy season, under towering thunderheads perpetually aflicker with mild lightning. The shops have whimsical names, like "Sporting-House," "Happy-Store," and "The Lively Place." It was said that most of the consumer goods of Java had been channeled into them, just as Jakarta had to stand by to sacrifice its electric current if anything should occur to threaten Bandung's power plant.

The town was spruced up and repainted in a fashion astonishing to the gentle Javanese; furthermore it was scrupulously sealed off. Whatever Bandung had in the way of a corps of professional ladies had been banished to some fifteen miles away. The roads were cordoned. A security system was introduced that required a file of passes and papers which reduced the normally torpid pace of the town to something often approaching immobility. Indonesia was taking no chances with its embarrassing quota of controversial celebrities; it could not be forgotten that rebel bands were all over the place as near as thirty miles from Gedung Merdeka, the Conference Hall of Independence.

Bandung was never built to accommodate these more than two thousand strangers, including one of the densest and most fretful concentrations of newspapermen seen for years, all lodging in rather gruesome congestion and whiling away the time spotting those of their number who were most palpably spies. Six hundred and fifty-five journalists were accredited to the Conference. Not all those accredited showed up. Not all those who showed up were journalists. Not all who were journalists did any journalism. And not all of those who did any journalism did it for organizations that could remotely be defined as journals. It became clear that there was representation of some very obscure interests indeed, and there was much curious, not to say fishy, activity. Anyone from foreign parts for whom no special classification could be found was issued a small rectangular badge marked press and released among the restless, sweating mob. One gentleman was caught distributing literature denouncing the Soviet tyranny in Turkestan; he was quickly arrested; by and by he was released, and soon was back in the pressroom distributing literature.

Even for the pure in heart, life in Bandung presented

131

many problems in a day that began with a breakfast, in the Dutch fashion, of cold pork and cheese, and ended in fatiguing pursuits of the more accessible dignitaries around the suburbs. The Indonesian rupiah clings to an exchange rate so grotesquely loaded against the foreigner that even the modest amenities of Bandung became fantastically expensive; everyone used the black market, which provided a rate some three hundred per cent better, and to which all prices were in any case related.

The Bandungese adored it; all day and half the night they jammed behind the armed guards applauding everyone, but particularly the stars—Chou, Gamal Nasser, Nehru. The collection of autographs was maniac, and for the delegates there was great advantage in being U Nu, say, rather than Sastroamidjojo. Besides the delegates the town soon began to swarm with parties of peripheral special interests—the Archbishop Makarios of Cyprus and the Grand Mufti of Jerusalem, armed respectively with arguments against Britain and Israel; the African National Congress, to whom this was a God-sent chance to argue their case.

There was a North African team denouncing the French, and the Malayan nationalists denouncing the British. There was Congressman Adam Clayton Powell from New York. There were Saudi Arabians roaming around who, disdaining all the womanish peace talk about them, attended each session with a .45 strapped handily under the arm, while in the lounge of the Homann Hotel the orchestra of listless Dutchmen fiddled for their new masters—either out of ignorance or cynicism they always seemed to play "Kashmir Love Lyrics."

The Counterfeiters

BY MAX ASCOLI

Our State Department should have no difficulty in recognizing the game Chou En-lai has been playing in Asia and Africa before, during, and after Bandung: Gracefully and thoroughly, with the ease of a great impersonator, he is producing in the two continents a striking replica of our Good Neighbor policy. Were there such a thing as diplomatic copyright, Chou En-lai would have to pay huge sums to Sumner Welles.

Truly, Chou En-lai's production of the Good Neighbor show has been a great hit. He has been deferential and reassuring, not only toward big India, but toward the weakest and most exposed of his neighbors, like Thailand and Cambodia. He has gone out of his way to humor his own Nicaraguas and El Salvadors.

It is not at all surprising to find such superb mimetic qualities in a Communist leader. For what is Communism if not a perverse rendition of western civilization, the attempt to present a phony copy as an improvement on the original?

There is no country or people today, no matter how primitive, that is not convulsed by a feverish eagerness to be westernized. When imposed from the outside on weak or defenseless natives, westernization was called colonialism or imperialism—names that have fallen into horrible disrepute. Now, under the guise of nationalism, there is no country that does not want to be westernized in its own way, full steam ahead, and adopt under some shape or form basic features of democracy and of industrialism.

But which is the type of western civilization more readily available? The genuine one, sometimes upsetting, sometimes naïve, yet endowed with an incalculable power of adapting itself to infinitely varying circumstances; or the other one, synthetic, imitative, and spurious, yet made alluring by its ready-made pattern, allegedly designed for universal adoption? It must be admitted that the two patterns, profoundly different as they are, manifest themselves in fairly identical objects —such as tractors or electric power and, in a few years, atomic piles. They both exhibit the ballot box, but in the Peoples' Democracies it is used strictly for purposes of decoration.

Our country, by universal consent the leader of the West, is the one most directly and vitally concerned with exposing the counterfeit. But rather than prove we are right, we seem to be satisfied when somebody—no matter who—says that Communism is wrong. When the representative of the Iraqi Government, probably one of the most authoritarian and racialist in the Middle East, got up at Bandung and said that the two great Com-

133

munist powers were imperialistic and aggressive, there was positive jubilation in our press. Truthtelling by improbable proxy seems to answer our needs.

This timidity shows a pusillanimous conception of these needs and of the role that should be ours, for it is the function of our country to be actively on the side of any nation hurrying toward the West, to give assistance whenever necessary and counsel against the countless pitfalls ahead. One of the most obvious pitfalls lies in the fact that national independence turns out to be a rather shaky, precarious thing when it is not buttressed by economic solvency.

Modern technology has made the formulas on how to reach westernization alluring and cheap. But the adoption of these formulas still exacts a price. Sometimes this price can be staggered. Sometimes to a certain extent—but never altogether—it can be made more bearable by loans of foreign money or of foreign skill. But the price can never be zero, lest this spurious and ultimately most horribly expensive form of westernization that is Communism prevail.

Modern technology and the universal popularization of skills allow the new nations of Asia and of Africa to catch up with the West in an astonishingly short time. Yet during this time, no matter how short, the going is hard. The nations that met at Bandung felt that their lot could be considerably eased if they could deal with westernization on a collective-bargaining basis.

If we do not assist these young nations individually and together, who can? Only we can understand the need for unity that prompted the Colombo powers to call the Bandung Conference. These new nations want to share their risks, and we should not be afraid to take up a large part in the underwriting. We must be patient in dealing with them and at the same time firm; constantly kind and occasionally tough; positive in our thinking and at the same time imaginative.

We should understand why, precarious as their growth is, the Asian and African nations are so afraid of war. We should reassure them and make it clear that for a reason of our own we are opposed to war as much as they are—our reason being that in peace, much better than in war, the spurious, malignant type of westernization is sure to be recognized for what it is and rejected.

A FEW JINGLES

Riviera Emperor

To destiny I will not bao,
   For I would sooner dai
    Than leave my croupiers
       hai and drai
And ngo to Vietnam nao.

            —SEC

Middle of the Road

In Gettysburg, the middle of the road
Is where you walk. The cardinals and jays
Flicker and twit impartially, and the toad
Frozen against the dull brown gutter stays
Still till the nearest tread. Whether to right
Or whether to left of the lane, the world is one;
Oak, laurel, berry bushes, the pale delight
Of sky through twigs, the early budding begun
Most tenderly. Here is the path of peace,
Where the only pull is toward all living things
And the only quarrels among the loud high geese
And the nesting birds, each claiming where he sings.

The middle of the road, excepting here,
Is a tight wire strung from fear to fear.

            —SEC

The Ghost Fleet

"A perfumed ship built by a Pharaoh nearly 5000 years ago to carry his soul to heaven was discovered today. . . . The poor fellah had a small clay boat."—New York *Times*.

There's a mighty fleet a-comin', Lord, of every shape
    and size,
An armada of the famous who will sail the rolling skies,
They're not ready for the journey, but the keels are
    bein' laid

135

And you'll recognize the sailors by the way their boats
  are made.

There'll be Churchill in a battleship of earlier design,
And Eden in an armored yacht, a vessel of the line,
There'll be Bevan in a tramp ship with a cannon in her
  bow,
And Attlee in a shabby but unsinkable old scow.

There'll be quite a lot of Frenchmen in a leaking *Liberté*
And Germans in flotillas of destroyers, all class-A;
There'll be Chiang inside a sampan with a Navy-surplus
  sail,
And Mao and Chou in carriers hard-bearing on its tail.

In a ship of huge displacement Georgi Malenkov will
  ride,
With a crew of groaning galley slaves and tritium inside,
And in its wake a brigantine a-flyin' the skull-and-bones
Will bear the raging cargo of McCarthy's soul—and
  Cohn's.

There'll be Ike aboard a schooner slow to catch the
  rising wind,
And Dulles in a ferry by conflicting currents spinned,
And the closest thing to Cheops will be Texas million-
  aires
A-racin' up to heaven in their new Chris-Craft corsairs.

But Lord, you may be happiest to welcome, still afloat,
The spirit of the *fellah* in his small—clay—boat.

—SEC

136

THAT MAN (FROM THE REPORTER'S NOTES)

Treason at Yalta

There must be men in Russia who are plain mad at That Man in the Kremlin, but cannot express themselves the way John T. Flynn and the rest of the Roosevelt critics do.

That Man, the Stalin-haters must think, sold Russia down the river at Teheran and Yalta. He was so bamboozled by the wiles of Churchill and Roosevelt that he left western Europe, the wealthiest and most industrialized part of the continent, to the Americans. When the war ended the Communists were by far the strongest elements in the resistance movements in France and Italy. And what did That Man do? He ordered the Communists to enter coalition governments and play the democratic game. Everybody knows what happened: After a couple of years, they were kicked out of the coalition governments. Now, the Communist Parties in France and Italy can neither play the role of the Loyal Opposition nor seize power themselves. They are trapped. And the worst is yet to come, for the trend has already started in several countries. The Communist Parties are going to be outlawed.

And what did he gain, That Man, at Yalta? He collected the wayward and underprivileged peasants of eastern Europe and now, as if that weren't enough, he has taken four hundred million famished Chinese off the American relief rolls.

But, of course, he was happy at Teheran and Yalta. The Tiflis seminarist strutted in his brand-new, brass-burdened uniform, proud to be treated as an equal by the descendant of Marlborough and by the scion of Dutch patroons. They got him. The Atlantic could have been the Soviet frontier, and now to hide from the Russian people the lands that should be theirs, he has rung down the Iron Curtain.

Incidentally, to top it all, a son of That Man is beginning to get his name into the headlines—Lieut. General Vassily Stalin. Junior was in command of the air squadrons that flew over Red Square on the last anniversary of the Russian Revolution.   —M.A.

137

That Man Again

The people in Moscow who loathe That Man in the Kremlin must be boiling mad these days. "Do you understand what he has done?" they ask each other guardedly. "Of course he didn't have the remotest idea that the American government and the Security Council would react the way they did. What kind of intelligence reports does he receive from abroad? He never understands anything that happens outside of Russia anyway. Otherwise how could he have let the United States gain control of the United Nations?

"The best he can probably do now is to sneak back into the U.N. again, riding on Red China's tail, and try to muddy the waters there. But it's too late. He set the alarm off, and now the Americans are wide awake. Until then everything was going our way. The Americans thought they were strong just because they were told of miraculous new weapons that could be made some day. They were talking of licking the pants off Joe Stalin, and they didn't even have enough strength to knock off the North Koreans. If we had only let them daydream for a couple of more years, our stockpile of atomic bombs would have been ready in 1952 or 1953.

"Now, in 1950, the lid is off. That Man isn't satisfied with being a generalissimo: He has to take up the job of American War Mobilizer. Sooner than we think, American power is going to be so great that we will have to respect it. For a long time the Americans have been talking of 'containing' us. Now he has given them no choice but to do what they have been saying all along.

"Isn't it really time for a change?"   —M.A.

That Man—III

The blood pressure of the Soviet patriots who hate That Man in the Kremlin reached an all-time high when U.N. troops captured Seoul. "See what he has done?" they whisper in dark corners. "He has given the West a chance to probe how much military strength we have and how much of it we can use. Instead of trembling, people in the West may even start figuring out what is wrong with our home front, why we have to keep so many people under arms, and what kind of arms we have. He has opened a gaping hole in the Iron Curtain, and now our enemies are getting a look at us.

"It had to happen some day. You can't get by forever on luck and breaks. Trotsky knew it all the time: *He's* a small man who got where he is because he acts, talks, and actually is like everybody else. His plodding, bureaucratic mediocrity covered up his conquest of power. His enemies could never bring themselves to believe, until it was too late, that our least brilliant and impressive leader could establish himself in the Kremlin.

"He can't afford having men of higher stature around him. The victorious generals of the Red Army have been sent to rot in provincial garrisons—or worse. The people he likes are old cronies from his home state, like Beria. Or if he can't find a Georgian, he'll take nobodies like Molotov.

"In ordinary times it might be all right to have a man like that at the heard of our country, but now our régime, our national existence, is in danger. Whether we like it or not, he is the one who makes the historic decisions—like invading South Korea. Now his bluff has been called. Harry Truman has put him in his place."

—M.A.

Troubles in the Kremlin

The arbiters of Russian destiny are sitting around a big table, in one of their all-night sessions. Gloom is in the air. Everybody is looking at everybody else with more than usual suspicion, but never for long losing sight of The Chief, whose face is drawn.

"The best thing we can do," one man says, "is sit tight and watch. Or rattle the saber at our borders, while our loudspeakers keep blaring peace, peace, peace, as they have these last few years, and then wait. The dissensions in the enemy's camp are working for us. I have all the evidence: Every day the Americans are getting more distrustful of the Europeans. The anti-American wave in Europe is mounting. The job of spreading confusion has been spontaneously assumed by people whom we don't control and don't pay. The left-wingers in England and the right-wingers in America are doing well.

The internal conflicts in the enemy camp will stop only if we are stupid enough to attack now."

Another man, who can scarcely control his indignation, speaks up: "All right, let's do nothing, plan nothing. Let's tell the millions of people we have mobilized in our armies, the millions of comrades in enemy countries whom we have trained to act, let's tell them all: 'Sit back and relax. Or keep in trim, take some calisthenics. Talk revolution but never try it.' Marx said that violence is the midwife of history. But there are men here who think that the world revolution can come painlessly, the way women bear children in America. Or perhaps a stork will carry the baby here and land it in our laps.

"Comrades, do you realize that though the Americans are quarreling their rearmament goes on? While their President and one of their generals make faces at each other, their steel production surges ahead. It is more than three times our production. . . ."

The discussion goes on and on, far into the morning. It keeps revolving around the same points:

"If we don't move, our people can't be kept for long under the tension we have imposed on them."

"If we move, we will give our enemies the unity they have lost."

"While we engage in this great debate between those who want to move and those who don't, guns and planes and tanks are rolling out of the American factories."

One shrewd man labors the point that the quarrels between Truman and MacArthur, Attlee and Bevan, De Gasperi and the left-wingers inside his party, that all these are just superb theatrical performances staged by the ruling circles of Wall Street. "They have only one purpose," the speaker concludes, with a dramatic sweep of his arms: "to make us divided and afraid to act."

This point makes everybody present stop and think. Then the discussion resumes, but with more harmony and about one topic—America. The consensus seems to be that America is unfathomable, unpredictable, beyond the reach of Marxist, or even common-sense, understanding. The great specialist on America speaks at length: "They talk too much for our good," he says. "Things are being printed there so dangerous that if they were known over here they could threaten our na-

140

tional security. We have to classify practically every American newspaper clipping we get. When you talk of Wall Street and its lackeys, do you know that Wall Street's own journal has consistently followed a pacifist policy since the Korean War started? Do you know that instead of talking like a bloodthirsty warmonger, one of the most powerful American generals, Omar Bradley, makes more propaganda for peace, talks peace with greater fervor than all our Stockholm high priests? He even manages to look like a Gandhi who happened to become a general."

The Chief, who hasn't opened his mouth, seems about to speak. "America," he mutters, choked by hatred. "The chattering sphinx."
—M.A.

A Voice from Hell

Probably it was all because we had read too much of Dante's *Inferno* just before going to sleep. Anyway, we had a nightmare:

"This is Joe Stalin speaking. Being here is what I bargained for ever since I left the Tiflis seminary. It's hot, it's hell, but here is where I belong. And how can I complain, considering the way things are going now aboveground?

"The American Comrades are stupid enough, but that's no obstacle to our progress there. Now and then they get themselves caught plotting and spying, but why do we enlist them if not to get them caught? Even the most valuable secret stolen by the ablest spy is not half as important to us as the way the Americans react to our plots.

"A plot is no good unless it has its built-in exposure. Like good wine, it improves by aging. A dormant spy or a dormant apparatus can sometimes be the best thing our money can buy—dormant while the clues to expose them are being kept somewhere until the time is ripe. A spy dormant for keeps—dead—can be even better than a live one.

"In most of the parts of the world we have not yet swallowed, we must be active in running things and show our hand. We have to get mixed up with nationalisms of all sorts; we have to reconcile our dialectical

141

materialism with all brands of religion and superstition in Asia and Africa, and prove that only Communism can satisfy all hopes and dreams. Sometimes the going is tough.

"But with Americans it is quite different. Just the words 'Communist conspiracy' are enough to make them jump at each other's throats. In other countries, we have to do our job of subversion the hard way, with mass organizations and riots and bloodshed. But in America we can always count on bringing about a maximum of confusion with a minimum of effort. In America just our shadow can do what is achieved elsewhere only by massive strength. If by any chance they show signs of turning sober, an old, over-age plot sets them agog again.

"Sometimes it gets rough down here—even for me. I sent millions of people into these pits, and they were all waiting when I came in. But nobody can prove I was wrong. Total evil in one country was enough to transform the lives of the living men we rule into something quite close to hell. As for the rest, we can afford to be patient, applying in each instance efforts proportionate to our means. Those Americans are wonderful. They go to pieces with so little stimulus from us!

"I knew all the time what I was doing and I liked it. I like it still—even when Trotsky is on my neck."

—M.A.

COMMENT ON THE ARTS

TV *and the Dramatist*

BY MARYA MANNES

On the evening of December 29, Robert E. Sherwood interrupted a reverie. The reverie concerned the great opportunities television offers to writers. The interruption was a one-hour television play, the first which this distinguished man had written of a series contracted for with NBC a year ago and awaited with high hope. For although it was not the first time a well-known American playwright had written for television—Saroyan and Faulkner had done so, as had Thornton Wilder and others—it was the first time a man of Sherwood's reputation had agreed to undertake a series of television plays at a fee heretofore never paid and with a freedom of choice never before so contractually granted. It was a sort of coming of age of a medium which has been arrogantly—and to their loss even more than its own—neglected by our country's intellectuals, who have gathered u₁ their creative garments about them out of reach of the masses, for fear, one supposes, of contamination.

Here was the irony and failure of Mr. Sherwood's first attempt, which he called *Backbone of the Nation*. For while he tried to show with it that there is no such thing as the "average, typical American family" (or life, or way), what he wrote was an average, typical television play. It was even below the quality of less heralded scripts: formless, cliché-ridden, unfunny, the points dulled, the bland conclusion justifying the very attitudes he had set out to rend. One could not help thinking two things: that Mr. Sherwood was deliberately condescending to the medium—stepping down from Olympus so that the little people would be less awed by his eminence—and that he had really not looked at television much. If he had, he would have found out what marvelous things a good playwright can do for it—and it for him. This was the reverie that his play interrupted.

I had been wondering, as I watched play after play on television, what it is that makes their best moments—

143

the high points—different from theater or motion pictures. And I had come to the conclusion that it is intimacy: intimacy with faces, with emotions, with words. There they are, these treasures, held in a very small world of space, with nothing between them and you but an electrical impulse. It is, in fact, the closest form of communication next to actual presence. For writer and viewer the physical distractions are gone: there is no problem of seating, of diction, of lighting, of scenery, of audience noise. You see and you hear the actor without such interventions, and the writer can write without deference to them. He does not need the constant action necessary to theater or movie pace. There is action enough in the talk between two people and the expressions of their faces; even in the talk of one, if the words are good.

Although the writer is limited by time, he is not limited by arbitrary divisions into acts. The thorn of the interrupting commercial has bled many writers, but I see no reason why it cannot be extracted by the concerted effort of the networks and the playwrights, who can surely convince the sponsors that it does more harm than good. In any event, a break need be no disaster to the writer who has discovered that he can pack as much into twenty minutes of television as he can into forty of theater. It is as if power of impact were in direct ratio to exigency of space. Cinemascope and wide screens notwithstanding, space means diffusion, contraction strength. The television writer should exult in this limitation as a painter exults in his. Both are frames which spur as they discipline the creative spirit, and those who reject such boundaries will find confusion rather than freedom.

Television is the place for the poet, the master of mood and of word. It is the place for implication, for simplicity, even for silence (a quality not yet appreciated on the medium). On television the small gesture can become the great act, the tentative phrase the grand statement. The writer need never strain for effect; the quality of his thought is effect enough.

I can see the day when television will be the home of certain kinds of writing and thinking that other media either spurn or brutalize: delicate works of the imagination which belong, truly, to this magic casement. Works of tenderness, fragments that would be lost in larger frames, could here be cherished for their very fragility.

But the writer for television must look at television. He may not find the key to his new home in the dramas themselves, but rather in the ordinary men and women who are the stuff of drama, telling their stories—often on programs of appalling crassness and bathos—to the millions they cannot see. Seeing them, hearing them, he will discover again—if he has forgotten it—how triumphant is the human being and how powerful is the word of truth. This is why the millions look at television, mesmerized. They are seeing themselves.

This communication—so direct and so limitless—is open to the thinkers and dreamers and creators of this country if they want it. The price is a television set and the humility to realize that if they wish to reach the human spirit (and what artist does not?), they must use all and every means. Of these, television is the most powerful yet devised. If they relinquish it, the wreckers will take over.

The Morbid Magic of Tennessee Williams

BY MARYA MANNES

It is one mark of the artist that he knows what he is doing. In Tennessee Williams's stage directions for the second act of *Cat on a Hot Tin Roof*, now playing to capacity audiences on Broadway, he writes: "I'm trying to catch the true quality of experience in a group of people, that cloudy, flickering, evanescent, fiercely charged!—interplay of live human beings in the thundercloud of a common crisis."

Not only in *Cat* but in the five other Williams plays I have seen and read, this aim has been realized. He *has* caught the true quality of experience, it *is* cloudy and fiercely charged, and the human beings *are* live and in crisis. I would except only one word, and that is "common." The crises of Williams are never common. They are the creation of a very strange and very special imagination, potent enough and poetic enough to impose itself on an audience and hold it in a common trance. He is a theater magician, invoking the lightning of emotion, releasing the doves of instinct, holding in fanlike suspension a brilliant pack of cards peopled with symbols and specters. This is as true of his latest play, *Cat*, as it was of *A Streetcar Named Desire, The Glass Menagerie, Summer and Smoke*. They fascinate. And it is the quality of this fascination, with its strange sequel of doubt, that I would like to explore and examine here.

Williams is as aware of this doubt as he is of everything he does. In his foreword to *The Rose Tattoo* he says: "So successfully have we disguised from ourselves the intensity of our own feelings, the sensibility of our own hearts, that plays in the tragic tradition have begun to seem untrue. *For a couple of hours we may surrender ourselves* to a world of fiercely illuminated values in conflict, but when the stage is covered and the auditorium lighted, *almost immediately there is a recoil of disbelief*" (italics mine).

He is entirely right about his own plays "in the tragic tradition," and he was wise not to call them tragedies. For I do not think real tragedy, springing as it must from common truth, leaves this aftermath. It leaves instead illumination and catharsis. And I doubt whether the emotional exhaustion that is the residual effect of seeing a play by Tennessee Williams—the feeling of having been stretched on a rack for two hours—is either illumination or catharsis. It is a shock treatment, administered by an artist of great talent and painful sensibility who illumines fragments but never the whole. He illuminates, if you will, that present sickness, which *is* fragmentation.

Take *Cat on a Hot Tin Roof*, now one of Broadway's critical and popular successes and the winner of the N. Y. Drama Critics' Award for the best play of the season. As brilliantly produced and acted as it is written, the play is about a crisis in a Delta plantation family brought on in equal parts by the refusal of the son, Brick, to sleep with his wife, Maggie, and by the imminent death from cancer of the father and patriarch, Big Daddy. Now cancer can be a tragedy and the rejection of love can be a tragedy, but the play is not tragic. It is a special and compelling study of violence: the violence of an obscene, gargantuan, perceptive man, Big Daddy, against his body's end, against his own frustrations, against the trap of his family; the violence of the alcoholic Brick against the woman and wife who "destroyed" his pure and noble relationship with another youth by suspecting its nature; the violence of the rejected Maggie in her attempt to recapture her husband's physical attentions. I say "attentions" because the only love in the play—and therefore the only tragedy—is that between Big Daddy and Brick, and the play's highest moment is the scene in the second act where the two men break through the agonizing block of communication and tell each other the truth. And the only reason that even this climax does not make the play important is that Brick's conflict has a very limited reference.

So for two hours the stage is full of screaming, violent, mendacious, bitter people, without nobility or purpose, thrashing in the net of their own errors and deceptions. And it is hard to believe that even Maggie's final lie—motivated as it is by passion and compassion—will ever bring her more than physical release. Unhappy people are not necessarily tragic. For two hours Williams's magic holds you transfixed. But after it is over even he has not been able to make you share his belief in the tragedy of Brick and Big Daddy, the only two of his characters for whom he has no scorn, with whom, indeed, he is most strongly identified. On the title page of the *Cat* script he quotes Dylan Thomas:

> And you, my father, there on the sad height,
> Curse, bless me now with your fierce tears, I pray.
> Do not go gentle into that good night!
> Rage, rage against the dying of the light!"

In these four lines is the tragedy two hours fail to yield.

Tennessee Williams comes nearest to the true quality of tragedy in *The Glass Menagerie* and *Summer and Smoke*. The conflict in each play is between flesh and spirit, between sensibility and sensuality, between illusion and reality. Alma in *Summer* and Laura in *Menagerie* are sisters. Gentle, remote, innocent and defenseless, their loneliness cries out for love and is denied. The men recognize in them the rare beauty of the ideal, yet turn in the end to the comfort of simpler women. Both plays are deeply poetic and very moving; each wavers on the line between pathos and tragedy. If they fail to cross it, it is again because of the very specialness

147

of the author's vision, that quality of private obsession which in turn gives his writing its particular evocative power.

Streetcar, like *Cat*, is another exercise in violence—more successful than *Cat*, I believe, because the disintegration of Blanche is a far more valid object of compassion than the malignant disintegrations of the Delta family. Blanche is a heartbreaking character, and her progressive insanity is only an extension of that gap in all of us between what we think we are and what we are. To be able to create both Blanches at one time is Williams's triumph; the agony of watching both is the rack upon which an audience is stretched.

Nowhere, in fact, have I seen a closer parallel to this poetic insight of Tennessee Williams than the clinical insight into the mentally ill given in a recent television documentary of "The Search" series. With the patients' full consent, the Tulane University Psychiatric Institute permitted one to see several patients undergoing treatment, from electric shock to analysis. A pretty young Southern woman spoke in the toneless, ragged whine of extreme depression, then with rising violence, and later —after shock—in her warm regional voice. Her lines might have been written by Williams: She was not far from Maggie the *Cat*. And a schizophrenic being questioned was like Brick in his dreadful, wary responselessness.

This is precisely what I mean about the "special," extreme nature of Williams's characters and Williams's conflicts. His people are mostly sick people. If they are not actually insane, like Alma's mother in *Summer and Smoke* and like Blanche in *Streetcar*, then they are wholly divorced from reality, like Amanda the mother in *The Glass Menagerie*, like Big Mamma and Brick in *Cat*, like nearly everyone in *Camino Real*.

If they are not divorced from reality, they are as savage and uncontrolled as Stanley in *Streetcar* and as Big Daddy in *Cat;* as mindless and grotesque as Serafina in *Tattoo* or the shiftless wife in "27 Wagons Full of Cotton," a one-acter now on Broadway in *All in One*. Offhand I can think of only three comparatively whole or rational beings in Williams's plays: the Gentleman Caller in *Menagerie*, John in *Summer*, and Blanche's sister Stella in *Streetcar*.

148

To read the plays is to discover also that Williams is as much a painter as a poet, not merely because his stage directions are visually very explicit—colors, shapes, and movements clearly defined—but because there is a strong affinity between his writing and a certain kind of painting. Although he mentions Chirico several times in suggesting stage effects, I think both Dali and Eugene Berman convey more the special quality I mean. In Dali, the shock effect of surrealism is the expression of violent aberration in terms of exquisite workmanship. He isolates sickness in a vacuum of false reality, giving fragmented dreams the illusion of wholeness. Because of his compassion and fire, because of his vastly superior perceptiveness, Williams is an artist as well as a magician, while Dali is only a practitioner of magic in painting. Yet an affinity remains, though Berman, with his hot Mediterranean reds and blues, his rich theatrical vision, and his pervading texture of ruin and loss, comes closer to Williams's sensuality of despair.

I have left *Camino Real* to the last, not because it was the least successful of all Williams's plays, critically and financially, or is the least rewarding to read, but because it is the most difficult one to describe or convey. It must be seen and heard, and its effect is entirely one of subjective response. You are either transfixed or bored by it, according to the degree of feeling or understanding you bring to it. "My desire," says Williams in his foreword to *Camino Real*, "was to give these audiences my own sense of something wild and unrestricted that ran like water in the mountains, or clouds changing shape in a gale, or the continually dissolving and transforming images of a dream."

Here is fragmentation with a will: a nightmare shot through fitfully with poetic and passionate flashes of truth; the kind of dream confused yet on the edge of revelation, full of fears and smothering catastrophe, that wakes you screaming. Full also of a kind of baroque humor and horseplay which is another facet of Williams's genius.

Again the surrealist image comes to mind, this time a series of doors opening on a vista of infinity. They never open wide enough to show what is beyond, but at least they open.

In his afterword to *Camino Real*, the playwright

149

affirms once more what he believes and does: "But the incontinent blaze of a live theatre, a theatre meant for seeing and for feeling, has never been and never will be extinguished by a bucket brigade of critics . . ."

He is right again. Williams creates the incontinent blaze of a live theater, and for this one must be profoundly grateful. He is one of the very few who do. And certainly no brigade of critics will extinguish the blaze.

But incontinent fires, bright and hot as they are, do not burn as long as contained ones. A theater is meant for seeing and feeling, but it is meant for knowing and learning too. Once Tennessee Williams controls his flame and deepens and broadens his vision, the spell he now casts over his audiences while they are in the theater will linger long after in their minds and hearts. And there will be then no "recoil of disbelief."

The Overtrained Audience

BY GODDARD LIEBERSON

Nothing sweetens the air at a concert quite so much as applause. Yet, in the last fifteen or twenty years, applause—this precious oxygen given off by audiences which, more than money, gives life to an artist—has been steadily discouraged, slowly stifled, suppressed, and deadened. Consequently, concert halls have become stuffier, and graveness of mien a prerequisite for him who fancies himself the intelligent concertgoer. The fun is gone, or going, and music has come to be worshiped instead of enjoyed.

It all began subtly enough: the unsmiling face of a violinist or pianist after a sonata; a reluctance to face around on the part of a conductor, or his refusal to lower arms at appropriate (which he considers inappropriate) moments; and sometimes even a hand lifted in a repressive gesture toward an audience which dares to express enjoyment with a tentative burst of applause.

Thus the great solo artist becomes a kind of reluctant professor of music, too serious to acknowledge his students; the conductor a monochromic, monolithic father figure, grim, repressive, demanding of obedience and love. Like an unsmiling, humorless Mr. Darling of "Peter Pan" he seems to say, "A little less noise there. Just

150

watch your decorum—we are worshiping the divinity Music—keep your feelings to yourself." But only saints are adept at private ecstasies, and to ask this from the music public is asking for much too much.

One wonders where the foolish concept of "serious" music began. Was it an attempt to guarantee a posterity that otherwise seemed lost? Yet *bon vivants* are kindly remembered: We honor Dante, but we also honor Boccaccio; we are grateful to both Marcus Aurelius and Petronius. And are we not correct in our suspicions that the artist who "seriously" strives to create "serious" works which will be remembered by succeeding generations is at once doomed to failure?

I cannot help but believe that what we now call "serious" music was once listened to in quite a different way, that concert rooms were neither study halls nor places of worship, and that the atmosphere at music-giving gatherings was one of great social fun. Indeed, one has only to look at an old print depicting Handel as the conductor of his own music surrounded by a conglomeration of audience, singers, and instrument artists to know that a concert for those people was a robust frolic, not unrelated to other robust frolics, and nearly as much fun. I should imagine that our jazz concerts of today would come closer to approximating what concerts then were. At these concerts, faces are smiling, the air is electric with enjoyment, the applause is lusty and grateful.

One wonders: How many years of repression have gone into forming our serious music audiences? It must have meant years of training, because the natural reactions to the exhilaration that music engenders are applause, dancing, even vocal expressions of joy. Wasn't there once a time when applause between movements of a symphony was not considered a coarse gaucherie? Today, the unhappy creature who involuntarily and ecstatically claps his hands together after the first movement of Beethoven's Fifth Symphony is the center of malevolent looks, whispered "sshs," and perhaps even spoken insults from close relatives who expected a little more sensitivity from a respectable fellow. It is all heartbreakingly unfair. Particularly since Beethoven, if he were alive and not deaf, would be delighted, I am sure, to stand and bow in acknowledgment of the applause.

And what joy for a contemporary composer if he were to hear an inadvertent burst of applause from an exuberant admirer!

Our generation, in all aspects of life, has completely rejected the fustiness of Victorianism save in this one area—the concert hall. There the clinging plush, the dim lighting (as if to suggest gaslight), the grim art that hangs on the walls, and, above all, the somber atmosphere, suggest that the antimacassar still lives, and that Alfred Lord Tennyson has crossed no bars.

Soon music will have become such a serious matter that it will entirely be left in the hands of experts. That is, unfortunately, the direction in which it is now moving. It is the responsibility of everyone concerned with music to re-establish its pre-eminence in the field of entertainment, as an essential social (of course, in the broad sense) activity. A good way to begin would be to convert our musical audiences to the concept of the enjoyment of music, and to leave study and worship in the edifices designed for their use.

Up the Ladder from Charm to Vogue

BY MARY MCCARTHY

"Will you wear a star in your hair at night . . . or a little embroidered black veiling hat? . . . Will you wear a close little choker of pearls or a medal on a long narrow velvet ribbon? . . . Will you serve a lunch, in the garden, of *prosciutto* and melon and a wonderful green salad . . . or sit in the St. Regis's pale-pink roof and eat *truite bleue?*"

It is the "Make Up Your Mind" issue: *Vogue's* editresses are gently pressing the reader, in the vise of these velvet alternatives, to choose the looks that will "add up" to *her* look, the thing that is hers alone. "Will you make the point of your room a witty screen of drawings cadged from your artist friends . . . or spend your all on a magnificent carpet of flowers that decorates and almost furnishes the room itself?"

Twenty years ago, when *Vogue* was on the sewing room table of nearly every respectable upper-middle-class American house, these sapphic overtures to the subscriber, this flattery, these shared securities of *prosciutto* and *wonderful* and *witty* had no place in fashion's realm. *Vogue,* in those days before *Mademoiselle* and *Glamour* and *Charm* and *Seventeen,* was an almost forbidden monitor enforcing the discipline of Paris. An iron conception of the mode governed its semi-monthly rulings. Fashion was distinguished from dress; the woman of fashion, by definition, was a woman of a certain income whose clothes spoke the idiom of luxury and bon ton; there was no compromise with this principle. Furs, jewels, sumptuous materials, fine leathers, line, cut, atelier workmanship, were the very fabric of fashion; taste, indeed, was insisted on, but taste without money had a starved and middle-class pathos. The tastefully dressed little woman could not be a woman of style.

To its provincial subscribers *Vogue* of that epoch was cruel, rather in the manner of an upper servant. Its sole concession to their existence was a pattern department, *Vogue's Designs for Dressmaking,* the relic of an earlier period when no American woman bought clothes in a shop. And these patterns, hard to cut out as they were, fraught with tears for the amateur, who was safer with the trusty Butterick, had an economical and serviceable look that set them off from the designer fashions: Even in the sketches they resembled maternity dresses.

As for the columns of etiquette, the bridal advice, the social notes from New York, Philadelphia, San Francisco —all these pointedly declined acquaintance with the woman-from-outside who was probably their principal devotee. Yet the magazine was read eagerly and without affront. Southern women, Western women with moderate incomes pored over it to pick up "hints," carried it with them to the family dressmaker, copied, approximated, with a sense, almost, of pilferage. The fashion ideas they lifted made the pulse of the Singer race in nervous daring and defiance (What would *Vogue* say if it knew?).

This paradoxical relation between magazine and audience had a certain moral beauty, at least on the subscribers' side—the beauty of unrequited love and of unflinching service to an ideal that is arbitrary, unsociable, and rejecting, like Kierkegaard's God and Kafka's Castle. Lanvin, Paquin, Chanel, Worth, Vionnet, Alix—

these stars of the Paris firmament were worshiped and charted in their courses by reverent masses of feminine astronomers who would come no closer to their deities than to copy, say, the characteristic fagoting that Vionnet used in her dress yoke or treasure a bottle of Chanel's Number Two on the bureau, next to father's or husband's photograph.

Like its competitor, *Harper's Bazaar,* and following the French dressmaking tradition, *Vogue* centered about the mature woman, the *femme du monde,* the sophisticated young matron with her clubs, her charities, and her cardcase. The jewels, the rich fabrics, the furs and plumes, the exquisite corseting, the jabots and fringe, implied a sexual as well as a material opulence, something preening, flavorsome, and well satisfied. For the *jeune fille* (so defined) there was a page or two of party frocks, cut usually along princess lines, in pastel taffetas, with round necks. In this Racinean world, where stepmother Phèdre and grandmother Athalie queened it, the actual habits of the American young girl, who smoked and wore lipstick, were excised from consideration. Reality was inferior to style.

Covertly, the assumptions of this period remain in force. Despite social change, fashion is still luxurious. It is possible to dress prettily on a working girl's or business wife's income, but to dress handsomely is another matter, requiring, as before, time, care, and money. Fashion is a craft, not an industrial, conception, exemplifying to perfection the labor theory of value. The toil of many hands is the sine qua non of fashion. The hand of the weaver, the cutter, the fitter, the needleworker must be seen in the finished product in a hundred little details, and fashion knowledge, professionally, consists in the recognition and appraisal of the *work* that has gone into a costume. In gores and gussets and seams, in the polish of leather and its softness, the signature of painstaking labor must be legible to the discerning, or the woman is not fashionably dressed. The hand-knit sweater is superior to the machine-knit, not because it is more perfect, but on the contrary because its slight imperfections reveal it to be *hand*-knit. The Oriental pearl is preferred to the fine cultured pearl because the marine labor of a dark diver secured it, a prize wrested from the depths, and the woman who wears Oriental pearls believes that they show variations in temperature or that they change color with her skin or get sick when they are put away in the safe—in short, that they are alive, whereas cultured pearls, mass stimulated in mass beds of oysters, are not. This sense of the accrued labor of others as a complement to one's personality, as *tribute* in a double sense, is intrinsic to the fashionable imagination, which desires to *feel* that labor next to its skin, in the hidden stitching of its underwear—hence the passion for handmade lingerie even among women whose outer clothing comes off the budget rack.

In spite of these facts, which are known to most women, if only in the form of a sudden anguish or hopelessness ("Why can't *I* look like that?"), a rhetoric of fashion as democracy, as an inherent right or manufacturer's guarantee, has swept over the style world and created a new fashion public, a new fashion prose, and a whole hierarchy of new fashion magazines. *Mademoiselle, Glamour, Charm*—respectively "the magazine for smart young women," "for the girl with the job," "the magazine for the B. G. [Business Girl]," offer to the girl without means, the lonely heart, and the drudge, participation in the events of fashion, a sense of belonging en masse and yet separately, individually, of being designed for, shopped for, read for, predicted for, cherished. The attention and care and consideration lavished on the woman of leisure by lady's maid, coiffeur, *vendeuse*, bootmaker, jeweler, are now at the disposal of the masses through the various Shophounds, Mlles. Wearybones, beauty editors, culture advisers, male and female confidants. The impersonally conceived Well-Dressed Woman of the old *Vogue* ("What the Well-Dressed Woman Will Wear") is tutoyered, so to speak, as *You* ("Will you wear a star in your hair? . . ."): and a tone of mixed homage and familiarity: "For you who are young and pretty," "For you who have more taste than money," gives the pronoun a custom air.

The idea of a custom approach to ready-made, popular-priced merchandise was first developed by *Mademoiselle*, a Street and Smith publication launched during the depression, which differed from *Vogue* and the *Bazaar*, on the one hand, and from *McCall's* and *Pictorial Review*, expressions of the housewife, on the other. Before the depression, there had been, roughly speaking, only three types of women's apparel: the custom

155

dress, the better dress, and the budget or basement dress. Out of the depression came the college shop and out of this the whole institutionalized fiction of the "debutante" shop and the "young-timers'" floor. These departments, which from the very outset were swarming with middle-aged shoppers, introduced a new category of merchandise: the "young" dress, followed by the "young" hat, the "young" shoe, the "young" petticoat, and so on. The "young" dress was a budget dress with status, an ephemeral sort of dress, very often—a dress that excited comment and did not stand up very well. Its popularity proved the existence of a new buying public, of high-school and college girls, secretaries, and office workers, whose dress requirements were very different from those of the busy housewife or matron. What these buyers demanded, for obvious vocational reasons, was not a durable dress or a dress for special occasions, even, but the kind of dress that would provoke compliments from co-workers, fellow students, bosses—a dress that could be discarded after a few months or transformed by accessories into the simulation of a new dress. To this public, with its craving for popularity, its personality problems, and limited income, *Mademoiselle* addressed itself as "your" magazine, the magazine styled for *you,* individually.

Unlike the older magazines, whose editresses were matrons who wore (and still wear) their hats at their desks as though at a committee meeting at the Colony Club, *Mademoiselle* was staffed by young women of no social pretensions, college graduates and business types, live wires and prom queens, middle-class girls peppy or sultry, fond of fun and phonograph records. Its tone was gamely collegiate, a form of compliment, perhaps, since its average reader, one would have guessed, was either beyond college or below it, a secretary or a high-school student. It printed fiction—generally concerned with the problems of adolescence—job news and hints, beauty advice, and pages of popular-priced fashions photographed in technicolor or Burpee-catalogue hues against glamorous backgrounds. Its models were wind-swept and cute.

Fashion as fun became *Mademoiselle's* identifying byword, a natural corollary to the youth theme. *Fun* with food, *tricks* with spices, herbal *magic,* Hawaiian pineapple, Hawaiian ham, Hawaiian bathing trunks, Hollywood playclothes, cruise news, casserole cookery, Bar-B-Q sauce reflect the dream mentality of a civilization of office conscripts to whom the day off, the two weeks basking in the sun during February or August, represent not only youth but an effortless, will-less slack season (*slacks, loafers,* hostess *pajamas*), quite different from the dynamic good time of the 1920's.

In the *Mademoiselle* play world, everything is romp-diminutive or make-believe. The beau is a "cute brute," the husband a "sahib," or "himself," or "the little fellow." The ready-mix cake "turns out *terrific*." Zircons are "almost indistinguishable from diamonds." "Little tricks of combination, flavor and garnishment help the bride and enchant the groom . . . who need never know!" Brides wearing thirty-five dollar dresses are shown being toasted in champagne by ushers in ascots and striped trousers.

Work may be fun also. "I met headline people on the Hill every day." Husband-and-wife *teams* do "the exciting things" together. And the work-fun of a reader-surrogate named Joan, *Mademoiselle's* Everygirl, is to be continually photographed backstage at "exciting" events, "meeting summer half way on a Caribbean island," meeting Maurice Evans in his dressing room, or gapily watching a chorus rehearsal. The word *meet*, in the sense of "coming into contact with or proximity of," is a denotation of holiday achievement. Resort news is eternal, like hotel-folder sunshine.

The strain of keeping up this bright deception is marked by the grotesquerie of adverbs ("Serve piping hot with a dash of wildly hot mustard nearby"), by the repeated exclamation point, like a jerky, convulsive party smile, and by garish photographic effects. The typical *Mademoiselle* model with her adolescent, adenoidal face, snub nose, low forehead, and perpetually parted lips is immature in an almost painful fashion —on the plane, in the Parisian street, or the tropic hotel she appears out of place and ill at ease, and the photography which strives to "naturalize" her in exotic or expensive surroundings only isolates her further. Against the marble columns or the balustrades, with fishing rod, sailboat, or native basket, she stands in a molar eternity, waving, gesticulating, like the figures in home movies of the vacation trip. ("See, there she is, feeding the pigeons; see, that's Mabel there by the azaleas.")

Another magazine, *Seventeen,* which from its recipes and correspondence column appears to be really directed to teen-agers and their problems, strikes, by contrast with *Mademoiselle,* a grave and decorous note. Poorly gotten out and cheaply written, it has, nevertheless, an authentic small-town air; more than half of its circulation is in towns under twenty-five thousand. It is not, strictly speaking, a fashion magazine (though it carries pages of fashion, gifts, and designs for knitting and dressmaking), but rather a home magazine on the order of *Woman's Home Companion.* How to make things at home, simple dishes to surprise the family with, games to play at parties, nonalcoholic punches for after skating, candies, popcorn balls, how to understand your parents, how to stop a family quarrel, movies of social import, the management of the high-school prom, stories about friendships with boys, crushes on teachers, a department of poems and stories written by teen-agers— all this imparts in a rather homiletic vein the daily lesson of growth and character building.

Pleasures here are wholesome, groupy ("Get your gang together") projects, requiring everybody's cooperation. Thoughtfulness is the motto. The difficulty of being both good and popular, and the tension between the two aims (the great crux of choice for adolescence), are the staple matter of the fiction; every boy hero or girl heroine has a bitter pill to swallow in the ending. The same old-fashioned moral principles are brought to bear on fashion and cooking. The little cook in *Seventeen* is not encouraged, in the *Mademoiselle* style, to think she can make "high drama" out of a Drake's Cake and a pudding mix; she starts her party biscuits or her cake with fresh eggs, fresh butter, and sifted flour. Her first grown-up jewelry is not an "important-looking" chunk of glass but a modest gold safety pin or, if she is lucky and an uncle can give it to her for graduation, a simple gold wrist watch.

And in *Seventeen,* strangely enough, the fashions, while inexpensive, have a more mundane look than *Mademoiselle's* dresses, which tend to be junky—short-waisted, cute, with too many tucks, pleats, belts, and collars for the money. The *Seventeen* date dress is not very different from the "young fashion" in *Vogue* or *Harper's Bazaar*. It has been chosen to give its wearer a little air of style and maturity, on the same principle that an actor playing a drunk tries, not to stagger, but to walk straight. The artifice of youth in the *Mademoiselle* fashions betrays the very thing it is meant to cover—cheapness—and the little short bobbing jackets and boleros and dirndls become a sort of class uniform of the office worker, an assent to permanent juniority as a form of second-class citizenship, on the drugstore stool.

In the upper fashion world, the notion of fashion as fun acquires a delicate savor. The *amusing*, the *witty*, the *delicious* ("a deliciously oversized stole") evoke a pastoral atmosphere, a Louis Seize scene where the queen is in the dairy and pauperdom is Arcadia. The whim, piquant or costly, defines the personality: Try (*Harper's Bazaar*) having *everything* slip-covered in pale Irish linen, including the typewriter and the bird cage; and "just for the fun of it, black with one white glove." The idea of spending as thrift, lately coined by *Vogue*, implies the pastoral opposite of thrift as the gayest extravagance. "There is the good handbag. The pairs of good shoes. . . . The wealth-to-spare look of rich and lean cloths together." A "timeless" gold cross made from old family stones, and seventy-dollar shoes are proposed under the heading "Economical Extravagances." "And upkeep, extravagantly good, is the ultimate economy. Examples: having your books with fine bindings oiled by an expert every year or having your wooden shoe-trees made to order. . . . And purely for pleasure: flowers, silver, and the price of keeping it polished; an Afghan hound, the collection, from stamps to butterflies, to Coalport cabbages, that you, or we, skimp for rather than do without."

The fabrication here of a democratic snobbery, a snobbery for everyone, is *Vogue's* answer to the tumbrils of Truman. The trend of the times is resolutely reckoned with: Today "the smaller collectors who have only one Giorgione" buy at Knoedler's Gallery, just as Mellon used to do. As John Jacob Astor III said, "A man who has a million dollars is as well off as if he were rich." (What a *delicious* sow's ear, my dear, where did you *get* it?) The *small* collection, the *little* evening imply the intimate and the choice, as well as the tiniest pinch

159

of necessity. *Little* hats, *little* furs, *tiny* waists—*Vogue* and the *Bazaar* are wriggling with them; in the old days hats were *small*. And as some images of size contract or cuddle ("Exciting too the tight skull of a hat with no hair showing"; "the sharp, small, polished head"), others stretch to wrap and protect: *enormous, huge, immense* —"a colossal muff," "vast" sleeves; how to have *enormous* eyes. By these semantic devices the reader is made to feel small, frail and valuable. The vocabulary has become extremely tactile and sensuous, the caress of fine fabrics and workmanship being replaced by the caress of prose.

The erotic element always present in fashion, the kiss of loving labor on the body, is now overtly expressed by language. Belts *hug* or *clasp;* necklines *plunge;* jerseys *bind.* The word *exciting* tingles everywhere. "An outrageous amount of S.A." is promised by a new makeup; a bow is "a shameless piece of flattery." A dress is no longer low-cut but *bare.* The diction is full of movement: "hair swept all to one side and just one enormous earring on the bare side." A waist rises from a skirt "like the stem of a flower." Images from sport and machinery (*team, spark*) give this murmurous romanticism a down-to-business, American twang and heighten the kinetic effect. "First a small shopping expedition. . . . Then give your mind a good going-over, stiffen it with some well-starched prose; apply a gloss of poetry, two coats at least."

The bugaboo of getting in a rut, of letting your mind, your figure, or your wardrobe become habit-ridden and middle-aged, is conjured up with a terrible seriousness by all fashion magazines and most vividly of all by *Harper's Bazaar,* which sees culture as a vital agent in the general toning-up process, tries to observe unifying trends and to relate a revival of interest in Scott Fitzgerald to Carol Channing and the cloche hat, and is the victim of its own orderliness in collating a mode to a movement.

Literature and the arts, in the middle and upper fashion magazines, are offered as a tonic to the flabby personality, a tonic frequently scented with the musky odor of Tabu or My Sin. The fiction published by *Harper's Bazaar* (*Vogue* does not print stories), to be conned by suburban ladies under the drier, belongs almost exclusively to the mannerist or decadent school of American writing. Truman Capote, Edita Morris, Jane Bowles, Paul Bowles, Eudora Welty, Jean Stafford, Carson McCullers—what these writers have in common, beyond a lack of matter and a consequent leukemia of treatment (taken by the *Bazaar* editors to be the very essence of art), is a potpourri of *fleurs de mal,* a preoccupation with the décor of sorrow, sexual aberration, insanity, and cruelty, a tasteful arrangement of the bric-a-brac of pathology around the whatnot of a central symbol. This fashionable genre of literary story is published in good faith by the *Bazaar,* with a positive glow, in fact, of high-minded, disinterested evangelism. The editors, to do them justice, are as honestly elated by the discovery of a new decadent talent as by the announcement of a new silhouette, a new coiffure, a new young designer.

For both *Vogue* and *Harper's Bazaar,* the regular discovery of younger and younger authors, of newer and newer painters, is a rather recent development and a concession to democratic principle. Society people to not read, and are not interested (ask a modern dealer) in any painters later than the Impressionists. (The theater is the only branch of art much cared for by people of wealth; like canasta, it does away with the bother of talk after dinner.) A society person who is enthusiastic about modern painting or Truman Capote is already half a traitor to his class: It is middle-class people who, quite mistakenly, imagine that a lively pursuit of the latest in reading and painting will advance their status in the world. It is for them and for their financial inferiors, students of interior decorating or the dance, bookstore clerks, models, assistant buyers and advertising copywriters, the photographs of Picasso drawing with a ray of light, reproductions of paintings by De-Kooning or Baziotes, stories by Carson McCullers, Peggy Bennett, or Speed Lamkin have moment. For all those engaged in competition for status, the surge of a new name forward anywhere, in any field, in astrophysics even, or medicine, is of intense personal reference and concern. Any movement in the social body, any displacement, is felt at once by every mobile member of the organism as relating to his own case, and the inside knowledge of these distant events gives poise and assurance—hence the relevance of the yearly awards given by *Mademoiselle* and other fashion magazines for achievement in science, medicine, human relations, and the like.

A writer for *Mademoiselle* expresses the position of those on the lower rung of the ladder very clearly when she tells about how exciting it is to live in Washington, and adduces as an example the fact that her husband, Bob, once rode on a plane with the U.S. special representative to Israel and another time "bumped into Henry Wallace and General Vaughan coming out of the White House the day Wallace had his farewell row with the President." Here the sense of being close to important events (itself vicarious) passes from the husband to the author to the reader. It is three removes off. What she likes about a certain Washington couple, she continues, is "that they always have interesting people around them, kicking around interesting ideas." And of her friends, in general, "What really roots them to the spot is that the work they do has intrinsic, social meaning." The concluding phrase, with its queer use of the comma, suggests that the intrinsic and the social are distinct and antithetical properties. But from the context it is plain that work that has intrinsic, comma, social meaning is work that is close to the big, busy, important things.

What has happened, in the course of twenty years, is that culture and even political liberalism have been converted by the mass-fashion mind, with its competitive bias, into a sort of Beaux Arts Ball. "A literary and artistic renaissance is what they're talking about over coffee at the Francis Scott Key, Martinis at the Press Club. . . . The Phillips Gallery . . . pace-sets with frequent shows of important contemporary artists, photographers. . . . At Whyte's Bookshop and Gallery . . . the important draw is. . . ." The idea that it's smart to be in step, to be liberal or *avant-garde,* is conveyed through the name-dropping of a Leo Lerman in *Mademoiselle.* To allude negligently to Kafka, Yeats, Proust, Stendhal, or St. John of the Cross in a tone of of-course-you-know-them is canonical procedure for *Mademoiselle* contributors, whatever the topic in hand, while the minor name here (Capote, Buechner, Tennessee Williams, Vidal) has the cachet of the little evening, the little hat, the little fur. The conception of a mass initiate involves an assembly-line production of minority objects

162

of virtu, and is producing a new conformity altogether dominated by the mode, in which late Beethoven, Boogie-woogie, the U.N., Buechner, Capote, FEPC, and *The Cocktail Party* are all equally important names to be spent. Contrary to the practice in high society, the *recherché* is more prized than the known great, and Shakespeare is a virtually worthless counter, which Mrs. Astor never was.

The conspicuous mass display of the bibelots of a curio culture is the promotional secret of *Flair*, the new Cowles magazine, with its first-naming of the New Bohemians, "Carson," "Truman," and "Tennessee," and its splashy collage of democrats and decadents—Margaret Mead and Salvador Dali, Simone de Beauvoir and Mme. Pompadour, Jean Genet and W. H. Auden, Thomas Jefferson and Angus Wilson, Barbara Ward and Franco Spain, Leonor Fini and the Middleburg Hunt, Cocteau and Mauriac. As an instrument of mass snobbery, this remarkable magazine, dedicated simply to the personal cult of its editress, to the fetichism of the flower (Fleur Cowles, *Flair*, a single rose), outdistances all its competitors in the audacity of its conception. It is a leap into the Orwellian future, a magazine without content or point of view beyond its proclamation of itself, one hundred and twenty pages of sheer presentation, a journalistic mirage. The principle of the peep show or illusion utilized in the cutouts, where the eye is led inward to a false perspective of depth, is the trick of the entire enterprise. The articles, in fact, seem meant not to be read but inhaled like a whiff of scent from the mystic rose at the center (flair, through Old French, from *fragrare*, to emit an odor: an instinctive power of discriminating or discerning). Nobody, one imagines, has read them, not even their authors: Grammatical sentences are arranged around a vanishing point of meaning. Yet already, in the very first, quite androgyne number, an ectoplasmic feminine *you* is materialized, to whom a fashion editor's voice speaks in tones of assured divination: "Fashion is Personal. . . . Seven silhouettes chosen from wide possibilities, not because they are extreme high fashion, but because they are silhouettes you might claim. . . ." There follow seven dresses in the current high fashion.

The cynicism and effrontery of this surpass anything previously tried out in journalism. And yet *Vogue* immediately fell into line with its own warm defense of the reader against fashion's tyranny. "Ignore the exquisite exaggerations of fashion drawings" when trying to determine the weight that is right for you; study yourself, know yourself, wear what is timelessly yours. Copy courageous Mrs. Carroll Carstairs, who wears the same beanies every year regardless of the milliners; or Pauline Potter, who carries the same custom-made suede handbag suspended from a jeweler's gold chain. To an experienced reader, this doctrine is merely a 1950 adaptation of the old adage about knowing your own type, a text that generally prefaces the suggestion that the reader should go out and spend a great deal of money on some item of quality merchandise. But beyond the attempt to push quality goods during a buying recession like the recent one, or to dodge responsibility for an unpopular mode (this year's sheaths and cloches are widely unbecoming), there appears to be some periodic feminine compulsion on the editresses' part to strike a suffragette attitude toward the merchants whose products are their livelihood, to ally themselves in a gush with their readers, who are seen temporarily as their "real" friends.

And as one descends to a lower level of the fashion structure, to *Glamour* (Condé Nast) and *Charm* (Street and Smith), one finds a more genuine solicitude for the reader and her problems. The pain of being a B. G. (Business Girl), the envy of superiors, self-consciousness, awkwardness, loneliness, sexual fears, timid friendliness to the Boss, endless evenings with the mirror and the tweezers, desperate Saturday social strivings ("Give a party and ask *everyone* you know"), the struggle to achieve any identity in the dead cubbyhole of office life, this mass misery, as of a perpetual humiliating menstrual period, is patently present to the editors, who strive against it with good advice, cheeriness, forced volubility, a psychiatric nurse's briskness, so that the reiterated "Be natural," "Be yourself," "Smile," "Your good points are you too" (*Mademoiselle*), have a therapeutic justification.

A characteristic running feature in *Glamour* and *Charm* is a newsy letter from the editors, date-lined London, Paris, New York, or Rome, a letter back home full of gossip and family jokes, the sort of letter one writes
164

to a shut-in. The vicarious here is carried to its furthest extreme: The editors live out for the readers a junketing, busy life in which the readers, admittedly, will share only by mail—quite a different thing from the *Mademoiselle* Everygirl projection. The delegation of experience from reader to editor is channeled through a committee of typical (*Charm*) or outstanding (*Glamour*) business girls—the Charm Advisory Committee, the Glamour Career Counselors—selected from all over the country, who are polled from time to time on problems of special interest and who not only keep the editors in touch with the desires of the readers but pass on, through the editors, their own superior know-how to the lowest members of the caste.

A publication of Street and Smith, *Charm* has a more vulgar tone than *Glamour*, which belongs to the *Vogue* chain. Its circulation, considerably smaller than *Glamour's*, larger than *Mademoiselle's*, seems drawn preponderantly from the West and the South, backward fashion areas, while *Glamour's* public is Eastern or urban, the differences being sharpest in the vicinity of New York, Philadelphia, Boston, and Los Angeles. *Glamour's* dresses are more expensive than *Charm's*. It is conscious of Paris, Italy, and London, and will illustrate, in the front of the magazine, the work of Italian craftsmen and French designers for their own sake, as objects of beauty and wonder. As in the old *Vogue*, the cultivation of taste, the development of a fashion sensibility which impersonally delights in the finely made and the rare, are, at least in part, the editorial purpose.

A letter from *Glamour's* editor to the readers in last year's Christmas number, suggesting that the American girl lives too much on dreams and illusions and proposing impersonal goals, has the gently remonstrative seriousness of a young woman dean exhorting her alumnae. Maturity and dignity are valued. Photographs of secretaries of well-known persons, photographs of successful woman who began as secretaries, a history of the secretarial profession emphasize the dignity of office work and give it status through history and a tradition. Serenity in work ("Why I Like My Job"—a contest) and at home are stressed to the point where this itself becomes an aristocratic illusion: an article called "These Gracious Customs" showing the cocktail party with hunt-breakfast silver; the inevitable wedding pictures with champagne, striped trousers, and a butler. Yet the general attitude of *Glamour* is sensible, without much side, and in its own terms idealistic, the eye being directed less downward toward the immediate bargain counter than inward toward self-examination and outward toward the great cities and fine artisans of the world.

With *Charm*, on the other hand, the nadir of the personal is reached: The Business Girl is greeted at her lowest common denominator. The editor becomes "Your Ed," the fun-fabulous-wonderful-sensational shriek ("Learn to make one fabulous dish. . . . Give your earrings a new locale. . . . Carry an umbrella as a costume adjunct. . . . DARE TO DO IT"), addressed to the insecure and the maladroit, echoes in a national hollowness of social failure and fear. A presumption of previous failure in the reader, failure with men, with friends, failure in schoolwork, is the foundation of the average feature: "This Little Girl Never Had Any Fun," "Stood Up."

A lead article on "Smiles" in the January issue points to the Roosevelt smile, the Mona Lisa smile, the Betty Grable smile, the Jolson smile, the Dietrich smile: ". . . people in the public eye have never underestimated the power of a smile: it's odd that *you* have so often overlooked it. . . . Though smiling is nicer as a *spontaneous* thing, you might, just in the nature of an experiment, start smiling as a *conscious* thing. Smile at your family . . . your husband . . . your employer . . . your young man. Smile deliberately at some point in an argument . . . at a break in the conversation. . . . Smile a while in front of your mirror." The article finishes characteristically with some hints about dentifrices and the art of toothbrushing. In another feature by the same author, the natural attractions of the bride-to-be are so despaired of that she is advised to apply a lip-coloring base before going to bed, spray the room with "fragrance," and even "steal" a sachet under the pillow.

A preoccupation with deodorants and "personal hygiene" becomes more and more noticeable as the economic scale is descended. Social failure is ascribed to a lack of "fastidiousness," a lower-middle-class fear that first reveals itself in *Mademoiselle*, where the likelihood of giving "offense" is associated with the male sex. "It's the rare man . . . who isn't considerably more

attractive when he uses some [toilet water or cologne]."
"A consistently fastidious, scrubby male is mighty nice
to have around the house. . . . If he doesn't mind tomorrow's garlic and you do, get him a bottle of the leaf-
fresh mouth wash that *all* men love on first gargle. If
he uses a deodorant—and more men could—keep his
brand on hand. If he doesn't, put a squeeze-spray version where he'll see it—it will appeal to a man's mechanical instinct."

The bridal number of *Charm* carries a feature ("His
and Hers") on bathroom etiquette, showing pictures of
a man and woman gargling, shaving, creaming, brushing
teeth, putting powder between the toes against athlete's
foot, using a deodorant (male); the bathroom is called
the *lavabo*. In the same number, a marriage article, "The
Importance of Not Being Prudish," contains the following advice: "You'll also be a silly prude if you squeak
like a mouse when he, thoughtlessly, walks into the bed-
room without knocking and finds you standing in your
bra and panties. Don't make like September Morn.
Respecting your natural modesty, he'll probably say he's
sorry, walk backward through the door. . . . (He
should have knocked . . .)." And another feature,
"Beauty Steps to the Altar," includes two "Secret Steps":
crayons to color your gray hair give a "natural, plausible performance. . . . And remember there are very
good preparations that make a secret of scars and
blemishes."

Thus, at the lowest fashion level, a most painful illusion-
ism becomes the only recipe for success. Admiration and
compliments provide momentarily the sense of well-being which, for the woman of fashion of the upper level,
is an exhalation of the stuffs and stays that hold her
superb and erect as in a vase of workmanship. For the
reader of *Charm* it is her very self that is the artifact, an
artifact which must be maintained, night and day, in the
close quarters of marriage, brought to a higher sparkle
for party evenings with the gang ("Your quips were a
tearing success; his gags killed 'em"), at the office, in
the subway ("Smile"). The continued tribute to be ex-
torted from others, which the *Charm* policy promises its
untouchables, if only they will follow directions, is laid
down as an American right, to be fought for, creamed
for, depilated and massaged for—more than that, as

duty, with ostracism threatened for slackers. Every woman, says *Glamour* categorically, can be fifty per cent more beautiful. It is the rigorous language of the factory in which new production goals are set yearly, which must not only be met but exceeded. "Mirror, mirror on the wall . . . ?" begs the reader. "You," answers the editor, "if you did your exercises, were the prettiest girl in the Republic."

The Ordeal of Henry Duffill

BY ROBERT GORDON

There was once a lover of music named Henry Duffill, whose tastes were both sound and generous. He had a fine high-fidelity system and a collection of more than five hundred superb records, ranging from Gregorian chants to Bartók. He subscribed to a symphony and a chamber-music series, and if he went to a concert he did not merely endure the Haydn symphony until the Richard Strauss began, nor did he leave after Haydn because he thought that music had ended with the eighteenth century. There was room in his world for both composers.

Henry's attitude toward new works by contemporaries was equally sane. He always listened to them very attentively, and if he enjoyed the piece he applauded with enthusiasm. If not, he clapped hands lightly in tribute to the performers for their honest and dedicated endeavor. In times when everyone was apparently supposed to choose sides and quarrel about something called "modern music," Henry kept his head.

But Henry had a weakness, and it led to difficulties. Under the delusion that the only way to understand music was to listen to it and that listening to music and actually hearing what was there was an activity calling for intense concentration, Henry never read program notes, popular books on music, or the backs of record covers. Had he done so he might never have gotten into trouble, for he would have become inured to one of the devices by which critics often try to scare listeners into a wholehearted acceptance of *all* modern composers—that of dwelling on the follies of past music critics who made the mistake of backing the wrong horses among the composers of their own day. Faced with a work about which he has nothing in particular to say, a commentator can always quote the long-departed critic of the Vienna *Zeitschrift für Musik* to the effect that Beethoven's Second Symphony sounded to him "like *Walpurgisnacht* among the water buffaloes."

Such quotations serve more than one purpose. They'll fill space; they enable one critic to make fun of another with no risk of reprisal; and, most important of all, if the critic has, say, a brother-in-law who is a composer, and whose twelve sonatas for basset horn and percussion have just been issued in a handsome recording by Egocentric Records, they help to create an attitude favorable to their reception. What better way is there to support the cause of contemporary music than by ridiculing those who resisted our established master-pieces when *they* were contemporary? Any contemporary composer may be another Beethoven. Why not play it safe and pretend that he is, even if his music does sound worthless? Why risk the scorn of future generations?

But Henry knew nothing of such matters. Hence his amazement when he first discovered some of the nasty remarks that had been made about his favorite composers. He found them in a book that his wife, with the best intentions, had given him for his birthday. It was by Philip Finletter, a matchless producer of record notes, and was called *Little Lives of Big Composers*.

Most of the book consisted of elegant biographies of the masters, which Finletter had reduced from the usual sources, particularly *Grove's Dictionary of Music and Musicians*. But the critic happened to have in his files a prodigious collection of surly comments by past critics, and these he sprinkled as seasoning throughout his book. When Henry read them he was dumfounded. It had never occurred to him that music he had always enjoyed could have stirred up so much hostility. Moreover, in his innocence and with the help of a few hints from Finletter, he fell into the trap and made the inevitable connection between the follies of dead critics and his own response to some of the contemporary music he had heard.

A week earlier, for example, he had nearly laughed aloud during a performance of Ignaz Gassman's "Etheriation for Mouth Organ, Timpani, and Theremin." Hadn't he been following in the footsteps of Bosworth Figgis, who a hundred years ago had written in the

169

Manchester *Blade* that the Oriental water torture was as nothing compared to an evening of Mendelssohn? The idea was a disturbing one, and gradually there formed in Henry's mind the image that was to haunt him for weeks to come—of a many-headed creature called Posterity, busily giving Henry Duffill the raspberry for not recognizing the genius that flowered in his own day.

Finletter's book soon had more definite results. A week after reading it, Henry was seen at a chamber concert that offered the world première of Sacheverell Netherbow's "Liquefaction in F Minor," written for six viols accompanied by centrifugal water pump. Afterward he was heard to remark on the "significant new tonal textures" discovered by Netherbow. At a later program he vigorously applauded Millicent Griffon's "Keyboard Sonata in Five Minutes," a piece written faithfully to the rule that no single key could be pressed more than once. On this occasion Henry observed to his protesting wife that "The rejection by modern composers of the musical rhetoric of the nineteenth century does not, as some reactionary critics assert, imply a new lawlessness. Witness Miss Griffon's rigid adherence to her new-found principle."

But Henry's attempt to avoid Posterity's derision was not without its cost. Music—all music—began to lose its savor. When, for example, he heard a contemporary work that he enjoyed, he was frustrated in his efforts to express the degree of appreciation that he felt, for honesty here would have exposed his hypocrisy elsewhere. And so he became nervous and truculent in his efforts to keep up a front. He gave up his frantic search for good recordings of the Haydn symphonies and instead brought home Egocentric's new limited edition of Ferris Ferris's "Sixteen American Prolusions for Banjo, Castanets, and Snare Drum." And when he belligerently insisted on playing them again and again, his wife developed such a sudden enthusiasm for P.T.A. meetings and sewing circles that for weeks they hardly saw each other.

What would have become of Henry had this situation continued we have, fortunately, no way of knowing. For one evening, at a concert of little-known eighteenth-century composers, the clouds were dispelled and he recovered his sanity.

It came about this way: Henry happened to be sitting next to Grayson Glossin, the critic of the *Times-Guardian*. Glossin was of an ostentatious temperament, and would sit with his notebook held high, writing his comments in such a large round hand that all those about him could read them. Henry, like the others who surrounded Glossin, was perfectly willing to behold the birth pangs of tomorrow's column, for little had happened since his reading of Finletter's book to destroy his faith in critics. The first selection on the program was Johann Gottwald's "Symphony No. 112 in C." Gottwald had been a member of the famous Mannheim school, and had produced a total of 174 symphonies, 83 oratorios, 29 Masses, 120 string quartets, 80 piano sonatas, and hordes of *divertimenti*, serenades, and German dances. He had also been officially endorsed as undeservedly neglected (*unverdient vernachlässigt*) by no fewer than six German musicologists. Naturally Henry was hopeful as the conductor raised his baton.

But his hopes were miserably disappointed. Almost from the beginning, with its twelve solemn C-major chords, repeated exactly, Gottwald's symphony revealed itself as one of those exercises that eighteenth-century composers wrote to keep their hand in. The slow movement consisted of twelve variations on a theme so inane that Henry couldn't remember it even after the interminable piece, with all its repeats duly adhered to, had run its course. He was all the more surprised, therefore, when he saw Glossin's newly minted comment to the effect that the slow movement "exhibited moments of bardic profundity strongly anticipatory of the later Chopin."

After the lugubrious minuet had galumphed up and down the C-major triad for what seemed a terribly long time, Glossin wrote: "A sturdy rustic dance, a true *Mannheim* minuet, lacking, perhaps, the wit and elegance of Haydn's or Mozart's achievements in the same vein, but nonetheless possessing certain foursquare virtues of its own." The finale was, if anything, worse than the other movements—a chatty pastiche of C-major passage work. Yet the audience applauded vigorously, the conductor bowed in genial self-satisfaction, and Glossin scribbled away in an ecstasy.

By this time, however, Henry was busy with thoughts of his own—thoughts that were to lead to the recovery of his pre-Finletter state of balance. He was coming to understand that if Posterity, as represented by Glossin and the rest of the audience as they applauded Gottwald's symphony, could be such a priceless idiot, it wasn't worth worrying about. For a delicious moment Henry identified himself with the angry listener at the symphony's 1772 première who had, according to the program notes, "derisively snatched off the composer's wig and placed it upon the rear end of the Elector Palatine's horse." No longer was Henry disturbed by the similarity between such responses and his own. Future generations, he thought, might applaud the works of Ignaz Gassman or Millicent Griffon, but there was no terror in this possibility. Folly, like good sense and good music, transcended the passage of time and the succession of generations.

Henry Duffill is once more a lover of music. He goes to a great many concerts and listens hopefully and intently when new works are played. If he enjoys what he hears, he applauds with enthusiasm. If not, he claps hands politely in tribute to the performers for their honest and dedicated endeavor. And when someone asks him if he likes Bartók or Berg, he says, "Yes, I like some of his work, for example . . . but some of it I don't like, such as . . ."

But when he is asked his opinion of Sacheverell Netherbow's "Liquefaction in F Minor," his answer is very much like the opening of Beethoven's Fifth: terse, elemental, and delivered *con brio*.

Movies: Throwing the Book Away

BY ROBERT BINGHAM

If the incredible words "From a Story by F. Scott Fitzgerald" had not appeared among the credits for "The Last Time I Saw Paris," I certainly wouldn't trouble you with a description of this abysmal film. Just another rotten movie would be soon forgotten. But the differences between Fitzgerald's story and MGM's movie set me to brooding about some of the other rotten movies I have seen recently—and about the deliberate preference for bad writing that makes them what they are.

It's not that there's anything sacred about Fitzgerald. Like the people he wrote about, Fitzgerald lived recklessly and foolishly most of the time. When he wrote recklessly and foolishly, as he did too much of the time, he was the naughty darling of the Gay Twenties, but he wasn't much of a writer. When he brought understanding and discipline to bear upon his own experience, however, he could write a book like *The Great Gatsby* or a short story like "Babylon Revisited."

Fitzgerald's story is about two days in the life of Charlie Wales. The time is the early 1930's, and the mood is one of sobering up after a long binge. The party—rich Americans in Paris—had lasted nearly a decade, and it had cost Charlie a great deal. ("I didn't realize it, but the days came along one after another, and then two years were gone, and everything was gone, and I was gone.") Charlie returns to Paris hoping to persuade his vindictive sister-in-law to give up custody of his nine-year-old daughter, so that he can begin at least some kind of meaningful life for himself.

The way Charlie had lost his wife is treated with restraint and evocative indirection. Here is very nearly the whole of it: "There was a scene at the Florida, and then he attempted to take her home, and then she kissed young Webb at a table; after that there was what she had hysterically said. When he arrived home alone he turned the key in the lock in wild anger. How could he know she would arrive an hour later alone, that there would be a snowstorm in which she wandered about in slippers, too confused to find a taxi?"

At the end of Fitzgerald's story, a bartender speaks:

"'I heard that you lost a lot in the crash.'

"'I did,' and he added grimly, 'but I lost everything I wanted in the boom.'

"'Selling short.'

"'Something like that.'

"Again the memory of those days swept over him like a nightmare—the people they had met traveling; then people who couldn't add a row of figures or speak a coherent sentence. The little man Helen had consented to dance with at the ship's party, who had insulted her ten feet from the table; the women and girls carried screaming with drink or drugs out of public places—

"—The men who locked their wives out in the snow, because the snow of twenty-nine wasn't real snow. If you didn't want it to be snow, you just paid some money."

MGM's movie is about ten years in the life of Charlie Wills. (Perhaps the writers hoped to salve their consciences by changing his name.) The time is updated to just after the Second World War, and the mood is that of a Dartmouth house party. All the wanton, childish emotions that Fitzgerald had come painfully to understand and at last to control—everything he wisely forbore to write very much about—Hollywood has prettied up and spread before us in Glorious Technicolor with Stereophonic Sound.

It's a movie in which you may very well find your eyes filling with tears, but when you get outside you will resent the tears—because they were about nothing. I do not agree with Marya Mannes, who wrote some time ago in these pages that television can produce a much more intimate effect upon its audience than movies. With television you are sitting in your own living room, and there are familiar references about to remind you of reality: The telephone may ring, the baby may cry, a commercial will surely interrupt, and if you get mad at the show you can turn it off or go into another room. But with movies—having paid a dollar or more to sit in temporary isolation in a dark theater staring up at the huge people on the huge screen—you are almost helpless to resist whatever tawdry emotions may be inflicted upon you.

Van Johnson as Charlie pouts handsomely throughout and learns nothing from his experience. It is difficult to believe that Elizabeth Taylor as his wife Helen is capable of understanding anything beyond the fact that she has been photographed in a number of pretty dresses. A few years ago just after a divorce Miss Taylor grew thoughtful and summed up her own talents better than any critic ever could: "I have a woman's body and a child's emotions." In "The Last Time I Saw Paris," then, we are surely given what the press agents would call the *real* Elizabeth Taylor. She is ably supported in her endeavors by the rest of the cast, the director, and the writers.

Tidying up after great writers is not, unfortunately, peculiar to Hollywood. The British have made a version of Graham Greene's *The Heart of the Matter* that is even more of a disappointment than what MGM did to "Babylon Revisited." More of a disappointment because for the most part it is a splendid picture.

174

Greene's book concerns Major Scobie, assistant commissioner of police in a West African colony. Scobie is a believing Roman Catholic, and his anguish challenges and tests not only the dogmas of that church but the ultimate beliefs of all Christians. He cannot bear to hurt others. And yet his very existence inevitably involves pain for his wife, for the girl who becomes his mistress, and above all for his God. Scobie finds it impossible to go to confession believing that he will sin no more and thus receive for himself the peace of absolution. He thinks he will be able to take all the pain upon himself by committing the worst crime a Catholic can commit —suicide. "This was what human love had done to him— it had robbed him of love for eternity. It was no use pretending as a young man might that the price was worth while."

And yet what man can judge such matters? On the last page of the book there is this dialogue:

"Father Rank clapped the cover of the diary to and said, furiously, 'For goodness' sake, Mrs. Scobie, don't imagine you—or I—know a thing about God's mercy.'

" 'The Church says . . .'

" 'I know the Church says. The Church knows all the rules. But it doesn't know what goes on in a single human heart.'

" 'You think there's some hope then?' she wearily asked.

" 'Are you so bitter against him?'

" 'I haven't any bitterness left.'

" 'And do you think God's likely to be more bitter than a woman?' "

The British movie has reduced Scobie to a middle-aged man with woman trouble. He is even saved from suicide by a conveniently contrived accident. At the end he lies smiling in the arms of his faithful No. 1 Boy Ali and mouths the Sunday-school words, "Tell Missus God makes it all right."

It is disgusting. Disgusting because the actors—Trevor Howard as Scobie, Elizabeth Allan as his wife, and Maria Schell as the other woman—are quite good enough to have played the story the way Greene wrote it. The photography is beautiful, the direction is sensitive, but somewhere along the line it was found expedient to throw away the entire point of the book.

The Trial of Jomo Kenyatta

BY SANTHA RAMA RAU

A dark, infinitely foreign face from the mountains of Kenya stared out at Americans from their newspapers a few weeks ago. The man's hair was ragged, the eyes flat, the expression altogether uncomprehending—an obscure Mau Mau terrorist, condemned to death by a British court, standing beside an English soldier in a neat uniform with bright buttons, gazing with that wild look into the camera.

It was all supposed to be over by now: the terrorism, Mau Mau, the military outposts in the forests and hills of Kenya. It was supposed to have ended a year ago with the trial and sentence of Jomo Kenyatta. As I looked at the newspaper picture the other day, I remembered again that extraordinary trial, what it had taught me about Africa, and how it has been the beginning, not the end, of one of the most turbulent problems in the world.

The trial of Jomo Kenyatta, the only African to emerge as anything approaching a national leader in that curious association of colonies, trust territories, and protectorates that makes up British East Africa, began with a certain degree of local interest in an obscure village in a wilderness on December 3, 1952. It ended four months later in a flurry of world-wide publicity, in the wake of a massacre, with the conviction and seven-year sentence of Kenyatta on charges of leading and managing the secret society of African terrorists known as Mau Mau.

To the people who were following with fascination the progress of the trial—the foreign journalists, the white settlers in Africa, the Labour Members of Parliament in England, the representatives of the Colonial Office both in Britain and in Kenya, and of course the Africans—the outcome was never in very much doubt. But the issues held such enormous interest and importance for Kenyans, whatever their race, that the circulation of the chief newspaper reporting the trial in Swahili (the closest thing to a vernacular *lingua franca* for Africans) more than doubled during those weeks; and as the tension grew through the months of the equatorial summer and autumn, both the weather and the Royal Family were superseded in the Englishman's small talk by details of the Kenyatta trial.

Perhaps to the outside observer most of all, the Kenyatta trial seemed an extraordinary, bizarre, and ominous affair, exposing as it did many elements of magic, witchcraft, Christian fervor, atrocities, politics, and, even more horrifying, the chasm of misunderstanding, fantasy, and ignorance between the races.

On October 21, 1952, Jomo Kenyatta was arrested in Nairobi, the capital of Kenya, and detained under the emergency regulations that had come into force to deal with the disturbed conditions in the colony as a result of Mau Mau activity. Specifically Kenyatta was charged with "management of an unlawful society, Mau Mau, which is dangerous to the good government of the Colony." With him were charged five other Africans, all members of the Kenya African Union.

The six men were all charged with conspiracy "by use of physical force or by threat or intimidation, to compel persons in Kenya to take an oath, or engagement in the nature of an oath, purporting to bind those taking it to act, or not to act, in any particular way." To the layman these charges are inclined to seem vague—which is not altogether surprising since Mau Mau itself is so ill defined. The one clear point was that they referred to Mau Mau procedure and organization. This conspiracy, the government claimed, was intended to promote disaffection and discontent in Kenya, and to cause friction between the races.

The Europeans in the colony put it more simply and more catchily—if less accurately. To them Mau Mau was an anti-European movement designed to kick the British out of Kenya by terrorism, murder of human beings, slaughter of livestock, and possibly, in the end, a scorched-earth policy. They called it "the African Stern Gang," or sometimes a "Ku Klux Klan in reverse."

The felonious activities for which the six men were arrested were supposed to have taken place between January 1, 1950, and the date of Jomo Kenyatta's detention on October 21, 1952. Actually, the secret society called Mau Mau has been known as a functioning if elusive organization since 1942. For ten years the authorities saw no reason to worry about Mau Mau. Sir Philip Mitchell, Governor of Kenya until 1952, declared about three months before Kenyatta's arrest, "You will even see it reported that East Africa is seething with African unrest—of all inexplicable nonsense!"

Relatively little was at first known about Mau Mau beyond the fact that it was confined to the Kikuyu tribe, one of the most advanced of East Africa's 220 tribes; that its members seemed to be mostly in the Rift Valley, the vast geological fault that runs like a monstrous trench through the plateaus of Kenya; and that its membership, enrolled by oath, was confined to men. Even now, after the murders and massacres attributed to Mau Mau, after the extensive publicity it has received, after the committees, officials, policemen, soldiers, and journalists have all inquired into it, Mau Mau still retains most of its original mystery. Nobody (not even the majority of the members themselves) even knows what the name means. Various guesses have included the possibility that Mau Mau was evolved from the initials of Member of the African Union, and a more fanciful idea that Mau Mau is a corruption of "miaow-miaow" because the terrorists sometimes left a strangled cat at the scene of an atrocity as a symbol of their society.

The most logical suggestion is that Mau Mau is an anagram of *Uma Uma*, which in the Kikuyu language means "Get out! Get out!" But even this has never been confirmed authoritatively. Jomo Kenyatta answered the question when it was put to him in the witness box by saying that he had "no idea what Mau Mau means." Nobody really knows the extent of Mau Mau membership. Estimates vary from ninety-five per cent of the Kikuyu tribe—which would amount to more than a million people—to only five per cent.

The purposes of Mau Mau have remained almost as obscure as the name. It has come to be pretty generally accepted (except by the more diehard of the white settlers) that one of the reasons for the rise of Mau Mau was the Kikuyu land hunger. The huge productive plateau straddling the equator in the middle of Kenya is known as the White Highlands because here the Englishmen who arrived around the turn of the century to establish Kenya as a colony ruled that no Africans or

Asians might own land, and that the Highlands remain White in the racial sense.

In the last fifty years the population of the Kikuyu tribe has grown enormously, largely because the white man, in a way, brought his own destruction with him. Epidemics and tribal wars, which had previously kept the population pressures at a perilous equilibrium, were extensively controlled by the newly arrived foreigners. The land set aside for the Kikuyu tribal reserves can no longer contain them. Even on the land that they have, they are forbidden to grow the better-paying crops such as coffee, sisal, and pyrethrum (a variety of marguerite from which is extracted an essential component of most insecticides).

Finally, as Dr. L. S. B. Leakey, the most distinguished authority on the Kikuyu and their customs, claims, it is firmly established in Kikuyu tradition that the White Highlands were leased, not sold, by the tribe to the foreigners. Now the Kikuyu want them back. Mau Mau was supposed to force land concessions from the British.

To the average white settler who has bought his farm in good faith with all the right legal documents, developed the land far beyond its previous state, invested his money, and made his home in the Highlands, this whole argument seems, naturally, to be the outrageous nonsense of socialists or malcontents.

Another version of the purpose of Mau Mau that is quite often advanced is that it is a strong and sudden return to magic and the old beliefs of the power of tribal chiefs and witch doctors. This is supposed to have come about as a reaction to the work and preaching of missionaries and the teaching the Africans have received in mission schools. Here, it is claimed, the encroaching foreigner broke down the security of the African in the rigid structure of his tribe and the compulsive fears and confidence in his religion of magic and terror without providing an alternative society that was close enough or comprehensible enough to the African, and without substituting a religion that he could understand.

Certainly to the average African, even if he can sort out in his own mind the conflicting sects and contradictory creeds of the different varieties of missionary in his country, the contrast between Christian teaching and ethics and the African place in the new Christian society

179

that has evolved in Kenya must be disturbing and embittering.

A more cynical explanation of Mau Mau is that it was conceived largely as a money-making concern. With the rise of the cost of living in Africa the compulsory Mau Mau entrance fee has risen from seven shillings to sixty-two shillings and fifty cents—about nine dollars, or six weeks' wages for an African. Somebody must be getting all this money for a relatively small output. Mau Mau in this case would be only a sort of gangsterism, an extensive protection racket.

The most idealistic version of Mau Mau is that it is a genuine nationalistic movement designed to get self-government for Kenya Africans, and that its terrorist aspects are an unfortunate by-product that grew up—against the wishes of the leaders—among the impatient elements who felt that there was no chance of receiving a just settlement from the British by peaceful means.

Still other explanations are that the present outbreak is an inevitable race war; that it is the revolt of the intellectual African against the British and their discrimination against the colored races; that it is the revolt of the primitive and savage African against the intellectual African, and only incidentally against the British; that it is a Communist or Communist-directed upheaval; that it is an anti-Christian movement, that the whole thing has been hysterically exaggerated and that Mau Mau is really no force at all.

When Jomo Kenyatta was tried, there was a good deal of evidence to back up every one of these conflicting theories. For each there was also a good deal of discrediting proof. Altogether it was rather difficult for the outsider to make out precisely what—in the broad sense—Kenyatta was accused of.

Defenders of the African cause were quick to claim that Kenyatta's arrest was simply an excuse to ban the Kenya African Union, the first organized and politically aware group of East Africans to flourish and gain support for their work. The other extreme felt that unless Mau Mau leaders were dealt with firmly, Africans would lose respect for British sovereignty and government.

Only this much at least was certain, out of all the conflicting theories and explanations: that Mau Mau contained elements of blind superstition, intimidation, and political aspiration accompanied with savagery, brigandage, and murder of the most horrifying sort. Because of these the Europeans anger against Kenyatta from the time of his arrest rose sharply.

When Kenyatta was first detained it would have been possible under the emergency regulations for the British authorities simply to exile or intern him without any trial at all. During the more explosive moments of the trial, and as the list of European murders mounted to a total of eight in those weeks, a good many of the people involved wished that the authorities had done just that, for the Kenyatta trial quickly grew into much more than the exile of a troublemaker.

Kenyatta was arrested in Nairobi, but because the police felt that there was danger of public uprisings and trouble in the capital if the trial were held there, he was taken up to the Northern Province. This is a vast desolate frontier region of Kenya where the tribes are supposed to be particularly primitive. It is a "restricted area," where nobody is allowed in or out without a police pass. It was to this area that troublemakers, Communists, and various political and criminal prisoners were exiled or held in detention. And it was in Kapenguria, a tiny village there, that the trial of Jomo Kenyatta was held.

The point at which world attention suddenly focused on Kenyatta was when no European lawyer in Kenya would handle his defense. It would have ruined his his practice. D. N. Pritt, a lawyer of considerable distinction, a Queen's Counsel, a Labour M.P. for fifteen years, a man who made his reputation on political trials and who is perhaps best known in the United States for his successful defense of Gerhart Eisler when he jumped ship in England, announced that he would take the case and became the chief counsel for the defense of Kenyatta and his five colleagues. Pritt, a red-complexioned man of medium height with an offhand manner, flew to Kenya and plunged at once into the tangle of misunderstandings and the great gap between cultures that would characterize the trial. Pritt was met by an enthusiastic crowd of Africans, many of whom, it turned out, had heard his title "Queen's Counsel" and assumed that Elizabeth II had so taken Kenyatta's cause to heart that she was sending her personal lawyer to defend him. The

181

next few days, however, made it clear that Pritt brought no such overwhelming authority.

Pritt's very first act resulted in an antagonism that quickly grew to fury among the white settlers as the trial progressed. He appeared before the Kenya Supreme Court to declare with angry bluntness that the indictments against his clients were "the vaguest allegations of conspiracy I have ever seen in forty-three years' experience" and to demand that the venue of the trial be changed to Nairobi, where he would have access to libraries, essential documents, and witnesses.

Pritt's fireworks made the Kenyatta trial news for most of the world and such a *cause célèbre* in Asia and Africa that several lawyers from India and West Africa joined the defense team. This, in turn, raised a number of complications. It became clear that the trial was no longer a private Kenya affair. Inevitably the position of all Africans was going to be discussed. Probably the presence of the British in Kenya, even in all East Africa, would be considered. A number of vaguely discreditable and definitely disturbing facts about life in Kenya were going to get an uncomfortably public airing.

The various defense lawyers ran immediately into one of the bitterest issues between the races. They met it first in the matter of living quarters. All of them except Pritt were, in the Kenya sense, colored. They could not therefore stay in hotels, in clubs, or in wayside inns. They couldn't eat their meals in European restaurants, or travel first class in trains, or get a drink in a bar. Eventually they all crowded into the home of an obliging Indian businessman.

Kapenguria itself is too small a village to have any public accommodation. All the people involved in the trial lived twenty-four miles away in the nearest town, Kitale. There, the one hotel and one residential club were exclusively for Europeans, and the color bar (or the "culture bar," a genteel phrase some of the Europeans insist on using) excluded all the defense team except Pritt.

The Kenya Supreme Court turned down Pritt's request for a change of venue, and in an atmosphere of growing tension and hard feelings the trial opened in Kapenguria on December 3, 1952. The setting itself added uncomfortably to the drama of the occasion. Kapenguria has no courtroom, so a little red schoolhouse, normally used for government-sponsored classes in agriculture, was requisitioned for the purpose, and the only large class-room was arranged as a court. The immediate grounds of the schoolhouse were surrounded by barbed-wire fences and enclosures to which Jomo and his five fellow prisoners retired for their luncheon recess. The specta-tors from the nearby farms and counsel, as if at a picnic, sat on the grass munching sandwiches and bananas and drinking coffee or warm Coca-Cola.

The surrounding area and the roads leading to Kapenguria were patrolled by armored cars and by special details of police. Occasionally, driving to the trial, one would see groups of men from the wild and primitive Suk tribe that lives in the restricted area. They would be standing on the roadside, watching enthralled as the daily procession of cars (more than would nor-mally pass that way in a month), each with its accom-panying fog of pinkish dust, swept by to Kapenguria. The strangers in turn stared at the Suk, naked except for the nodding ostrich feathers in their headdresses and their beads or bracelets made of copper wire stolen from the electric lines across the country. A newspaperman told me of seeing a Suk girl wearing only what was ap-parently her most cherished household possession, an aluminum teakettle, on her head. Sometimes the mutual scrutiny became embarrassing, and the Suk, as is their habit when they are shy, would cover their faces with their hands. In a few seconds the cars would be gone.

Inside the cheerful, humdrum little room the antago-nisms, the loyalties, the tensions, and the rancor were so vital as to change the quality of the air one breathed. About fifty spectators could be seated comfortably in the room at the scratched school desks with the scrib-bled figures of old calculations on them, the carved initials, the doodles. In front sat the prosecutor, A. G. Somerhough, large, round-faced, balding, with the culti-vated Englishman's sense of humor and sarcasm, a pop-ular man in Kenya for his distinguished war record, his work on the trial of the war criminals in Germany, and, more recently, for the ability he had displayed as the second-in-command to the Attorney-General of the col-ony. Both he and his blond, handsome assistant wore the conventional formal black coats and striped trousers—startling and incongruous in the equatorial sunlight.

Next to them at the defense tables the lawyers were more informally dressed in tweeds and lounge suits. In front of them and to their right was the witness box. At the end of the room was the low dais where R. S. Thacker, the magistrate, sat in his robes and wig with his back to a blackboard and under a colored print of the young and smiling face of the Queen. To the left of the audience, on a long narrow bench set against the wall, guarded by two tall askaris in their uniforms of navy-blue sweaters, khaki shorts, and red Moslem fezzes, observed by several English CID men both inside the room and from the veranda, sat the six prisoners, looking unexpectedly short and shabby. Through the windows, across the barbed wire and the patrol cars, you could see the tall silver eucalyptus trees, the blue air of the high country, and the incredibly beautiful foothills of Mount Eglon.

Naturally most interest centered on Kenyatta himself. Throughout the trial, except for moments of intense emotion in the witness box, he seemed entirely at ease, sometimes amused. In the weeks that followed, his corduroy golf jacket, suede shoes, and colored shirt all became a familiar part of the trappings of the court. He is a stocky man with an ugly, powerful face. As the magazines and newspapers were soon to prove, he can be photographed to look either like a frog or like one of the more impressive and saintly Biblical prophets. He has a short, sparse beard and a big, curving mouth which shows uneven yellow teeth when he smiles. His nose is broad and his hairline receding. It is his eyes that transform his face, his admirers claim, into the dedicated countenance of a righteous leader. They have been described variously as hypnotic, flashing, brilliant, mesmeric, cunning, and blank. An Englishman once described him as "part mountebank, part Hampstead intellectual," but all the same he is just about the only African whose name is known throughout East Africa and who has devoted friends and followers among the most educated and the most backward of the Africans. Perhaps his most famous asset is a formidable gift of oratory.

When he spoke in public he drew audiences of thirty

to fifty thousand. Throughout Kenya people knew his voice, his speeches, and his mannerisms—so much so that one story ran that a sort of code had been established between him and his audiences. He always carried a stick with an ivory handle carved to resemble an elephant head. Another prop was a large ring in which was set a white stone about an inch in diameter. The rumor went that he used these props to indicate to his audience where he meant his words to be taken seriously or as the exact reverse of what he was saying. In the course of his trial this question of his sincerity in his public speeches became one of the more important aspects of the case for the Crown.

I suppose it is always the way with men who capture the imagination of crowds of people that they not only represent a number of diverse things to different people but that they are themselves represented in many conflicting and contradictory ways. The impressions and stories about Kenyatta are endless. He appears as the intellectual and also as the rabble rouser. Sometimes he is the dedicated patriot, at other times the devious traitor. He is described as selfless, almost an ascetic, yet one of the early prosecution witnesses in his trial called him the "heaviest drinker in the world."

Even the "facts" of his life allow for so much guesswork and interpretation that a baffling amount of contradiction exists. He doesn't, for example, know when he was born. His passport, based presumably on how old he seemed at the time he got it, makes him fifty-nine. He is by blood a Kikuyu, and was educated in one of the Church of Scotland mission schools, but beyond that, he says, he was "self-educated." Certainly his formal education was interrupted for a considerable period, for right after he left school in 1914 he went to work as a laborer on a farm in the White Highlands. In 1922 he began the political work which so consumed his interest that by 1928 he was devoting almost his full time to it. He earned a living by working as a meter reader for the municipal water board of Nairobi. In 1929 he went to Europe on money raised for him by the Kikuyu tribe. Already they recognized him as an important force.

Europe changed Kenyatta's life radically, although just what he did in the seventeen years he was there remains for the most part obscure. By his own admission he visited Moscow twice and spent altogether nearly two years at the Moscow University. He also spent some time at the London School of Economics, where he, like so many other students from various colonies and parts of the British Empire, fell under the influence of Harold Laski. He received a postgraduate diploma in anthropology in London and wrote as his thesis the semi-autobiography that was published as a book, *Facing Mount Kenya*. During this period he married an Englishwoman and had a son by her. He already had a Kikuyu wife.

In 1946 Kenyatta returned to Kenya. To all black Africans educated abroad, the return home is a disheartening experience. In Europe they have been treated as equals, if not actually lionized by the people they have met and worked with. Back home they are again thrown back to the irritations and insults of the color bar, and the more concrete grievances of lower pay and lesser jobs and virtually no possibility of economic advance, all countenanced by law and jurisprudence.

I suppose it must be assumed, in the light of Kenyatta's conviction, that he returned from England and immediately became the manager of Mau Mau. It is also assumed that the extensive job of founding African schools independent of the foreign missions—to which, ostensibly, he gave all his time that was not taken by the semi-political activities of the Kenya African Union—was really an elaborate way of establishing underground channels for spreading Mau Mau propaganda. When he was arrested these schools were either closed down or had been placed under strict supervision to purge their staff of Mau Mau teachers, and the Kenya African Union, already suspect as an organization, virtually ceased to function. Kenyatta's friends announced hotly that its suppression, not Mau Mau terrorism, was the purpose of his arrest.

To the spectators in the court, almost every day there was some new excitement, usually of a melodramatic sort. The prosecution's case, however, was entirely concerned with Mau Mau and fell into three broad sections. The first was intended to show that Kenyatta had taken and administered the Mau Mau oath; the second that on the occasions when he had denounced Mau Mau he was insincere and that his real policy, along with the
186

policy of the organization of which he was president (the Kenya African Union), was anti-European and pro-Mau Mau; and the last that he had allowed himself to be idolized, with his name blasphemously substituted for Jesus Christ's in hymns; and that these actions were consistent only with his role as manager of Mau Mau.

The first few prosecution witnesses—all of them Africans—set the mood for mystery, magic, and barbaric rites. They were the ones who claimed to have seen Kenyatta take the Mau Mau oath himself and administer it to others. All begged Thacker to withhold their names from the press because they were afraid of reprisals. They were all kept in a specially guarded encampment, for it was not considered safe to allow them to live in their villages. To a question of whether these witnesses needed such elaborate protection because they were committing perjury, Somerhough replied acidly and with considerable effect, "It isn't a question of witnesses committing perjury but of committing suicide."

Among them the witnesses established what became the classic description of the ceremony of the Mau Mau oath taking: the walk through the banana-leaf arch, the eating of the sheep's meat, the touching of the mucus and liquid from the sheep's eye to the lips, the payment of sixty-two shillings and fifty cents. One of them explained that the ritual had taken place in his village and he had been forced into participation against his will. His flat, rather surly account was curiously evocative of the evening in a hut three years earlier.

"I saw a lamp inside burning low," he testified. "It was practically out. I felt my hands seized by a man and I was told by him: 'Take off your boots and if you have any money get rid of it.'" The man was joined by Kenyatta. "He said, 'You have got to go in. . . .' As they pushed me in they tried to calm me down, saying, 'It is nothing bad.' I was taken back into the house where I had been told to take off my boots. There were two rooms in it and a lot of people were present. There was a lot of murmuring. I saw an arch of banana leaves and other things. Jomo Kenyatta took hold of me and passed me with him through the arch.

"We stood side by side on the far side of the arch. I heard a murmuring of voices saying, 'Eat this meat . . . Eat this meat. . . . If you sell our country or our people, may this meat destroy you.'

"Because I was angry I did not bite it, but it was rubbed hard against my lips. I was told again, 'Eat this meat. If you ever sell our land to the Europeans, you will die.'

"Again I was told, 'Eat this meat and you will pay sixty-two shillings and fifty cents. Unless you do, this meat will hate you and cause you to die. . . . If you ever disclose the secrets to any person not belonging to these secrets, may you be hated by this meat.'"

Throughout this ceremony, the witness said, Kenyatta was beside him and "was having done to him what was being done to me."

It must have occurred to a good many people who saw the trial or read about it that this whole question of oath taking and the government stand on it could create considerable confusion in the minds of the average uneducated Kikuyu tribesmen. Clearly the government considered the articles of the Mau Mau oath described by the witnesses wicked and worthy of punishment, though, to reverse the situation, an Englishman commits himself to many of the same things. An Englishman, for instance, cannot sell land in the White Highlands to anyone of another race; he too would be considered a traitor were he to "sell his country or his people"; and presumably he too lives under the threat both of punishment and of social ostracism.

Besides the commandments to which a Kikuyu was sworn under the Mau Mau oath, the manner of his swearing apparently aroused considerable disgust deepening to utter revulsion among the Europeans. Yet, fantastically enough, even more drastic ceremonies were condoned or initiated by the government authorities. In a ritual that undertook to release Kikuyu from their Mau Mau promises, which was officially called a "cleansing ceremony" but which became more popularly known as a "de-oathing," the authorities were looking for a ceremony so powerful that it would undo even the terrifying Mau Mau oath.

The procedure was, accordingly, intensified. Instead of simply touching the mucus of the sheep's eye to the lips, in the de-oathing one had to eat the eye, the theory being that a stronger witchcraft would destroy the weaker magic. This routine so upset Members of Parliament in England, who deplored the using of barbarism to defeat barbarism, that the more extreme forms of the de-oathing had to be suppressed. However, the ritual of de-oathing continued in a milder way.

One such ceremony that I saw was officially sponsored in a part of the Kikuyu tribal reserve where there was supposed to be an extremely high incidence of Mau Mau influence and membership. It was conducted by a fully qualified witch doctor wearing his regalia of ostrich plumes and scarlet jacket over rather patched and worn clothes. He was decorated with safety pins and carried the traditional quiver full of arrows. He performed the de-oathing ceremony with one of the magic *ithikari*—sacred stones which have seven holes in them to represent the seven orifices of the body. The man who was being cleansed placed the end of a sliver of bamboo in each hole. Holding the ends of the seven sticks, he repeated the oath of loyalty to the British government. The oath followed very closely the pattern of the Mau Mau's. It must be puzzling for the ordinary Kikuyu to decide just where foreigners stand on the question of witchcraft.

Soon after the opening of the trial an African acquaintance of mine pointed out to me a news item in a magazine. It described a Mau Mau "court" which was discovered while it was in session by some of the members of the Kenya African Rifles, a regiment that had been called up to help maintain law and order, and a few administrative officials. Thirteen Kikuyu members of the "court" were arrested, and among their confiscated paraphernalia were a rhinoceros whip and a white furry cap worn by the judge. "Look," said the African, "here in the Nyeri district it is a white cap and a whip. In Kapenguria it is a wig and a gavel. One is magic and one is British justice. Who should tell the African the difference?"

There must have been yet another source of confusion for many people in the fact that all the prisoners and many of the early witnesses who were in the box for having taken an oath were immediately put on oath again. To those of them who had accepted Christianity, possibly there was no doubt of which was the higher oath. To others who had felt betrayed by Christianity and who had specifically renounced its conventional form before they ever came to trial, the issue was less

189

lucid. What in such cases constituted perjury? Which oath or loyalty should a Kikuyu abide by? What, in the end, is the power of an oath beyond the willingness to be bound by it or the threat of what will happen to you if you aren't? In most of Kenya there isn't even a social stigma attached to going to jail—it is popularly known as "visiting King George's Hoteli." The work is light, and there are the advantages of fairly good food and secure shelter.

To the stranger in Kenya the puzzling point is, which of all the laws that seem to surround the African does he consider binding? I asked this of an African friend of mine and received the answer, "The law with the biggest stick behind it." This in turn left me—as possibly a good many Africans are left—with a tricky question of judgment. Who has the bigger stick? Mau Mau or the British government? Missionaries or witchdoctors? One's neighbor in an African village or the European on a big farm or in a distant town?

These objections may well seem specious to the Englishmen accustomed to the truism that a court does not administer justice, it administers the law. To the African without the great tradition of British justice to comfort him, I imagine that this seems at best arbitrary and at worst complete chaos. In either case it is certainly open to the political interpretation that the British, having established themselves in Kenya and wishing to preserve their position there, have enacted laws to protect that position and enforce them to ensure that it remains protected.

The Mau Mau, in any case, were apparently following a similar pattern. By whatever means they established their power, once it was established they too enacted their laws and enforced them. Their actions too were deeply motivated by political exigencies, however inchoate. Early in the trial the whole question of the political significance of Mau Mau and the involvement of the Kenya African Union came to the surface when Prosecutor Somerhough put into the witness box three deviationists, officials of one of the branch offices of the Kenya African Union who testified that Jomo Kenyatta had appeared to speak at a public meeting in their part of the country. They asked him why in his speech he had not openly denounced Mau Mau. Kenyatta, they said, had evaded the question, and eventually they were forced to close their branch of K.A.U.—presumably for being unwilling to support pro-Mau Mau policies.

Here was the direct implication that East Africa's only large, serious, well-organized, and actively functioning native political organization was not only deeply sympathetic with the aims of Mau Mau (whatever they might be), but was actually the main channel for the spreading of subversive propaganda and a front for its wilder methods. Kenyatta himself, of course, made the flat assertion from the witness box, "I say that K.A.U. has no connection with Mau Mau."

It might occur to the observer that there is something deeply unhealthy about a situation in which all the African politicians of stature are concerned with Mau Mau, and, further, that the solution has to be more fundamental and more searching than simply the imprisonment of such political leaders. The Europeans could answer with justification that no political rapprochement was possible until Mau Mau and its leaders were destroyed, that Mau Mau itself was the clearest indication of the African's political immaturity and the continuing need for British government in Kenya.

The Kenya Independent Schools—Kenyatta's special baby and one of the chief branches of activity of the K.A.U.—also came heavily under attack. These schools were designed to meet the African's enormous enthusiasm for education, which needed more outlets than the missions or the government could provide. (The European and Indian schools were not open to Africans.)

Now it was suggested that these schools, too, were used as channels for propaganda, that many of the hymns that were soon to become famous in the emerging testimony were first taught and sung to the schoolchildren. These hymns substituted the name "Jomo" for "Jesus" and "white people" or "the British" for "the wicked"; they spoke of Kenyatta as "the Saviour." All this was blasphemous—that is, if you happened to be a Christian. The hymnbooks that were produced over and over again in evidence contained passages like "The hearts that are brave were made brave by Jomo" and, more ominously, "The judgment will be delivered by Jomo." When Somerhough read from one of the hymns an extract that ran, "The love of Jomo Kenyatta is very great, he gave himself to become an agitator for our land," the prisoner interrupted fiercely and banged his fist on the edge of the witness box. "You are after my blood, my friend," he said. "I am not an agitator. The word means a fighter with words and demands." Somerhough represented a large part of Kenya's European opinion when he replied. "There is not much difference."

One of the early witnesses, a girl who had overheard a Mau Mau ceremony, established the connection between the atheistic sentiments of the hymns and Mau Mau. Among the fragments of conversation that she had overheard at the ceremony were, "I know there is no God," and "Jesus Christ they talk about is an Englishman." Her uneasy comment in the witness box was, "To my mind Jesus Christ is the son of God and right to the end of the meeting I had no joy in my heart because of this."

Sitting in that classroom, looking out at the sunlit hills, at the farms which are ordered and productive only because some Englishman has fought the forest, cleared the land, set up his homestead, and adopted Kenya as his country, it is easy to understand the bitterness the settler now feels at the suggestion that he is a wicked imperialist exploiting the native and should now go home.

Kenya, these Englishmen had always thought, was different. It wasn't a colony in the usual sense of the word. The men who followed Lord Delamere to Kenya considered themselves genuine pioneers. They made farms out of the wilderness; they made a nation out of scattered, warring tribes; they created a country in which they planned to live and which they hoped to bequeath to their children. Apart from their loyalty to the Crown, they considered themselves entirely separate from the Englishmen in other parts of the Empire who performed their tour of duty—even if it lasted twenty-five years—but then returned to England. Those people were colonists. Here, in Kenya, they were settlers.

Without them, they felt, the young Masai warriors, their bodies smeared with red ocher, living off fresh milk and cow blood drunk from a reed inserted in the vein, would still be raiding the Kikuyu villages, stealing the women and cattle and slaughtering the men. Without the settlers, East African agriculture would still be a primitive scratching of the soil, for they are the ones who had made Kenya a smiling and a lavish country. There would be no written language, no schools, hospitals, or roads. No central government ever existed before them, no public services, no towns, no police force.

"It may sound patronizing," an English friend told me, "to people who haven't lived here, but we *are* better for the Africans than the Africans are for each other."

Some settlers call the anger and ferment that have resulted in Mau Mau "ingratitude"; others simply accept it as an instance of the savagery that is so close to the surface of the East African character.

I think that nobody who travels in Kenya can help being impressed by the good intentions of the government, and if he visits the countryside, by the magnificence of the achievement of the pioneer white settlers, however outdated their opinions and their way of life may seem. But like nearly all the Englishmen I met in Kenya, these settlers lacked only the quality that is chronically lacking in whatever one means by the English character—an understanding and compassion for the other person's sensitivies. Much that is confusing in Kenya life, so many minunderstandings, such deep and genuine bafflement between the races, such a hopelessness of explaining or accepting purposes and motivations were crystallized during the trial of Kenyatta. The trial was punctuated with a series of these extraordinary moments.

On one occasion Pritt lost his temper with an African witness and asked rhetorically, "Do you always think everyone who doesn't agree with you is Mau Mau? Do you think I am Mau Mau?"

"I don't know," the witness replied seriously. "You come from Europe."

The prosecution called Kenyatta himself as the last witness on its list. He was questioned for ten days. During this long, frustrating examination, when Somerhough tried to establish that he had never openly denounced Mau Mau, the accused replied that he had. "The curse," Somerhough said, "was not a strong one and it had a double meaning."

Kenyatta replied that as far as he was concerned there was no longer or stronger curse.

Somerhough said that he understood that the earth was one of the most sacred things on which a Kikuyu could take a curse.

Kenyatta looked puzzled and pointed out that the fifty thousand people he had been addressing at the time could not put a single piece of earth to their lips, and further that the earth oath was an oath to deny or accept something, not a curse. The strong curse, the one that he had used, had been handed down among the Kikuyu for countless generations.

Somerhough, at the end of his patience, asked, "That is the strongest thing you could have done? Translated in *Baraza* [the official Swahili paper] as 'Let Mau Mau go and be hanged'?"

"The translation has not the same meaning as the Kikuyu words to the Kikuyu people," Kenyatta answered, making perhaps a larger generalization than he realized about the state of affairs in Kenya.

Again, after denouncing Mau Mau in a public speech, Kenyatta was supposed to have said, "Now let us all take a pinch of snuff." Again, in a fog of semantics and half-understood psychology, there was a fruitless exchange about whether or not Kenyatta had made such a comment, and if he had whether it meant the same to the Kikuyu tribesman as "Take all this with a pinch of salt" would mean to an Englishman.

Certainly the whole world of curses and their ritual was foreign to the foreigners there. It was rather more surprising that even the language was foreign to Kenyans. But most frightening of all was the chasm between the two minds, the two races, and the two worlds.

Yet again, in questioning Kenyatta about an inflammatory anti-British speech he had made, Somerhough asked him, "Did you say the English had relieved you of the slavery of the Arabs and then ask who purchased the slaves from the Arabs?"

"Yes, I did."

"Did you say that before the English relieved you of Arab slavery, they themselves used to carry away slaves in a ship called *Jesus*?"

In effect, Kenyatta answered that he had.

"Do you know [Somerhough was getting angrier] when the English abolished the slave trade in East Africa?"

"Whether they did or did not, did not prevent me relating a historical account of the slave trade.

"Even if they abolished Arab slavery we were put into worse slavery. Our land was taken away and we were put to forced labor."

Somerhough protested: "This is not an answer; it is a speech."

"The wages given to our people were so low that we lived in a sort of serfdom." The intensity of Kenyatta's voice rose. "Formerly a man could walk and feel like a man. All that was changed and we were subjected to the color bar and all kinds of humiliations. . . . If slavery was abolished, a new kind of slavery was introduced. When you have taken somebody's land . . ." He stumbled over his words. "Leaving him . . ." His voice broke off. "I can't go on."

"Go on," Somerhough said with infinite sarcasm, "I am hanging on your lips."

Briskly Kenyatta recovered his composure, "I hope you do not fall," he said in a cool voice. "If you had to change places with an African and live like him for a week—or even two days—I bet you would not stay there. You think they are happy but they are not."

Meanwhile, tensions built alarmingly between the Englishmen themselves and continually exploded in quarrels in the courtroom and in the jeers and anger of the spectators. Pritt claimed that he was working in "Cloud Kikuyuland" where the normal laws of evidence have no meaning. After one of Pritt's half-audible insults, Somerhough protested furiously, "How dare you, sir! It is intolerable and impossible! I cannot go on."

Pritt had his own grievances. "I have been exasperated in this case but I have tried to go on."

Thacker, the magistrate, deeply distressed and caught between the two, plaintively made his statement. "I am not used to dealing with abuse and have little training in it. . . . There have been occasions during this trial when I have felt it almost impossible to go on, and this is one of them."

In a way he was the most pitiable figure of all, trying the last case of his career, suffering from toothache, flying to his dentist five hundred miles away on weekends and during recesses, guarded night and day by English bodyguards because, as an acquaintance of his

put it, "If he convicts them the Mau Mau get him."
Laboriously he took longhand notes on the interroga-
tions, asking counsel or witnesses to repeat things occasionally that he didn't catch, exhausted from the long
strain of the trial and of the steamy atmosphere of conflict.

In the little Kapenguria courtroom the trial had become an abortive and unsatisfactory political battle in
which few points were made but everybody's bitterness
deepened. The rift between the races grew wider. The
testimony at the trial seemed to be clarifying no issues
and demolishing no barriers. Near the end of his days
on the stand Kenyatta said, "The disease of the heart
cannot be cut out with a knife."

After the long succession of witnesses and the special
drama of Kenyatta in the box, after all the turbulent
questions that had been raised, Pritt's defense seemed
short and relatively flat. It consisted mostly of contradictions of what the prosecution witnesses had claimed.
Witnesses who were supposed to have been at oath-
taking ceremonies described earlier in the trial appeared
to testify that Kenyatta had not been present. For the
one prosecution witness who testified he had been
present to see Kenyatta administer the Mau Mau oath,
Pritt produced ten to say he was lying. To refute the
prosecution witness who had connected Kenyatta with
the Mau Mau initiation ceremony, Pritt produced eight
men with contradictory evidence.

One woman whom Pritt called to the box was obviously rattled by the whole procedure. She claimed
that the statement she had made for the prosecution had
been extracted by threats and force. A police officer,
she said, had threatened to take her up in a plane and
drop her out.

Why, if the statement was false, had she allowed her
thumbprint to be put to it? (But that she should feel
that a thumbprint should have any authority was open
to question.) Well, her hand had been held by force. To
her, clearly it all seemed quite reasonable. "I wanted to
be released and go away," she said. "I wanted to be
returned to the place where I lived." But most of the
spectators must have sympathized with Thacker when
he said it was a very peculiar position. "I cannot follow
the African mind, I'm afraid," he added sadly.
196

"The question," an English lawyer who had practiced for some years in Kenya remarked to me, "should be, 'Does the African mind follow Thacker?' In court," he. continued, "as you watch these solemn black faces listening to English questions, translations, interpretations, the whole elaborate business of English court procedure, what on earth do you suppose they make of it?"

I asked him what is the biggest stumbling block in legal forms to most of the Africans. "The laws of evidence, I think," he answered. "Especially what is hearsay and what isn't. You ask a man how he knows something, and he says, 'The Chief told me—how else would I know?' You tell him, 'But in that case you don't *know*, you *heard*.' He doesn't understand at all and says, 'But I just explained, I know because the Chief told me.' Of course," he added, "when you reach philosophic concepts like 'a reasonable doubt' you're really lost." Most Africans, he assured me, think in terms of testing innocence by ordeal.

How, I asked him, would they react to the Kenyatta trial—surely they didn't see it as an elaborate ordeal to test him.

"The purpose of a trial like this wouldn't, in their minds, be to establish guilt or innocence. Everyone would know that Kenyatta was Mau Mau. To them the only remaining thing is to settle how much he has to pay—how many goats or cattle."

However it may have appeared to the Africans, the Europeans for the most part didn't seem too surprised by all the shifts and contradictions of testimony. Such, apparently, was only to be expected from Africans, and only added another sort of mistiness to an already obscure situation.

Pritt, in his final address to the court, which he read in a monotone at breathtaking speed, used the general obscurity to claim that there was never a real case against his clients at all. In fact, he said, the prosecution had never really decided just what the charges against Kenyatta were. He flung a series of questions calculated to disturb almost anyone in Kenya. If Kenyatta was charged with managing Mau Mau, then the prosecution's job should be to show just what it was that he was managing. Why, and in what fashion? In what office? With what policy or with what documents? Was

197

he the sole manager? Was he just one of a number of members of the management? And, of course, at the heart of all these questions was a problem of very long standing: What was Mau Mau?

Not only, Pritt continued, were the charges "vague and woolly," but the evidence produced by the prosecution was designed to show that Kenyatta was sympathetic to Mau Mau, that he had not denounced it forcibly enough, that he was anti-European, or even, to push it to its furthest limits, that he had taken the Mau Mau oath. Of course, Pritt said, the defense claimed that most of this was untrue, but even if it were true, " . . . the charge is not of being friendly to Mau Mau or of lacking in zeal in discouraging Mau Mau. The charge is of managing Mau Mau."

As to the political aspects of the case, Pritt insisted that Kenyatta had never said or written anything in contradiction of the published statements of the moderate and constitutional policy of the Kenya African Union. Obviously, he indicated, the answer was that the government did not wish these Africans to carry on propaganda of the sort demanding "more land for the Africans," as this would tend to be embarrassing to the British.

One by one Pritt checked off the points made against his client in the prosecution's case: the points about the oath taking which he felt had been refuted by the testimony of his witnesses, then the evidence of the three deviationist K.A.U. officials, who, he said, were "almost as obsessed with Mau Mau as a Washington politician is with Communism." These men had demanded that Kenyatta denounce Mau Mau, which he had done; the rest of their evidence could not be credited.

On the various occasions that Kenyatta had spoken in public against Mau Mau there was no evidence that he was not sincere. And as for the various songbooks, hymnbooks, and exercise books that had contained verses in praise of Kenyatta, well, the accused could not be held responsible for anything that anybody thought fit to write about him, and the fact that some of the documents were found in his house certainly did not prove either that they were his property or that he had any connection with them.

That, said Pritt, was the whole of the case against Kenyatta in this "very important political prosecution."

Clearly, he concluded, Kenyatta and the other five accused should be acquitted.

Somerhough, immediately on beginning his final address, protested that Kenyatta's trial and prosecution were certainly not "political"; however, "it would be a fair retort to say that the court had heard a political defense."

But it was when Somerhough began to reply to Pritt's "Where?" "Why?" and "How?" that the true and very broad political aspects of the case emerged. The answer to "Where is Mau Mau?" was simple, said the prosecution counsel. Mau Mau was in Kenya. This was, of course, altogether too simple for some of the observers of the trial to swallow without any mental chewing. It stated a fact without either answering the question or accepting its real, and to Kenyans extremely important, meaning.

The answer to "Why?" was slightly more complicated. "If the Crown were asked why it has suggested that these people should have managed and controlled Mau Mau, the answer would be 'the lust for power.' It must be that, and can't really be anything else." (Of course it could be something else. It could be several other things ranging from nationalist fervor to gangsterism.) "It has increased their prestige and increased their hold on the people so that they could exercise more power."

Possibly unintentionally, Somerhough by this statement made it clear that this was, after all, a political trial. Possibly unintentionally, he had suggested that the danger of Kenyatta and the other five accused lay in their increased prestige. If participation in Mau Mau had given them greater standing with their own people, then the political strength and use of such an organization became obvious, and Mau Mau appeared as much more than the amorphous and inexplicable thing that Somerhough himself later described as "a purely barbaric movement accompanied by circumstances of revolting savagery."

The answer to "How?" was, again, Somerhough continued, fairly simple. Mau Mau was run largely by propaganda. Africans were told that they had been robbed of their land. They were encouraged to drive out the Europeans, and in the hymnbooks designed to spread

199

the propaganda there were "fantastic allegations about slavery and that sort of thing." But the real damage was done to the "simple African" who was being taught to feel he had grievances.

Immediately after this, Somerhough tacitly accepted the political and emotional power of those grievances—imaginary or otherwise—in his comment that if you can find people "to follow their leaders and do as they are told, obey the orders of the leaders and to come when they are called, then you are building up an army of persons who are bound to you by a strong sanction. This sanction appears to have reached a strength which it is very difficult for a European to comprehend." To the foreigner the striking point was that it is a sanction that for the Kikuyu, at least, superseded both their previous emotional ties of loyalty or affection to the Europeans and their political ties to the government.

Kenyatta, Somerhough concluded from his replies to Pritt's queries, was the only man with the "personality and the education" to manage an organization of the scope of Mau Mau.

Later in his speech, Somerhough came to the heart of the tangled situation in Kenya that had made the trial such an extraordinarily bewildering series of cross purposes and muddles, and in a way diagnosed the sickness of most of Africa. We maintain that Mau Mau can only flourish in an atmosphere of hatred between the races. It is no good telling Africans to drive out Europeans, or to tell Europeans to do likewise if they like each other. Neither party will listen to you. The only soil in which Mau Mau could flourish would be in soil poisoned by racial hatred."

Among the Africans of various shades of political opinion to whom I talked in Kenya, certainly none would have disagreed with Somerhough. They might, however, have wondered where the poisoning of the soil had begun. In colonization or in Kikuyu land hunger? In economic grievances or in anti-European propaganda? In the color bar or in Mau Mau?

During the month that Thacker spent considering the evidence and the cases of the defense and the prosecution, Kenyatta's case remained in the news and in the horrified conversation of Kenyans. New Mau Mau conspiracies were discovered. Some of the remaining

African leaders who were Members of the Kenya Parliament and had always been represented as moderates were imprisoned after a dramatic night raid in Nairobi. This inevitably emphasized the political ill-health of the entire colony. Some days before Thacker gave his verdict, Mau Mau's biggest and most senseless atrocity took place. A hundred and fifty Kikuyu were killed in one night in one of the African locations called Lari. Their villages were burned to the ground, and the people who tried to escape from the blazing huts were chopped to death with the *pangas, simis,* and *rungus*—the three typical varieties of knife—of the waiting terrorists. One story said that the massacre had been planned in protest against Kenyatta's conviction and sentence, which the Africans had anticipated, but something had slipped up and the timing had been entirely misjudged. Another rumor said that Thacker had delayed giving his verdict because he was afraid, if the mistimed massacre was any sample, of the carnage that might result.

Another news item in the month before the verdict concerned Pritt's departure from Kenya with the honors given him by the Nairobi Africans—a stool, a robe of colobus monkey skins, and a fly whisk—the traditional equipment of an African tribal elder.

Most of the Europeans of Kenya seemed to feel that Pritt had only contributed to the worsening of the situation; that he had so played up the race war and political angles of the trial that he had really done the Africans a disservice and made it much harder for them to deal in a friendly and equitable way with the Europeans in the future. But I think an African I talked to about this spoke for many of his countrymen when he said, "It is very wonderful for us to see an Englishman fight so bravely on the side of an African."

Eventually, protected by soldiers and Sten guns, Thacker gave his verdict in the Kapenguria schoolroom. For Kenyatta and the other five accused, the sentence was seven years' hard labor—the maximum he had the the authority to impose, though even that, he said in the course of his speech, was "quite inadequate" for what Kenyatta had done.

Kenyatta replied that he and his colleagues were not guilty and did not accept the magistrate's ruling. In his opinion the purpose of the trial was simply to strangle the K.A.U., "the only African political organization which fights for the rights of African people." The world, he said, was meant for human beings to live in happily. Consequently he would continue to object to racial discrimination and would continue to demand—in a constitutional way—the return of African land and eventual self-government. "I am not," he said, "asking for mercy, but that justice might be done and that injustice against the African people should be righted."

Thacker, apparently despairing of any solution for Kenya's problems, said, "I am sorry to say I don't believe you."

Early in the trial Pritt had said, casually, "It is more important to fight this case than to win it." Now, a year later, it is clear that in one way or another the case is still being fought—before the Privy Council in England and in the mountains of Kenya. Nobody in Kenya or the world can now accept that the Kenyatta trial and sentence have meant the end of Mau Mau. It is much more probable that they have marked the beginning of perhaps one of the most inflammatory chapters in history—the political and emotional self-assertion of the Africans in the eastern, central, and southern countries of their immense continent.

The Eagles of Swaziland

BY ROBERT ARDREY

His name was Jan De Villiers. The De Villiers are an honored race in South Africa. Their French Huguenot ancestors came to the Cape two and a half centuries ago. They established vineyards and orchards, and the villages around Franschhoek. They came up against the Dutch, were utterly defeated, and became, to all intents and purposes, Afrikanders.

So Jan De Villiers is an Afrikander, just as are the De Wets and the Den Heevers and the Oostehuizens and the Van Aardts. Jan is twenty-six, blue-eyed, brown-haired, and slim. He is a professional driver for a safari outfit in the Transvaal, and it is his job to find photogenic lions for Americans such as myself.

"You haven't lived," a friend in New York had said,

"until you've gone to one of these African game reserves and had a lion scratch his rear against your fender."

"You haven't lived," a friend in London had said, "until you've parked your car beside an African river, and here's a dozen or so nervous antelope a hundred feet ahead, and over here right under your window is a lioness stalking the antelope and using your car as a screen."

I look with suspicion on such proceedings. My experience with North American animals consists of regular contact with two house cats (*Felis domestica*), some tropical fish, and a canary of agreeable disposition. Whether I have lived is a question that seldom concerns me; whether I shall continue to do so seems as a rule of greater interest.

In Africa, however, the time came. I had been stalking politicians in Johannesburg, the Free State, and through the Parliamentary jungle of Cape Town. In spite of all better judgment, I came to long for the four-legged animal and the dark magnificence of a fabled continent. So it was that I took my choice, paid my money, and slept my last night in a Johannesburg hotel bravely and truly dreaming of unfriendly leopards.

At four in the morning I found myself staggering blindly around my hotel room while a porter put tea on my table. The safari people believe in rousing you early even when it isn't necessary. It's a wise move. The city-bred American must condition himself from the first instant to the African carnivore's most discouraging habit: the hours he keeps.

At five, on Eloff Street, I met Jan De Villiers. It was too dark for us to see each other. I stowed my 30-30 Kodak aboard his Chevrolet.

"What'll we see?" I said, trying to keep my voice natural. "Buffalo? elephant? lions?" I kept away from leopards.

"If you have read the literature," he said, "you will know that Kruger Park abounds with wild life of all descriptions."

Kruger Park lies between the Transvaal and Portuguese East Africa, three hundred miles east of Johannesburg. It is low veld. In March, at the end of the rainy summer season, only one section is high enough to be free of malaria and open to the public. We arrived at Pretorius Kop, the rest camp, in time for lunch.

"Rest till four," said Jan, austerely. "The game will be resting. There's no point in going out."

"I can't wait," I said.

He looked at me gloomily.

I went to my rondavel. The round hut has influenced considerably the more sophisticated African architecture. My cabin had brick walls, a conical thatched roof, and a veranda. I looked at the thick bush a hundred yards away, wondered how tired the animals were, and went in and locked my door.

At four we were on the road. We circled a rocky hill slowly.

"There's been a pride of lions living here this summer," Jan remarked.

Tensely, I watched the rocky slopes. I inspected the flat-topped African trees. We saw nothing. Suddenly there was a crash in the brush and I dropped my camera and the gray haunches of an animal resembling a compact cow vanished into the undergrowth.

"Wildebeeste," said Jan, sourly. "You have now seen game."

His face seemed drawn. I looked at him suspiciously. We left the hill. We drove eleven miles before we came to the crocodile. Once Jan pointed out a speck beside the trunk of a distant tree. He identified it as a baboon. My eyes are not what they once were, and I did not see it. Once I caught a sunny flash from a hillside a mile away.

"Zebra," said Jan, with some admiration. "Very good, boss."

Once he slowed the car to a stop and looked raptly at a tree.

"Ficus sycomorus," he said.

"Where?" I said, frantically, pointing my camera and wondering about the light.

"The tree," he said.

We came to the crocodile. There was a little draw and a small stream. Half a dozen cars were in line at the bridge. It is a rule in Kruger Park, as in most game reserves, that one cannot get out of the car. People leaned from the windows with cameras. "Crocodile!" shouted someone triumphantly. We waited our turn.

The crocodile lay on a rock a hundred yards away. It

was a baby, three feet long, and resembled in no small degree one of our less impressive Florida alligators.

"Jan," I said slowly, "you and I are going to have to have a long talk."

There was a line of cars behind us waiting to see the crocodile, and so we had to drive on. We stopped under a tree.

"*Combretum imberbe,*" he said. "Leadwood. Very heavy."

I got out cigarettes. A green flash zoomed through the trees.

"Meyer's parrot," he said.

"Jan," I said.

He leaned his forehead against the steering wheel. He closed his eyes. Then he straightened himself, and he fingered his four-in-hand tie which he wore even when hunting lion, and he took a cigarette.

"It breaks my heart," he said, very low. I lit our cigarettes. A variety of shrike flew past. It grows a long tail in the mating season. "No one has seen a lion around Kruger Park in two and one half weeks. There is a family of four cheetah. It's possible we may see them, but since everyone else in the park is trying to see them, this family of cheetah are becoming embarrassed and are reluctant to show themselves."

"Good God," I said. And suddenly I wanted to see a lion.

"I could cry," he said. And for a moment I thought he was going to. "I pick up somebody like you in Johannesburg. Next Tuesday it will be somebody else. They have shown you the literature, they've taken your money, and who is to find the lion? *I* am to find the lion—"

"Look here," I said hastily, "I don't really care about seeing a lion." I did, of course, by now. I cared enormously about seeing a lion. But I thought he was going to cry, and he seemed fifteen years old. "I understand. It's luck. And it's the wrong time of year—"

"Oh, yes," he said. "The wrong time of year. Then the right time comes, and the animals come, and the people come, and here is this lion and forty cars lined up to observe, and you can't get a picture that doesn't look like a parking lot. Oh, I tell you sometimes at night I dream of eagles, and I wake up and say I cannot face another safari; it breaks my heart. I am going back to the eagles even though I can't make a living."

"Look," I said, "don't worry about me. I like trees. All I wanted was to get out into Africa. Parrots and things. I love birds—"

"You do?" He whirled on me, with an amazing fire. He must have seen something in my eyes. The fire died. "That's not fair, boss."

"What is all this about eagles?" I said.

He started the car. "If we move along, we may see some very fine buck," he said, most formally. "It will be dark soon. We have to be in camp."

"Turn that thing off," I said. "Tell me about eagles."

"I train them," he said, reluctantly, almost sullenly.

"Train eagles?" I said. "How long have you been training eagles?"

"Ten years," he said. "Since I was fifteen. Till a year ago. There is no money in it. A man must grow up."

"I don't understand," I said slowly. "I never heard of training eagles. I don't believe it." He reached for the starter. "I'm sorry," I said, quickly. "I believe it. Where did you start doing this?"

"At the Cape," he said. "Where I grew up. In the Valley of the Wagonmakers."

"I have been there," I said.

Jan De Villiers turned towards me, and there was a moment.

"Paarl? Franschhoek?"

"Paarl and Franschhoek," I said.

"You know, then!" he said. "The Drakensteins! The mountains above the orchards, and Paarl. There are streams in the mountains, and fountains high above the trees, and little places where the eagles are!"

I nodded. I didn't know, but neither could I speak.

"Oh!" he said. "One starts out with hawks, of course. This is falconry. One reads the books. They tell you how. In the valley you catch a hawk. Stake out a pigeon, a living pigeon, and there is a black net of fine threads. The hawk swoops for the pigeon, and he is caught. It is great fun, but it is nothing to eagles.

"Eagles!" Jan repeated, and he looked out of the car window at the sky. "Yes. The day comes, boss. You look up at the mountains from the valley and you say, I can

206

do it with eagles. Up in the mountains you lie in the little places. You watch. For months that is all. You observe the golden eagle. Then—like for the hawk, but stronger—you lay a trap. And lo! it is all so simple. You have caught an eagle."

A herd of gentle brown impala came delicately into the road. I scarcely saw them.

"You must bind him quickly," said Jan. "The golden eagle. He fights the traps. He may hurt himself. Bind him, bind him quickly all over like a mummy, so he will not be hurt. And take him home. There free him."

The lovely brown antelope, shoulder high, surrounded our car. They nibbled at the bush, raised their great oval ears.

"How do you free him?" I said.

"In black dark," said Jan. "Or with a hood about his eyes. You stand him on your arm. He grips it. He cannot see. He cannot fly. He will lose his balance but for your arm. Your arm is his security. Now feed him. Feed him the very finest meat, meat you cannot afford for yourself. In a very few days, remove the hood. He will stay with you. But for months you must carry him on your arm."

"How much does he weigh?"

"Ten pounds. The martial eagle more."

"What happens to your arm?"

"It grows strong."

The sun was leaving the gray green leaves of the thorn trees, and the cassia, and the bird plum. All in an instant they became black lace against the paling sky. A red-headed francolin hawked at us from the tall grass. An impala, a slim young buck, stepped daintily across the road to join the feeding herd. He held his horns high.

"Once—once!—I trained a martial eagle." The young Afrikander watched the slim young buck. He spoke very low. "It was on a farm, in the Orange Free State. Golden eagles are playful. They tease you. Not the martial eagle. How he would drop from the sky, in one long zoom! On a jackal. The hawk kills with his beak, the eagle with his claws. I'd approach the dead jackal. Mwe —that was the name I called my martial eagle—he would leap from the jackal to my arm. And look away.

"He would ignore me. On my arm, he would look

away while I picked up his kill. I would give him his reward—a bit of meat far better than the dead jackal—and he would take it in his terrible beak, and still ignore me, and turn his piercing eyes away across the veld. What did he look at? I don't know.

"Golden eagles will tease you. They will pretend to fly away, and while you are not looking they'll come back and knock your head off. It is all a joke. It is also dangerous. On the leg of a golden eagle one must put a bell, so you can hear him coming, or you will end up in hospital.

"Not the martial eagle. To have put a bell on Mwe? Oh, no. That was not our relationship. He would follow me about the Free State farm, flying from tree to tree, yet never seeming to see me. Not till I put up my arm and faced him would he come. Then—like that—from half a mile he would come."

We watched the herd of impala move slowly away into the darkening bush. A hornbill with a great absurd yellow sickle of a beak dropped down on a branch of the leadwood tree and regarded us. The sky took fire. Tier after tier of flat-bottomed cumulus clouds caught the spreading conflagration.

"Where can one see a martial eagle?" I asked.

"In the mountains," he said, motioning to the south. "In Swaziland."

"What happened to Mwe?" I said.

"Who can know?" said Jan. "Often I took him out in the fields for a joy ride. I would raise my arm, and for a moment he would stand there, all dignity, ignoring me, looking away across the veld. Then—off! Circling into the sky, higher, higher. Here was an eagle with an eight-foot span. How high must such an eagle fly to disappear entirely, straight above?

"I have good eyes. I would say to myself, this time I will see him to the top. And I would lie down on my back while he rose, circling, circling. I would watch, watch, watch. Now he is as small as a hawk, as a night-jar, as a sparrow, as the tiniest insect. And then—it is always the same. He is a remembrance. I have lost him again. I have lost him to the blueness, and the mystery.

"Always it is the same. I cannot tell you, boss, the sadness with which I rise from the ground. This time, I think, I have lost him for good. Why should he come back?

208

"Yet always I stop at the gate by the farm. And I raise my arm, and wait. And joy, joy! there he is! Mwe! Always! The beggar! He could see me when I could not see him! Down he comes, out of the blueness in long, slow sweeps. And now he is on my arm again, ignoring me, looking out across the veld. My heart bursts. We go to our dinner."

"Always?" I said.

"Always," said Jan. "Always—but once."

Nowhere but in Africa are there such sunsets. While you count perhaps to thirty the sky burns out, and there is left only purple smoke.

"I was twenty," said Jan. "That was five years ago. It is still a very great temptation to look for Mwe, wherever one goes, in all Africa. Like an awful voice it comes to me, sometimes in most unlikely places—'Stand! Look up! Raise your arm! Mwe is up there, up there in the blueness, you cannot see him but he can see you! Raise your arm! He is waiting.'"

I sat in silence. A breeze chattered through the leadwood. The hornbill flew away. The impala moved in the dark brush. Jan started the car.

"We must get back to the camp," he said. "It is the rule. We're late."

There were two donkeys standing on my veranda. It was too dark to take their picture. Jan and I agreed that on the following morning we would hunt leopard. It would be a clear night. There would be a heavy dew. The leopard, who dislikes getting his feet wet, would follow the roads. We would get out early, and our chances would be excellent provided that we were the first car on the road.

At four-thirty lights began to come on in the rondavels at Pretorius Kop. Ours was the first. At quarter to five, in complete darkness, we were at the gate. By five-thirty, when the gate was unlocked, six losing cars stood behind us. In the dry months when game and guests are plentiful, one must sometimes get up at two to be first at the gate.

At eight o'clock, after two and a half hours of eyestrain, we had seen three giraffes, a few wildebeeste and zebra, more impala, and a wart hog.

"Let us get the hell out of here," I said. "I want to go to Swaziland."

We spent the night in Barberton, last lovely town in the Transvaal. At dawn we entered the Protectorate. We climbed rocky red roads. We passed through gauzy clouds, and cool young pine forests planted by the English. We climbed once more, to the top of the world, to where the sky turns a royal blue, as before dawn, yet the sun stands high and likewise the moon. Beyond and below us lay Africa, bold in its purples, shimmering in its greens, endless, patternless, empty of all but legends.

Jan was pointing down into the valley. He seemed unwilling to speak. And I could see them, the two, circling at leisure, flirting with the flimsy clouds, turning all of sunlit, silent space to their own best advantage.

"Eagles," he said, at last.

A LITTLE BUSINESS

Italy's Oil Rush and That Man Mattei

BY CLAIRE STERLING

Rome

When Italy's Prime Minister Mario Scelba visited the United States at the end of March, he made it emphatically clear that he had *not* come to discuss oil. Before he left he had made it clear to Parliament that he would not touch on that subject with anyone in the United States—not with the State Department and not with the American oil companies. This may seem strange since there is nothing essentially evil about oil. Moreover, the question of who should have what rights over Italian oil is causing serious tension between Rome and Washington, and neither country can afford to leave it unsettled much longer.

Recent discoveries make it appear that Italy has enough oil in its subsoil not only to meet its own requirements but also perhaps to become an exporter of oil.

One reserve in Sicily, discovered by the Gulf Oil Company in 1953, may have enough to cover Italy's needs for a century by itself. Until lately, this Ragusa deposit was thought to contain a relatively small quantity of oil spread over an area of perhaps two square miles. A more extensive survey now indicates that the area may be fourteen square miles. Although U.S. experts are cautious about making estimates, Italians, with exuberant optimism, think there may be a recuperable reserve of seven hundred million tons in Ragusa. Italy uses only eleven million tons a year. Just a few days ago a new strike was made in Sicily—this time at Agrigento.

The oil in Ragusa is like Venezuela's: commercially usable but not high grade. Gulf has just found what looks like a much more important deposit in the Abruzzi region on the Adriatic coast. It has not yet been measured, but the first well drilled is comparable, in the excellence and abundance of its crude, to the wells of legendary Kuwait. Geologists on the spot are talking in terms of billions of tons. Experts of the Standard Oil Company of New Jersey have long believed that the

211

Po Valley in the north of Italy contains the richest oil beds in Europe. They still think so despite the fact that none of the wells dug there has proved to be rewarding.

All this oil has fired imaginations in poverty-stricken Italy. People here have started thinking of their country as a new Texas. The new and still unmeasurable wealth can make Italy's chronic depression a thing of the past. So the Italians dream. And they would like to have that dream come true today.

Lack of natural resources has always been Italy's worst handicap. At the present time coal and oil imports account for half of Italy's $750-million annual trade deficit. An ample domestic supply of fuel could not only lower production costs and retail prices but could also encourage private investment and new industry and provide cheaper transport. (Gasoline costs about eighty cents a gallon, of which about fifty cents goes for government taxes.) With cheaper oil, new programs of road construction and motorized agriculture may become possible. The royalties could finance needed social reforms. Some day Italy's trade deficit might be eliminated.

That's what could happen. It isn't necessarily what *will* happen. And, of course, nothing is going to happen unless the oil can be gotten out of the ground. Very little is coming out at present.

The questions before the Italian government are standard in any country where oil is found—particularly where the country happens to be poor. Does Italy have the capital, equipment, and technicians to exploit the oil that has already been found and to find more? If not, should Italy invite foreign oil companies in to do the job? And if foreign companies are given concessions, can they be asked to produce all the oil the Italians want—or at least enough to make Italy self-sufficient? Finally, could the Italians be sure of getting a sizable share of the profits?

There are two sides to all these questions, and the arguments advanced by the American oil companies are far from unreasonable. After all, there are some other parts of the world—indeed, of Europe—where oil is being found these days. The oil companies are perhaps somewhat oversensitive whenever the words "cartel" or "price

212

fixing" are mentioned. But certainly there is enough competition all over the world among private oil companies, nationalized oil concerns, and wildcatters of all sorts to make the American oil companies worry at the prospect that some day oil may become a drug on the market. Moreover, the American companies have learned from bitter experience in more than one country that from nationalism to nationalization is only a short step. In Italy as elsewhere they have reason to fear the Communist brand of nationalism.

In Italy the conflict has sharply divided Italian politics. On one side is Enrico Mattei, forty-eight-year-old head of the new state natural-gas and oil agency, ENI, who has the backing of a large portion of the Christian Democratic Party, at least half of Scelba's Cabinet, the Social Democrats, Republicans, and Independents on the Left, and, out of sheer malice, the Communist Party. The other side is represented by a group of American oil companies headed by Standard Oil of New Jersey and backed by the U.S. State Department, another section of the Christian Democratic Party that is led by its aging founder, Don Luigi Sturzo, the other half of Scelba's Cabinet, and the big Italian trusts.

Mattei and Standard Oil are old antagonists. They first clashed in 1946, when natural gas was found in the Po Valley. Standard Oil had exploration rights in the Po and had spent a lot of money there ever since 1891. But it was Mattei who found the natural gas. After leading the Christian Democratic partisans in the north, Mattei had been assigned in 1945 by the Liberation Government to be head of AGIP, the state corporation formed by Mussolini to find and exploit petroleum. Since AGIP, like Standard Oil, had found nothing, Mattei had been ordered to liquidate. He ignored the order, gambled on a spectacular break, and won.

The discovery of natural gas in the Po Valley in 1946 led to three thousand requests for concessions. The two main contestants, however, were AGIP and Standard Oil. Both asked for exclusive rights in the area, and Mattei won again.

One reason for Mattei's success in the fight over the Po Valley was that AGIP had struck oil at Cortemaggiore in Lombardy. This was only two years after the Italian government had decided to abandon its search for oil as hopeless. In 1947 it had offered to sell its mining plants, together with concessions, for only one million dollars. No Italian or American company saw fit to accept the offer.

Although the deposit at Cortemaggiore didn't turn out to be a large one, it was enough to decide the dispute over natural-gas concessions in the Po Valley. Standard Oil, after all, was an outsider and had found nothing. Mattei was an Italian who had found enough to become a national hero. In February, 1953, the Italian Parliament voted, with the approval of all eight parties, from neo-Fascist to Communist, to put AGIP under a new state corporation called ENI, headed by Mattei, with exclusive rights to all the gas and oil in the eighteen thousand square miles of the Po Valley.

A few months later, the government introduced Bill No. 346, designed to open the rest of the mainland to exploitation by private companies, both Italian and foreign. Since the regional government of Sicily had done the same for that island in 1950, the passage of the bill would have meant that more than two-thirds of Italian territory—much of it highly promising like the Adriatic coast—would be reserved for private enterprise. Mattei's fears that the bill would jeopardize his exclusive rights in the Po Valley were borne out when the Americans reopened the debate that had already been settled by an Act of Parliament. The resulting conflict has kept the bill bottled up in committee ever since.

The debate over the Po was reopened at a press conference in Rome last June, where Eugene Holman, chairman of the board of Standard Oil of New Jersey, said that the Po Valley had the most promising geological terrain in Europe, that neither ENI nor any other single company could explore it adequately, and that "it might be well to open exploration of the Po to free Italian and foreign initiative," which would share profits with the government on a fifty-fifty basis.

Holman's thesis was picked up first by *Fortune* magazine for July, 1954, then by *Newsweek, Time,* the New York *Herald Tribune,* the *Wall Street Journal,* and most recently the Rome *Daily American,* an English-language paper devoted mostly to sports news, gossip columns, and comics.

The main point advanced in all these articles was that

Mattei's monopoly in the Po Valley constituted the biggest single obstacle to large-scale American investment in Italy. *Time* said that "to U.S. businessmen trying to do business in Italy, Enrico Mattei is the biggest and clearest symbol of what is wrong with Italy's economy. . . . E. N. I. has neither the capital nor the equipment to explore the Po Valley properly." The solution, said *Fortune,* was to reduce ENI's authority to go into new ventures, deny it any tax favors, and limit it to "a modest Po Valley area."

Several of the articles suggested that Mattei's only genuine supporter in the Christian Democratic Party was Budget Minister Ezio Vanoni (allegedly because both were passionate fishermen); that the politicians, journalists, and economists who defended him were either his paid employees or Communist agents, or both; and that the Communists were his principal supporters.

These American charges aroused bitter reactions in Italy. Of course Vanoni is a firm supporter of Mattei, but so are many other Christian Democratic leaders. In fact, so is Amintore Fanfani, secretary general of the party and heir apparent to the Premiership. Mattei's economic power is so great that no Christian Democratic politician can be indifferent to it unless he has access to some other sources of support.

Apart from members of his own party, Mattei's defenders include such well-known anti-Communists as Social Democratic Vice-Premier Giuseppe Saragat, the Republicans' former Cabinet Minister Ugo la Malfa, and the Liberal economist Ernesto Rossi, whose lifetime work has been attacking monopolies. The Communists take Mattei's side in this dispute because "ENI represents a precious weapon against the assault of foreign imperialism," as *L'Unità* has put it. But at the same time they attack him for refusing to recognize any Communist union among his fourteen thousand employees and for being one of the biggest sources of campaign funds for the Christian Democrats.

These anti-Mattei articles in the American press were widely quoted in Italy. Italian journalists noted particularly that two of the publications concerned are owned by Henry Luce, husband of the U.S. Ambassador to Italy. Editorial comment grew sharper as reports leaked from the Prime Minister's staff to the effect that the

State Department was reluctant to discuss any other serious economic matters with the Italians "until this oil business is settled." "Certainly," the independent weekly *Cronache* observed, "*Fortune* doesn't represent an official point of view. But people tend to confuse husbands and wives, and they listen to those of evil intentions who claim that America, in general, wants to get her hands on Italian petroleum." Mrs. Luce herself has been increasingly explicit. At the beginning of March she said in an interview that there must be "political safety" to attract foreign capital, and that in the case of Italy "much depends on the government's oil policy." Irate articles in the left-wing press and indignant speeches from left-wingers in Parliament followed the Ambassador's interview.

All these American pressures have helped to make Mattei the outstanding personality in Italian public life since the end of the war. There can be no doubt, however, that his own achievements are more than enough to justify both his popularity and his reputation as a tough-minded and rather unusual kind of Italian.

Mattei is a self-made man in the most aggressive American pattern. He is proud of having risen from being the son of a *carabiniere* to become one of the most powerful men in Italian industry and politics. Before he became the head of ENI, he had already reached a measure of success in private business. Now, however, as the near-sovereign head of a state-owned industrial complex, he can afford to challenge on their own ground some of the most powerful Italian monopolists. Even his enemies find it hard to deny that Mattei has done very well in the field of natural gas. Not only was he the first to discover it, but he has found enough of it to save Italy $60 million a year in coal imports. More than that, he has developed ENI into the only profit-making state corporation in Italy. ENI's capital investment is now close to $100 million, and it does a gross business, through its various subsidiaries, of $400 million a year; the net profit of ENI alone, as a holding company, was almost $4 million last year.

Mattei's companies are described by *Fortune* as "tidy," his operations "technically sound," and his staff "thoroughly competent." With the help of this staff, as well as his high credit standing, he has built more than
216

two thousand miles of gas pipeline; acquired a fleet of twelve tankers, half ownership—with Standard Oil and Anglo-Iranian—of three big refineries, and full ownership of three others: gone successfully into the manufacture of such by-products as lubricants, asphalt, soap, and electrical energy; secured the assistance of Union Carbide and Phillips Petroleum to build Europe's largest factory for the manufacture of synthetic rubber and nitrogen fertilizer; plunged briskly into such allied ventures as manufacturing gas tanks, promoting a string of sleek modern motels, and planning long-distance express highways; and so modernized his AGIP service stations as to win twenty per cent of the retail gasoline market against stiff competition from Esso, Caltex, and Shell.

This performance has not endeared him with private Italian monopolies like Montecatini (chemicals), Edison (electricity), and Pirelli (rubber) who because of Mattei have first known the bitter taste of competition. Some of these majestic firms have had not only to compete with him but also to become associated with him in some of his ventures. To millions of Italians he has become a hero.

Against his past successes, however, must be set the fact that he has failed to find any more oil in his vast and promising domain, whereas an American company has found a lot of it elsewhere in Italy.

There are many other valid criticisms of Mattei. He is a proud and arrogant man. His accounting to the government is elusive, his decisions are arbitary, and to a large extent he has become a law unto himself. He has no qualms about admitting that he has broken at least eight thousand local ordinances to get his pipeline through small communities without permits.

A few years ago, Mattei "invaded" the gentle town of Cremona, which was "strategically" necessary to connect the gas field at Lodi, near Milan, with the important industrial center of Bergamo, farther to the northeast. If Mattei had filed a legally drafted document with the mayor of Cremona asking for permission to lay his gas pipes through the city, the debates in the town council, in the press, and perhaps in Parliament would have lasted for months, if not for years. Mattei discarded that line of approach. Taking command of a team of three hundred workmen and technicians armed with picks and spades, he stealthily approached the outskirts of the city one night after its inhabitants were asleep. In a few hours Cremona had been cut in two by a trench, with piles of paving high enough to block all wheeled traffic.

The police made no effort to interfere with public works so impressively organized that they looked perfectly lawful. But there came a moment soon after dawn when the first trucks laden with fresh produce, milk, and fruit from the country ran into an unfamiliar obstacle. They jammed the narrow side streets, blocked all traffic, raised a deafening din, and started bewildering rumors among the sleepy population. It was then that Mattei called on the bewildered mayor, apologizing to him for the "mistake" his employees had made and offering to give orders for an immediate stoppage of work on the trench. In the face of what was in fact a threat to leave the town's pavements in an appalling state, the mayor begged Mattei to go on laying his pipes, have the trench filled in within twenty-four hours, and go with God.

Given half a chance, Mattei will plunge into practically any business venture that is even vaguely connected with generating power. Wherever there was a reasonable prospect of finding natural gas—in the Marche, in the Abruzzi, in Lucania, in Sicily, or even in Somaliland—he has started digging, ready to repeat on a smaller scale what he had already done in the Po Valley. Last year he took over the bankrupt Pignone factory in Florence, and as part of the deal got the government's interest in the Larderello works, fifty miles away, where natural steam erupting from the earth is used to generate electricity. Thus he extended his domain over a large part of Tuscany. This man who has learned so well how to harness the forces of nature strikes anyone who deals with him as a force of nature himself—a force that is still unharnessed.

Mattei is notably public-relations-minded and is not stingy when it comes to using money for the molding of public opinion. Of the estimated $2 million he is said to have spent for promotion last year, some went for ordinary retail advertising, but some was also spent to extend his domain. He is said to have made a generous contribution to the campaign for a "little ENI" in Sicily.

Moreover, Mattei the fighter of monopoly has given an extraordinary evidence of price fixing in the commodity that he controls as a monopoly—natural gas. His price is pegged by law to the international price, including taxes, which amounts to three times the cost to his agency. When the international price went down by a third in 1953, Mattei got the government to raise taxes on it sufficiently to keep his own price at the old level. The profits are plowed back to finance further gas and oil explorations. Some of this cash is needed to develop his own gas supply, but the greater part, allegedly, is being spent in the hope of making another spectacular discovery. Though he may succeed, he is financing his explorations with money that might otherwise have represented a saving to both producers and consumers. For this he is attacked bitterly and often—by the Communists, incidentally, more than by anyone else.

These criticisms are minor, however, compared to his failure to find new oil deposits. He has failed not only in the Po Valley, where no one else might have done any better, but also in Ragusa, where AGIP once drilled a well and abandoned it only a few miles from the present Gulf site, as well as in the Abruzzi, where there is an abandoned AGIP well only a few hundred yards from Gulf's new discovery.

This might be no more than bad luck. The same thing happened to Anglo-Iranian in Kuwait and to Jersey Standard on the site later found to have the second biggest deposit in the United States. The question is whether the Italian state can afford to finance bad luck. Oil prospecting is one of the most technically complicated, expensive, and speculative ventures in the world. Independent oil experts say Italy would have to put up at least $150 million for barely adequate exploration of the subsoil, and the risk would still be forbidding. Four-fifths of all the exploratory wells drilled in the world are dry, only six in a hundred pay the cost of drilling, and only one in a thousand hits a really big deposit.

It was because big companies are willing to take such risks that France, for example, gave Standard Oil concessions of 1.7 million acres not long ago. The same reason was behind Sicily's decision in 1950.

The choice for the Italians is thus not between a state

monopoly and the kind of energetic, competitive free enterprise that could do so much to develop Italian resources. Most of the concessions that don't go to ENI will go—as many have already gone—to private giants like Montecatini and Edison, which are among the most solidly entrenched in Europe, in partnership with the American oil companies. The choice is thus between two sets of monopolies, both rooted in the Italian economy. The logical solution advocated here by many fair-minded people is to have the production and the pricing of oil conducted by both sets, one exerting its countervailing power on the other.

But many Italians fear that what the American oil companies are primarily interested in is discovering oil deposits—and then sitting on them.

The American companies deny that they would have any interest in keeping the better part of Italian oil underground as a reserve. They point out that most of the big international companies are competing for the Italian retail market, and all of them want to protect or improve their marketing positions. The advantage of using domestic crude, with its minimal transport costs, would be obvious, especially after so much money had been spent to locate it.

The critics of American companies point out that the example of Gulf in Sicily is not reassuring. Alone or in partnership with Montecatini, Gulf has concessions of a million acres in Sicily. Since it opened the Ragusa deposit in November, 1953, it has drilled only four wells in this entire area and its agreement with the regional Sicilian government promises only twenty-two more for production purposes in the next three years. True, Gulf's exploitation rights weren't confirmed until last fall. Nevertheless, a commitment for twenty-two wells in three years is not much in a zone that American geologists admit privately might justify a thousand.

Gulf may be waiting for the Sicilian elections next June—and who can blame it? If the Communists win, they could expropriate all the oil lands on the island; they have been pouring money and agitators into Sicily for months, with "oil imperialism" their most useful campaign slogan.

The Sicilians' enthusiasm over the discovery of oil two years ago is gradually turning into disillusion. The fact

that Gulf found the oil where AGIP had failed is already
half forgotten. The Ragusa wells haven't given work to
more than forty manual laborers, and the trickle of oil
coming out so far has brought no visible wealth to the
island. There will be important royalties some day. The
regional government expects eventually to collect $15
million a year, which is a fifth more than its present
budget. But that's several years in the future. It isn't
hard to persuade Sicilians at the moment that they
could do better on their own, and the walls of Ragusa
are already covered with very explicit invitations to the
Americans to go home.

There is a parallel danger on the mainland, where,
also alone or with Montecatini, Gulf has exploration
rights for half a million acres in or near the Abruzzi. But
it has no rights to produce. Even with a temporary permit, it would be justifiably unwilling to go into big production unless and until its investment is guaranteed by
law.

Until Bill No. 346 is passed, therefore, the Italians
aren't likely to see much oil coming out of the Abruzzi.
And, of course, the longer they have to wait, the more
suspicious they will become.

Obviously, the circle has to be broken. It's hard to
break, however, not only because of the feud between
Mattei and the Americans but because the bill itself is
so poorly drafted.

The bill has been described by Ernesto Rossi in the
Liberal weekly *Il Mondo* as a "monstrous abortion," and
its weaknesses have done more than anything else to
push Italians like Rossi—who has attacked Italian state
monopolies in the past with devastating effect—into
taking Mattei's side. It permits concessions of up to
750,000 acres to one group, more than seven times the
limit for American government-owned oil lands in the
United States; allows any company finding oil to keep
its entire original concession, whereas the United States
allows only a fifth and puts the rest up at public auc-
tion; requires no production commitment in sizable
quantity; and leaves the fixing of royalties to the discretion of a state board that might be easily manipulated
by lobby pressure. Finally, it is so loosely worded that
it could be interpreted as including the Po Valley along
with the rest of the mainland.

In the last few weeks, both sides have shown some signs of willingness to compromise. Mattei has accepted the principle of "free competition" in the rest of Italy, though he still wants exclusive rights in the Po Valley. His group has let it be known that there will be no further effort to block the oil bill's passage, provided it is amended to bring it more in line with American—or even better, Canadian—laws covering oil concessions.

While the American firms haven't endorsed the amendments, at least they are toning down somewhat their campaign for the Po. Some of them seem rather embarrassed by the extent of U.S. government pressure. When Mattei was in the United States last February, Henry Luce gave a party at the Waldorf in his honor. It is reported that Luce asked Mattei to write an article for *Fortune*. Then Mrs. Luce's interview at the beginning of March gave a new impetus to left-wing diatribes against "American oil imperialism."

Yet it should be clear by now that the gentle and understanding way of handling Mattei is likely to be far more successful than blasts against him from the American press or the American government. Some significance may be found in the sympathetic attitude of the British press toward Mattei—a sympathy that some people say is shared by the Anglo-Iranian Oil Company.

There is undoubtedly at present a greater willingness on the part of the U.S. companies to reduce tension and ultimately reach a compromise with Mattei. Gulf isn't in the fight for the Po Valley, and although Standard Oil has only made a tactical withdrawal and not given up on eventually getting into the Po, both admit that they would be willing to invest and explore elsewhere in Italy if some kind of law were passed that made the development of Italian oil, with all the investment that is implied, predictably profitable.

Inevitably a compromise must be reached between those Italian monopolies which are backed by American companies and that Italian monopoly which is named Mattei. The *carabiniere's* son can no longer be treated like a usurper, a freakish product of the postwar era whom sometime in some shady way somebody is going to "get." All attempts at "getting" Mattei have been dismal failures so far. His hold on the people's imagination is constantly increasing. His gigantic horizontal and vertical combination of business ventures is efficiently run and pays good dividends. But, to use the terminology of contemporary international politics, Mattei must be "contained"—perhaps in his own interest. Out of reciprocal containment "coexistence" can come, and be highly profitable for everybody concerned, including the people of Italy.

With their rich experience in the domestic affairs of many nations, the American oil companies can be of great assistance in helping the Italian monopolists to work out their differences with Mattei. The best thing the U.S. government can do to hasten the agreement is to keep quiet and avoid stirring up Italian nationalism. After all, Mattei is not a Mossadegh. He wants to increase his nation's wealth, not keep it underground.

The compromise must be reached between the economic powers, and when that is done the Italian politicians will quickly pass a workable law. Then at last Italy will start getting oil out of its wells.

Can Government Be "Merchandised"?

BY WILLIAM LEE MILLER

A prominent member of the "Dewey team" complained after the Governor's first eighteen-hour television show, in 1950, that it was disgraceful that the distinguished Governor of a great state (I think that's the way it goes) should have to appear in such a public-relations stunt. An advertising man who helped to arrange the "telethon" quoted Jimmy Durante in reply: "Dem's da conditions dat prevail."

Da conditions seem now to prevail even more, for public-relations men and their close relatives, advertising men, have moved into politics in a big way. Their activities, which hitherto have included tasks like creating memorable headgear for candidate Kefauver, devising such edifying slogans as "You never had it so good" and "The voluntary way is the American Way," and figuring out new places to print the phrase "I Like Ike," have now come to include the planning of entire campaigns and even, most recently, the conduct of government.

223

Governor Dewey may owe an extraordinary debt to such professional public relations, for it is said that after his defeat in 1948 an exhaustive investigation of his public personality by an advertising agency led to the redesigning of his mustache. Whether it was this singular service or the hundred thousand votes he admitted the telethon had gained for him, something plainly ended whatever scruples he may have had about public relations in politics, for in 1952 he used all kinds of props and all kinds of twists and hammered it up on each new television production number his advertising agency worked out for him. His question-and-answer programs with prearranged questions from selected ordinary people, his comedy programs about "Harry's Haunted House," and his commentary programs on which he was Deeply Shocked each week at what the Democrats had done showed how thoroughly the distinguished Governor of a great state was willing to accept the admen's judgment as to the conditions that prevail.

A public-relations man may defend his new role in politics by saying that he just takes good political ideas that haven't gone across and makes them go across. The editor of *Tide*, an advertising and sales trade publication, remarked during the past campaign, ". . . advertising . . . demonstrated beyond question that it can sell a good idea as successfully as it can sell a good product."

But this statement omits the rather important fact that it can do the same for a *bad* idea. And advertising is not simply neutral as to whether the idea is good or bad, but has a bias within it. I don't mean whatever biases there may be in advertising men and agencies as a result of their relation to the business community and its politics. I mean the bias in the nature of advertising itself. It is this bias of which some public-relations men in politics seem most spectacularly unaware. They seem not to see that the media over which you say something and the devices by which you say it alter what you say.

The advertising man tells the politician to make the argument quick and simple, without any unpleasant complexities. ("VOICE: Mr. Eisenhower, what about the high cost of living? EISENHOWER: My wife, Mamie, worries about the same thing. I tell her it's our job to change that on November 4th.") He says the appeal must be basic and unmistakable. ("The farmer's farming every
224

day, making money and that ain't hay. CLAP! CLAP!
Don't let 'em take it away!")

Qualifications must be carefully subordinated to
clear, positive, unequivocal promises. ("VOICE: Mr. Eisenhower, can you bring taxes down? EISENHOWER: Yes.
We will work to cut billions in Washington spending,
and bring your taxes down.") The opposition between
the two parties must be made dramatic and absolute.
("They'll promise you the sky. They'll promise you the
earth! But what's a Republican's promise worth?") Fearful and tragic events are to be associated with the Opposition. ("VOICE: General, the Democrats are telling me I
never had it so good. EISENHOWER: Can that be true
when America is billions in debt, when prices have doubled, when taxes break our backs, and we are still fighting in Korea? It is tragic. It is time for a change.") Familiar symbols of home and prestige must be associated
with the client. ("The Democratic party took apples off
the streets and put apple pie on the table. Whenever
history puts them to the test, Americans will always
choose the best.") The advertiser tells the politician that
examples should be memorable, whether or not they are
illuminating or representative. ("VOICE: General, just
how bad is waste in Washington? EISENHOWER: How
bad? Recently, just one government bureau actually lost
four hundred million dollars and not even the FBI can
find it. It's *really* time for a change.")

Clem Whitaker, partner in the California advertising
firm of Whitaker and Baxter, which conducted the
American Medical Association's successful multi-million-
dollar campaign to eliminate national health insurance
("socialized medicine") from the alternatives politically
available to the American people, is one of the most out-
spoken of the new public-relations men in politics. Whitaker has drawn up an apparently definitive list of the
grand strategies of political campaigns built on public-
relations techniques: ". . . you can interest voters if you
put on a fight. No matter what the fight, *fight for something*. . . . You may wonder if that is the only technique
in campaigning. It isn't the only one. There are two. The
average American also likes to be entertained. . . .
He likes the movies and he likes fireworks and parades.
So if you can't fight, put on a show!"

A public-relations man in politics may say he is only

doing better what politicians have always done. But though the "old-style" politician often did oversimplify and sloganize and appeal to fear and greed, he does not seem to have done this quite so systematically or so effectively as the modern advertisers in politics. He did not have the dominating control of the sources of opinion that the modern national "mass media" advertiser can enjoy. And he had a restraining set of pressures on him to which some of the political advertising men do not seem to be subject; at least he had to pay some attention to facts. His campaigns may have lacked moxie, but he had to deal with interests of his constituents, which were real and which were independent of his manipulation. He could not, as a memorandum from one public-relations firm advised its agents to do, create situations of reality; he had to fit his actions to a reality that already existed. He could not engage in what public-relations man Edward L. Bernays has described as the "engineering of public consent"; he had to let the public engineer its own consent.

But Clem Whitaker has said that managing campaigns, now becoming "a mature, well-managed business, *founded on sound public relations principles,* and using every technique of modern-day advertising," is "no longer a hit-or-miss business, directed by broken-down politicians."

It's hard to see just how the public will be helped when a "broken-down" politician is rebuilt by Mr. Whitaker's ten million pieces of printed matter, 650 billboards, and 18,000 smaller posters.

And these new PR men themselves may not necessarily be an improvement over even the "broken-down" politicians. No politicians, for instance, could have the adman's freewheeling auxiliary relationship to politics, thinking up slogans at "brainstorm meetings" for clients with the money to pay for them. The politicians were potential public officials and as such had to shape their relationship to the public to some extent in accord with their ability to act as a part of a government. Many of them, in their quaint, broken-down way, have had a genuine interest in public policy. Occasionally one could even discern, in some of them, an honest conviction. They rarely approached the immaculate amorality of the political public-relations man who, admitting that his candidate did not know anything about anything, said, "Let's consider this campaign clinically. After all, you don't criticize a brain surgeon's technique just because he operates on a criminal."

The public-relations man tends to work backwards, from desired effect to technique to content. If present tendencies continue, we may get political campaigns tailored to fit the requirements of public relations and then government tailored to fit the requirements of the campaign.

Clem Whitaker has a consoling thought to offer on this score: ". . . whatever technique we use, in the end we always come back to Lincoln's fundamental—public sentiment is everything. If sometimes we go to extremes to create that sentiment, we can recall that some of the greatest statesmen in American history went to extremes, too." Going to extremes has testimonials from top-brand-name statesmen, and never mind whether Mr. Whitaker's extremes are quite the same as Mr. Lincoln's.

It is a bit hard to tell at this distance just what Lincoln meant by his statement "public sentiment is everything," but it is clear what Whitaker, who quotes it fondly, means. He means that public sentiment is *everything*. Other facts of the political world, such as the structure of Congress, the size of armies, the location of oil, national beliefs that run deeper than the mood of the moment—these are not very important, and can easily be controlled by the proper manipulation of public sentiment.

Even a new character for a candidate can be created synthetically, by a nickname, a slogan, the right profile, or a redesigned mustache. Unfortunately for the public-relations man, however, the realities behind the illusions he builds sometimes do break through to spoil things. The candidate's character cannot always be entirely concealed by his public-relations man. This exasperates Mr. Whitaker: ". . . an automobile . . . can't object to your sales talk, and if you step on the starter, it usually runs. A candidate, on the other hand, can and does talk back—and can sometimes talk you out of an election, despite the best you can do in campaign headquarters."

Mr. Whitaker explains that public-relations campaigners like himself have a problem with a candidate's "willingness or unwillingness to hew to the line on the

227

plan of strategy which has been worked out . . . his ability or inability to measure up to the character you give him by your carefully-prepared build-up." Apparently some old-fashioned candidates still want to hew to their own line rather than the adman's, and present to the public the character God gave them rather than that given by Mr. Whitaker's "carefully-prepared build-up."

Some public-relations men in politics tend to substitute illusions of their own devising for existing facts. Then, too, they may hold the view of the public's role in politics exemplified by this statement of Leone Baxter, Mr. Whitaker's partner in "Campaigns, Inc.":

"It's because the public relations profession, and its allied professions, know something about presenting abstract ideas, in attractive form, to masses of people who are too occupied with their daily lives to think analytically on their own account, that the average man today is in a position to know more about the trends of human affairs than ever in history. . . . You are helping him to understand your clients and their problems, their ideals. You are helping him to be a better citizen."

The techniques by which some public-relations people help us to be better citizens now include the saturation radio-TV spot campaign, brought to the service of the nation in last year's Republican campaign. The plan for this operation, HOW TO INSURE AN EISENHOWER VICTORY IN NOVEMBER, listed these advantages of concentrating the spot announcements in the last three weeks: "1. It gives maximum effectiveness of penetration and recall without becoming deadly to the listener and viewer; 2. It delivers the maximum just before the election; 3. It occurs at too late a date for effective Democratic rebuttal." (Since this memorandum makes the regrettable slip of calling the Democratic Party by its name, it must have been another agency which struck a blow for decency in government by deciding that Republican orators should henceforth call the Democratic Party the "Democrat" Party.) The spot-campaign people were concerned with higher things, a "special, all out effort to switch forty-nine counties in twelve states and with it the election to Eisenhower." When I asked the head of the advertising agency that handled the Democratic Party's account about this saturation spot campaign, he seemed worried only that I might think the Republicans had stolen a march on him. "We had the idea for a saturation spot campaign long before the Republicans," he protested, "but we couldn't get the money."

Another way the public is brought to understand the client's ideals is by hearing them whether it wants to or not. For example, the Republican advertisers are well satisfied that they made a net gain last year over the Democrats by purchasing the higher-priced time already allocated to top TV performers. A man who arranges such political programs explained it to me: "A viewer tunes in to see Arthur Godfrey, but in place of Godfrey there is our program, and since there *are no top programs opposite Godfrey* he has to come back to us!" Thus is the public "delivered" to be taught about trends in human affairs.

To one outside public relations and its allied professions, capturing, delivering, and saturating the public would appear to be rather the opposite of helping it to know human affairs and understand ideals. In a way it would seem that the better the public relations, the wider the gap between the public's emotional approval of the client and the public's rational understanding of the reasons *why* it approves of the client. The advertising man's habit and purpose is to go beneath the reason to build strong emotional attachments to what he is selling, by associating it with all good symbols, relevant or not. Thus, it seems from the pictures in the advertisements that toothpaste has not only brightened the young lady's teeth but also papered the walls, straightened the room, and introduced her to a smashingly handsome young man. The advertiser's victim automatically calls the toothpaste's name when she goes to the drugstore.

An advantage of such techniques to the candidate is that he can now do "scientifically" what politicians have always had to do in fumbling, uncertain ways. He can say something without saying it. His advertising can systematically create an impression that goes well beyond any direct claim he would make and have to stand by. The most striking example of such public relations is the treatment of the Korean War by the Republicans last year, and in particular Mr. Eisenhower's "I-will-go-to-Korea" speech. In millions of American homes, voters had a deep and emotional *impression* that Eisenhower would end the Korean War, but the Eisenhower forces could rightly say that they never directly made any such claim. It was a triumph of the manipulation of public sentiment.

If public sentiment continues to be manipulated in this way, the public may choose world policies simply because they are recommended by some telegenic personality who has a good-looking, cloth-coated wife, born on St. Patrick's Day, and a little dog named Checkers.

The public-relations man says these are the conditions that prevail, and we might as well accept them. But it is possible that the conditions are not quite that prevalent. In the 1952 campaign the Republicans were selling the public something which it very much wanted to "buy," a change and a hero. By evoking distaste in some quarters, the "Ike" advertising may even have helped the Opposition. In the face of the overwhelming odds, the significant evidence about public relations from the 1952 campaign may come from the other side, on which an unknown, running against the hero and against the tide, still managed to gain a respectably large vote. And he did that without a big public-relations ballyhoo.

The two most remarkable appearances of that campaign, an acceptance speech and a concession of defeat, were made without benefit of advertising. No format was tested at an agency, no gimmicks were devised for audience effect. There were no make-up men to arrange each eyebrow, no production men to supervise the camera angles, no charts to tell the audience when to laugh or cry. The words that were spoken were the speaker's and the feelings that he evoked were real and spontaneous, for there is no public relations that can take the place of the honest words of an honest man.

The Eisenhower movement, born and nurtured in the smooth new world of public relations, is the biggest client yet persuaded of the prevailing conditions. Not only from Governor Dewey and his team but also from the alert businessmen who flocked to the banner, the crusade came to understand how tough a "selling" job the Republicans had, and how useful modern "scientific" selling practices could be for such a tough job. During the primary campaign Senator Taft complained that some top executives, even against their own inclination, were supporting Eisenhower on the advice of their

230

corporations' public-relations men. Of the convention at which Mr. Eisenhower was nominated, *Tide* wrote in its snappy, underlined newsletter: "The *Republican convention* next week will almost be *a convention of advertising and public relations men*. An amazing number are attending . . ." A group of public-relations men, called the "Eisenhower-Nixon Research Service," takes credit for the first big Eisenhower victory, for it gave the "Fair Play" amendment its felicitous name and planned the triumphantly successful build-up of public support of the Eisenhower side in that crucial convention fight.

During the campaign the same group chose, named, and pushed the "captive candidate" theme against Stevenson, but this was only one of many public-relations groups working for Eisenhower. Three advertising agencies had a hand in the campaign: the Kudner agency, which was originally given the Republican account; Batten, Barton, Durstine & Osborn, which joined the crusade early in September and came to handle all radio and TV for the General; and the Bates agency, one of whose executives thought up the much-debated saturation spot campaign.

But the Eisenhower movement did not stop its use of public-relations techniques on Election Day; the "conditions" apparently "prevail" not only for campaigns but also for governments. An article on "The GOP's 'PR'" in the *Wall Street Journal* late in February said: ". . . the Eisenhower forces already have a fair claim to the title of the most-public-relations-conscious-administration in history. . . . This heavier-than-ever accent on 'scientific' public relations techniques crops up all over the place. . . ."

The *Journal* story concentrated on the Eisenhower-Nixon Research Service, now renamed the Research Associates, and their proposal of a "carefully-calculated, Government-wide effort to cultivate the public" with methods which the *Journal* reporter said were "reminiscent of those employed by a private company . . ." The plan was presented in a "fascinating brochure . . . handsomely gotten up in a black loose-leaf notebook, with cellophane-covered pages, a gaudy lay-out, and the word 'Confidential' stamped on the front," which was reported to have found its way to the bedside table of the President and also to Vice-President Nixon and Postmaster General Summerfield.

A more recent story in the *Wall Street Journal* reported that "Eisenhower & Co. have opened a new sales department right in the White House. The new division of the Republican Administration is headed by a man President Eisenhower privately calls 'the greatest salesman in the world'—the Seattle mortgage banker, Walter Williams . . ." Mr. Williams, who is also Under Secretary of Commerce, will try in this new job "to 'sell' the President's policies to the public—and tout his achievements." As the *Journal* story observed, ". . . the Eisenhower forces, a lot of them former businessmen, simply believe in a little salesmanship."

This salesmanship was nowhere more evident than in the President's TV report in June to the people of the nation he governs. It was planned, rehearsed, and presented under the graciously donated professional supervision of B.B.D.&O.

Tide reports that Bernard C. Duffy, head of B.B.D.&O., said of the campaign last fall that Republican strategy centered on merchandising Eisenhower's frankness, honesty, and integrity, his sincere and wholesome approach. The strategy by which the candidate was "merchandised" was used again in June to "merchandise" the President. B.B.D.&O.'s best techniques of television advertising were employed to bring the President and his Cabinet to the people, to tell them about how the roof was not leaking. It was as though, having created during the campaign the TV character Likeable Ike, his sponsors found it expedient to continue the installments of his adventures. *Advertising Agency* magazine quoted Mr. Duffy's satisfied comment: "One of our best shows."

This adman's "show" did not insist that the public make the hard and controversial decisions about world policy. Instead the implied view of the public was that of a docile, harmonious family, waiting to be told a few fascinating facts about its government by Likeable Ike and his swell friends. Government appeared as a merely technical and administrative matter: "What you're concerned about is that the house is in good order"—about which there is, of course, harmonious agreement. "Now, everybody helps to do that, everybody in the family." Yes, everything is being well handled by these dandy people we have in government: "Since government is just people, you have seen the kind of people that are trying to solve these things for you."

There was no suggestion that there might be at stake profound problems of value about which the public had to decide. Herb and George, and Mr. Benson, who was a farmer himself, and Mrs. Hobby, whose job was a woman's in the home, read their lines, sometimes going into detail about the problems selected for discussion, but the detail served more to show their seriousness and competence and perhaps the romance of government than to provide a genuinely illuminating discussion.

All through these edifying discourses ran the homey advertising gimmicks—the basket of mail from which "we get our ideas"; a letter from a lady in Pawtucket; 8 to 1 approval of the entire program; a chart showing Mr. Benson's travels; a mention of Derby, Kansas, and Limestone, Maine. The "points of interest" described so chattily were all assumed to be completely under control by the genial and efficient new managers of the business—"I'm going over to Bermuda to meet with some of our friends and talk over these things"; "Well, now, of course, George, we know we're going to stop this"—and the public can rest easy, assured that "We've done something and are now doing things to repair the holes in the roof and keep the fences mended." All that was left for the viewing public to do was to say, "How nice!"

Bill Tyler, who writes a column in *Advertising Agency* magazine called "Copy Clinic," had the following illuminating comment:

"Undoubtedly the most effective commercial of the month was the President's TV appearance around the first of June. . . . it closely followed the pattern of an agency new-business solicitation. The President let each department head, armed with slides, present the story of his branch of the business. Then he wrapped the whole thing up in a masterful manner and asked for the order. As a TV salesman, we think you will agree, Dwight Eisenhower has few peers. . . ."

Members of the Eisenhower Administration themselves sometimes seem to conceive the relationship of the government to the people in advertising terms. The *Wall Street Journal* quoted this statement from a high official, which the President is said to endorse, explaining the new White House sales office: "We all suddenly realized we were busy manufacturing a product down

233

here, but nobody was selling it." One of the President's top aides sent a memorandum to all government personnel who deal with foreign policy just before the President's important April 16 speech to the American Newspaper Publishers Association. The memorandum described an elaborate plan to publicize the speech around the world, and it called this promotion of a major address of the President of the United States "merchandising-in-depth."

The differences between selling a product in a market and choosing public policies in a democracy may not be immediately apparent to some advertising people. The consumer acts as an individual and can defend himself against high pressure and the gullibility of his neighbor —by consumer resistance or buying different products. But the citizen *must* live under the government that he helps to select, and it can make ultimate claims upon him. The political issue is the health and direction of the whole community, not just the satisfaction of an individual consumer's desire.

It remains to be seen how much the Eisenhower Administration will continue to "sell" its policies with carefully devised "new," "positive," and "dynamic" slogans, even though the policy may be old (our "dynamic" European foreign policy), negative (cutting the Air Force budget to get "more defense"), actually confused ("trade, not aid"), or nonexistent (the "liberation" of eastern Europe). At first the crusade seemed to have taken advertising techniques even into the formulation of national policy itself, as in the remarkable trust our new foreign affairs people had for a while in "psychological warfare." Somebody needed to explain to the new Administration that advertising and public relations had to be secondary to real political action. Apparently the committee headed by William Jackson did just that for the foreign-policy information field.

What we may now need is a similar criticism of the Eisenhower Administration's relations to the American people. It might say to the Republican Party that what is needed (if I may try my hand at a little sloganizing) is not a better selling job but a better doing job.

A WAY FOR AMERICA

What Price Peace?

BY MAX ASCOLI

"There is no longer any alternative to peace." "War would present to us only the alternative in degrees of destruction. There could be no truly successful outcome." In these last few months the President has been harping on this theme in impromptu talks, in press conferences, in formal addresses—literally every time he had a chance to say what was weighing most heavily on his mind. General Eisenhower is no recent convert to belief in peace. But lately his knowledge of what nuclear destruction entails, compounded by his unique experience as a practitioner of war, has so haunted him as to make him sound at times like a peacemonger.

With his message to Congress on the Formosan situation, the President has started moving from the generic to the specific, from the formulation of his strategic aim to the listing of the tactical measures to be taken if the aim is to be reached.

That there is no alternative to peace in our days is an absolute truth. But unilateral acknowledgment of this truth can result in a disaster as horrible as its verification. Now more than ever, it takes two to establish peace: the democracies and the Communists. And the price must be paid by both sides. The President, with his message, has made his opening bid. It is a momentous event, for it implies the abandonment of old taboos and a new system of relationships with Communism. It may also imply the breakup of the Republican Party.

The occasion for the President's message arose from imminent danger in an area that since the end of the war has been the soft underbelly of the democracies. To face Communism in Asia we have a frail facsimile of NATO, doubtful or weak allies, and a dismal record of non-containment. Of all the soft spots in Asia the softest is Formosa.

The difficulties the President has to face inside his own Administration and party in trying to stop Communism are at least as great as those that are set in his path by neutral or unreliable Asian governments. Indeed, it is the strange allegiance of some of the Republican Congressional leaders to the weakest and most synthetic of all these governments that has made them resigned, if not eager, harbingers of preventive war. Nor are Congressional leaders the only victims of this pro-Chiang infatuation. The record of Admiral Radford is well known. So are the speeches of that improbable diplomat Mr. Walter Robertson, who recently stated that Chou En-lai comes no closer to representing China than William Z. Foster does to representing America. Yet these are the men on whom the President must rely for the conduct of his Asian policy: Senator Knowland is the leader of the President's party in the Senate, Admiral Radford is his chief military adviser, and Mr. Robertson is the high-ranking expert on Asia in the State Department.

The President's dilemma was extraordinarily irksome: With the Chinese Civil War kindled anew, he could no longer delay. He had to announce his terms for the establishment of peace where peace was most endangered. Under no condition could he turn from a near peacemonger into a preventive warrior. Part of his embarrassments he can blame on himself, for they come from his 1952 decision to play the game of politics as an orthodox Republican. Since then, however, he must have learned enough about politics and statesmanship to realize that the best a leader can do, when surrounded by men he cannot shake off, is to use their ambitions and prejudices for his own purposes.

What the President had in mind had become known several days before he sent his message to Congress: It was a cease-fire. That could only lead to the neutralization of Formosa. Only then would the Allied and neutral powers stand by us; only then could the line be drawn behind which we would not fall back. The President of course knew that the opposition to neutralizing Formosa would be equally vigorous in Peking, in Taipei, and on the Republican side of Capitol Hill.

This is probably one of the reasons why he announced his new Asian policy in a message to Congress. He knew he could count on Democratic assistance, and indeed it is doubtful whether he would ever have advanced his cease-fire proposal at the end of his message were it not for the fact that Congress now has a Democratic majority. The idea of a cease-fire to be reached through the U.N. is of Democratic origin, and is still considered by many Republicans either as an inconsequential pious fraud or shameful appeasement.

General Eisenhower has started a movement on two fronts. Through the U.N. he seeks to initiate a process of negotiation that may ultimately make Formosa's independence an international and not an exclusive U.S. responsibility. At the same time, he envisages broader military action for the defense of Formosa and the Pescadores, and announces that "unhappily," to prevent Communist attack against Formosa and the Pescadores, we may be compelled "to take into account closely related localities and actions"—which probably means that some of the offshore islands may be defended, and that preventive bombing of the mainland of China may be ordered. It is even more probable that the mention of "related localities"—Quemoy and Matsu —was made for bargaining purposes on the theory, as a high government official put it, that "You have got to have a little something when you negotiate with Orientals."

The President's message was designed to elicit the cooperation of the U.N., of the Democrats, and of the Knowland Republicans. These last have their own particular reasons to be elated: The President, contrary to what has been stated by some of his critics in the Senate, has not now joined the preventive warriors, but he has made a tentative, preventive declaration of war against the only enemy Chiang's friends are spoiling to have the United States engaged with in battle.

Will Red China comply and through aggression or overt preparation to attack make itself responsible for war? Will war then remain limited to the defense of Formosa? Will it be fought with conventional or unconventional weapons? The China Lobbyists are far from being in agreement on these points, and indeed the Chinese Nationalists are much less sanguine than their American friends. One thing, however, is certain: By raising all these questions, hopes, and fears, the President has paid a very heavy penalty to maintain for a while longer a semblance of party unity.

The President is taking an extremely serious gamble that has probably been made unnecessarily risky by past hesitancies. Since he came to the White House General

Eisenhower has used his power so sparingly that now he needs a vote of Congress to act as President of the United States.

But this is the time when, rather than criticize the President for what he failed to do in the past, we should make every effort to understand why he has acted as he has, and to remove as many as possible of the obstacles that stand in his way. Sir Anthony Eden has already started doing this by proving that interallied solidarity has not been broken in one of the areas where it was most endangered. The Democrats in Congress have acted with an equal sense of responsibility—particularly those among them who elicited from the President the declaration that he alone has the authority to take "any decision to use United States forces other than in immediate self defense or in direct defense of Formosa and the Pescadores."

The Allies, as well as patriotic Americans of all parties, have clearly understood that something even more important than the defense of Formosa is at stake. To break the Formosan tangle we need the U.N.; if a political alternative to war is to be found, there is no by-passing the U.N.

In the near future the U.N. action which the President has invoked can build up enough pressure to make imperative the gentle liquidation of Chiang Kai-shek and the establishment of true self-government for the Formosans under U.N. trusteeship. The course on which the President has recently entered, risky as it is, can turn out to be a healthy and successful one if the U.N. and interallied action develops vigorously and acquires ever-increasing momentum so that Asia and the whole world may be given a greater measure of peace.

To reach this aim it is imperative that some degree of understanding and co-operation with Soviet Russia be established, for the United States and Soviet Russia would be the protagonists and also the major victims of a generalized nuclear war. At present only these two countries have influence enough to stop the civil war which has ravaged China for over thirty years.

When the action at the U.N. starts paying dividends, when the very nearness of war makes it compellingly clear to both sides that there is no alternative to peace and that binding multilateral agreements for the reduction of armaments are imperative—then the gamble that the President has taken will start paying off. The greater his success, the more likely he is to acquire the freedom of action he needs to shed his most troublesome aides.

The President must be praised for having taken this gamble. The Chief Executive of the United States cannot reduce himself to playing the role of inspirational leader. But he will have to be extremely skillful, firm, at times even ruthless. For the indecisive, the hesitant, is at the same time the most reckless among gamblers and the one who cannot win.

Back to Fortress America

BY MAX ASCOLI

The recent moves of Soviet diplomacy have been generally interpreted—particularly by our government spokesmen—as evidence that the position of strength we have achieved has started "paying off." In fact, it is said, Soviet Russia is so anxious to have this strength of ours weakened that it is willing to pare down its own. Secretary Dulles recently told the nation over TV that the sudden Soviet change of mind over the Austrian peace treaty and on negotiations with the West in general was a reward for our "policy of strength and firmness and the standard of moral principles." As to how we got all this, he had a homely explanation: "You keep on steadily, steadily, keeping the pressure on, and all of a sudden you get a break." That was a memorable TV show, a milestone in government by television. Who will ever forget how effectively the flat words of Secretary Dulles were counterpointed and dramatized in the changing expressions on the President's face?

Others have said that the new course of Soviet diplomacy has been determined not only by our virtue but also by economic difficulties inside Russia, particularly in agriculture. Or maybe the Russians are worrying over China's power and ambition. All this spreads glossy smiles of self-congratulation over our leaders' faces. Only the visit to Belgrade of Bulganin and Khrushchev seems to arouse some uneasiness and brings little or no ethical solace to official Washington—although the point could be made that our assiduous search for another Tito has finally "paid off," since the men who rule Russia today are such good national-Communists, or Titoists, that they feel duty bound to pay a respectful visit to the proto-Tito of them all.

It may be advisable to explore at least another possible interpretation of the New Look that Soviet diplomacy has adopted—a New Look that may have been tailored to fit not Russian but American weaknesses and internal troubles. It is the part of wisdom to assume that our adversary knows us well and uses his knowledge to inflict on us the greatest possible harm.

It may be assumed that Soviet diplomacy first works on our allies, then waits for the predictable American reaction to our allies' behavior, then goes back to work on our allies again. There can be no doubt that Russia's primary aim is to unhinge the Grand Alliance. Particularly since Stalin's death there is mounting evidence that the Russians have been steadily pursuing this wedging process, which lately has "paid off" rather well—for them. They have literally plagiarized the major proposals that France and Britain have been advancing for the last two years at the disarmament negotiations, and now they advocate the principle that reduction of conventional and unconventional armaments be gradual or, as it is said, "phased." They now subscribe to the notion that until the outlawing of nuclear weapons has been completed, a victim of an atomic attack is entitled to retaliate with A- or H-bombs—if it happens to belong to the atomic "haves."

In widening any crack there may be between the atomic haves and have-nots, Soviet diplomacy has done a precision job. Since it became known that any war in Europe would be fought with atomic weapons, peace has become ever more desperately cherished by our western allies, on whose cities democratic or Communist bombs may be exploded. Peace has acquired a new connotation on the Continent: no atomic air bombardment, no shooting of atomic guns. The presence on their soil of American air bases and atomic batteries does not make the Europeans comfortable.

For each European nation, Soviet diplomacy adds something like an extra dividend to the notion of peace. For the French, it is no atomic war, plus the prospect that German rearmament, after all, may never take place. For the Germans, it is no atomic war, plus unification. For other countries, like Italy, it is no atomic war, plus relaxation of internal tension. Since this tension is mostly contributed by the local Communist Party, the Russians can quickly deliver an installment on this extra dividend. In Italy, although with some bitterness and internal quarrels, the Communist Party can even agree to let its strength dwindle and Nenni slip out of its clutches.

The American reaction to the Europeans' anti-atomic peacemongering is of a nature that anyone who knows our country could easily predict. Do our allies stick by us or not? irate people ask. How can they impose on us a limitation in the use of the weapons we produce? The contagion of neutralism in Europe as well as in Asia is particularly bewildering to us, and indeed it is surprising that our spokesmen have, so far, reacted rather blandly to it. For Soviet-sponsored neutrality actually is nothing but one more bogus extra dividend offered by Russia to any nation anxious to gain an exemption from war—irrespective of the capacity the nation may possess to make its neutrality respected or of any multilateral agreement on the part of the major powers to guarantee it. Yet the idea of a neutrality belt from Finland to Yugoslavia does not seem to alarm our President. In a recent press conference, he stated that Austrian neutrality will be an armed one, like that of the Swiss, who, he said, "would fight to the death for it." This was a remarkable piece of news, of which the Austrians themselves had no inkling.

There are, however, much fiercer American reactions to be expected in the weeks immediately ahead, while the consultations prior to the meeting with the Russians go on. It may then become clear that some of our allies, aside from flirting with neutrality, take kindly to the idea that American bases may be reduced—or removed. A number of people here may snap back that if this is what the Europeans want, they can have it. Some military experts may suggest that, after all, as the range of our bombers increases, the need for foreign air bases proportionately diminishes, and moreover the era of intercontinental guided missiles may be just around the corner. If we have no reason to keep our soldiers stationed abroad, then the lodestar of American diplomacy, "enlightened self-interest," clearly shows us the way: Let's get back home, save money, and mind our business.

Quite a number of different forces are pulling us in this direction, and the Communist influence on most of them is negligible or nonexistent. The blundering verbosity of some of our political and military leaders has frayed the nerves of our allies and heightened their resentment at the moody, nagging character of our diplomacy. Our emphasis on the purely military aspect of the alliance and on the atomic side of our military preparedness has created a mood in many nations that is becoming crystallized into two ideas. One is neutrality, the other is the wish to gain the greatest possible independence of America. The Russians have done their bit to further the first idea by housing neutrality in a very central European location.

As to the second idea, the Russians have reason to be satisfied when they see how greatly unwilling Congress has been to lower trade barriers and eliminate racial discrimination in our immigration laws. By studying both allied and American politics they can measure the many forces that are pushing and pulling us back to Fortress America. Can there be any doubt as to their desire to keep the peace, at least until the process is finally consummated?

There is, of course, Asia. There the Fortress has an outlying string of bastions, thousands of miles away. The suggestion that we might pull back from the most insignificant, untenable Asian outpost is considered even worse than appeasement—treason. But there, too, we may have to reckon with the stubborn determination of our major antagonist to use not only the seduction of neutrality and the verbiage of peace but actually to keep peace. Bandung proved that a bit of patience, a stint of all-around smiling, can get quite far. Our Asian antagonist, the Chinese, might disconcert us by *not* pulling the two triggers—Matsu and Quemoy—that some American high officials have put within their grasp. In Asia neutralism is, if anything, even rifer than in Europe, and the Communists at any time can launch an Austrian experiment in some border nation, no matter how tiny: Cambodia, for instance.

In Asia as well as in Europe, a condition of peace is developing—a condition that our antagonists assiduously cultivate, for they see in it the best possible guarantee of our undoing. This peace may prove to be for our nation, and indeed for our civilization, as ruinous as war. But this ruin cannot be prevented by war. All the prospects of warfare, nuclear or psychological, limited or unlimited, have been exhausted in the process of talking about them—incessant, reckless talking, made in the name of the most peaceful-minded people on earth, yet insistent and plausible enough to deject or scare our friends.

The Communists, we can assume, know better. They foster the kind of neutrality that keeps every nation isolated, disarmed, and soft. They must rejoice, seeing America dragged to the conference table by its allies, represented by men in constant dread of criticism from their own party, reluctant and unprepared to answer Russian or, for that matter, allied proposals—save by stressing the supreme importance of the NATO military alliance, the twelve German divisions, and the ring of imitation NATOS in other parts of the world. The Russians hope that the sorely tried bonds which still hold the Grand Alliance together may snap and the power of our country be safely locked up in Fortress America.

I do not say that this is what is bound to happen. But I do say that this is what may happen because of the way our foreign policy has been conducted during the last few years—and not necessarily since the Republicans came into power. The danger that this may happen despite our vaunted position of strength and despite our virtue must be taken into account before considering what the program of our government should be in the coming round of negotiations.

The Miracle

BY MAX ASCOLI

And yet it happened: There was a miracle at Geneva. There is no trace of miracle in the fact that the leaders of Soviet Russia and the West did not indulge in any verbal equivalent of spitting in each other's eye, nor is there proof of supernatural visitation in the Four-Power document that concluded the Conference. The miracle was strictly an American one, evidenced by the U.S. delegation. It was wrought upon the same men who, before reluctantly going to Geneva, had summoned all their skill as devil's advocates to forewarn the nation against the illusion that anything extraordinary, or to any extent momentous, could be expected to take place at Geneva.

Yet, in spite of all the mobilized anti-miracle squads of the American Government and of the American press, it happened. We are freed now from the horrible servitude the Russians had imposed on us: that of being the main guarantors of that condition of no-war, no-peace which the Russians had first introduced into the world at the end of the war and then confidently had entrusted to our care.

It must be admitted that our government, both under Republican and Democratic leadership, did a good job at that. It hated this role, but couldn't help playing it: Nothing else could be done. It could only arm and arm, producing in ever-increasing quantity weapons it dreaded to use. Even the growing realization that the weapons we as well as the Russians possessed would result in planetary suicide, even the awareness, as the President has said that "there is no longer any alternative to peace," was not enough to stop the drift. For what was *this* peace to which we were stuck without alternatives? We could scarcely counteract international Communism with a Deminform. We, the least empire- or revolution-minded of all peoples, found ourselves pitted against the most imperialistic, revolutionary power that has ever set out to subjugate the world.

Since 1945, there have been several attempts at peaceful settlement with the main Communist empire. But the armament race in which we were forced to engage after the Korean aggression in 1950 had resulted from the conviction that attempts at peaceful settlement with the Communists were futile. The armament race, of course, increased tension, and tension made the prospects for peaceful settlement even more remote. We could not trust peace, and we could not trust war. This double nihilism suited the Russians' scheme for long-protracted or—as Trotsky put it—permanent revolution. For a nation like ours, this nihilistic policy was a product not of malice but of despair. The Russians, on the other hand, could well indulge in their "peace offensives" while arming as fast as we did—or faster, as their recent production of warplanes showed.

There can be no explanation for miracles, for if the causes that bring them about could be traced, there would be no miracles. All one can do is to gather some evidence as to the fact, and from this viewpoint perhaps the best possible evidence that a miracle occurred at

244

Geneva can be found in the statements of Secretary Dulles, who notoriously was the Doubting Thomas of the American delegation. Back from Geneva, he said at his first news conference, "We believe that the principle of non-recourse to force is valid not merely for the United States and its allies, but that it is valid for all."

Mr. Dulles, a man quite conversant with legal and political theories, may perhaps sometimes be inclined, like many professional theorists, to give an over-forceful formulation to his ideas. Yet even granting this, it is certainly astonishing that the man now propounding the non-recourse-to-force principle is the same man who, not so long ago, formulated the theory of instant, massive retaliation against Communist aggression, and never defined the kind of aggression that called for retaliation "instantly, by means and at places of our choosing." Is it possible that Secretary Dulles has moved from an eye-for-an-eye-and-tooth-for-a-tooth position into one near Gandhi's?

What happened to Secretary Dulles is that—like other members of the American delegation, and first of all, the President—he realized at Geneva that we can talk peace without fear of helping the Russians or of precipitating war. He said in the same press conference: ". . . for the predictable future, we can subject our differences to the patient processes of diplomacy with less fear that war will come out of them." Until Geneva, the plight of our diplomacy, or rather the reasons why we did not have much of it, came from our feeling—not without foundation—that negotiations with the Communists on any subject, be it disarmament or Germany, entailed most certainly a waste of time, and probably the risk of war. During these last ten years, no wound opened in the international community has ever been healed, anywhere. This is true even where Communism was not involved, as in Palestine and Kashmir. Ours has been the era of the progressive debasement of what used to be called peace, the era of permanently precarious armistices and cease-fires.

No wonder the diplomatic colloquy between ourselves and the Russians was reduced to an exchange of roars and the flexing of muscles. Again, the Russians thrived on this state of things. They did not lack countless mouths speaking lies for them all over the world, while we were tongue-tied.

At Geneva we found our tongue. We had things to

245

say, and a world-wide audience hung on our words. Whatever was said by our leaders is far less important than the fact that we could speak freely, and that the response to what we had to say was overwhelming. It was a response to specific demands, compellingly asked of our representatives by the public opinion of mankind. At Geneva, our delegation found out that it could talk peace about fairly specific and crucial problems, such as Germany, the satellites, the reduction of armament, or international Communism, without either serving Russia or risking war with it.

At Geneva it happened that the vaguely idealistic, somewhat vaporous expressions of international goodwill voiced by our President generated a universally felt, irreversible reality. Our President is fond of talking about a new spirit, moral forces, power of good. What he says in this vein usually carries, for it has a ring of obvious sincerity. But at Geneva something more happened. Over and over again, the President spoke about "a new spirit that will make possible future solution of problems which are within our responsibilities," new frameworks within which hitherto insoluble conflicts may be tackled and disposed of. At Geneva these ideas did something more than carry. They took. The spontaneous rhetoric of Ike Eisenhower turned immediately into a hard, durable fact on which it will be very difficult for Communist trickery or American politicians' shilly-shallying to make a serious dent. This was the miracle of Geneva.

We can only guess at some of the causes that brought this thing about. Certainly it helped that both we and the Russians found ourselves standing in a position of strength. The attitude of our two major allies, who needed orientation but not orders from our government, greatly contributed to give solid backing and concreteness to the President's exhortations. But unquestionably and most of all, there was in Geneva the irresistible pressure—inarticulate yet unmistakable—of the human race, which does not want to court extinction for the sake of verifying ideologies.

The consideration of all these complex or universal forces in no way must detract, however, from the personal credit which is due to the President. There is an element of greatness about him, a power for creating some kind of unity and of harmony among people he is associated with, no matter how broad the association may be. Indeed, it may be said that the broader his sphere of action and the greater the multiplicity of elements, the more effectively the peculiar talent of Ike Eisenhower functions. When, back from the NATO command, he set himself to harmonize the G.O.P. and took a my-party-right-or-wrong position, he was driven to crusade against fellow Americans whose patriotism he had no reason to question, and suffered in public promiscuous association with men beneath his contempt. But whenever he has acted as the leader of the whole nation, and particularly since the Republicans lost control of Congress, he has proven, for all the imprecision of his language, that there is still power of leadership in him on most specific occasions when leadership is demanded in the conduct of foreign affairs.

At Geneva he was at his very best. He did not crusade against Bulganin, Khrushchev, and company. On the contrary, he was so generous as to declare that these men were equal to him in their devotion to peace. He dealt with them as if they too, in spite of their militant godlessness, had a conscience. There was no surer means to bring them under his spell. Above all, in his own way, he gave voice to the common sense of mankind—which is exactly the role of our nation in this World.

Now, however, there is no time to waste. The miracle of Geneva, which the President, more than anybody else, embodied, is something quite alive and quite pressing. Geneva is only the beginning of a series of conferences. It marks only the very first step out of the deadly no-war, no-peace swamp, and for a long time to come the world will have to be satisfied with a patchwork of international settlements—each, it is to be hoped, less shaky than the one that went before.

Now American diplomacy, as Secretary Dulles has said, can start playing its role, no longer fettered by the desperate nihilism of the pre-Geneva era. It is a new and to a very large extent an unprecedented game that our diplomacy must play, and an enormous amount of thinking and doing is necessary if peace and freedom are ultimately to prevail in the world. However, it is good to think that there has been a beginning, and that the main role in this beginning has been played by our country and our President.

247

REMEMBER SPAIN

Spain: U.S. Loans and God's Good Rain

BY CHARLES WERTENBAKER

Madrid

On the morning of January 25 a few thousand students of the University of Madrid, who had been given a convenient holiday, gathered in the broad Paseo de Recoletos, which had been conveniently cleared of traffic. Photographs published later in Spanish newspapers show a well-dressed, cheerful mob, prominently displaying a standard with the slogan GIBRALTAR ESPANOL. The students proceeded across the Castellana (which is seldom called by the name that most of it now bears, Avenida del Generalissimo Franco) in the direction of the British Embassy. Traffic policemen looked on benignly.

A couple of days earlier there had been a smaller demonstration in which some stones had been tossed through Embassy windows. But that crowd had been short of ammunition. This morning, conveniently, a truck loaded with bricks of a convenient size happened to pull up at the right moment. Broken glass soon began to fly, from windshields as well as windows.

Since the demonstration was of the character officially described as "spontaneous," police were on hand to make a show of trying to keep order. Witnesses disagree as to exactly at what point the police became too zealous, but it is generally understood that they went so far as to charge the students on horseback and that the students then directed their brickbats at the police and that the police retaliated with clubs and that quite a few on both sides, not to mention some innocent bystanders, were badly bashed. At the height of the excitement, the students were shouting present-day Spain's most hated epithet, *"Rojos!"* Naturally, no pictures of this part of the demonstration appeared in the Spanish press. Nor was it mentioned that during the early part of the demonstration Foreign Minister Alberto Martín Artajo had waved encouragingly to the students from his office window.

According to the Government's embarrassed explana-

248

tion, eighteen of those arrested came from "outside university life" and several had "political-social records." Since in the absence of a denial these may be presumed to have been members of the Falange, which organized the demonstration and of which Francisco Franco is Caudillo, it is hard to see how this absolves the Government of its double responsibility.

Foreign correspondents were mostly content to file the facts, without underlining the cynicism of a Government that incites its young men to riot with one hand and attacks them for doing so with the other. It would seem, however, that the students were underlining this when they shouted "Reds!" at the police. Some of them may have brooded on it further as they sat in cells or lay in hospital beds instead of gathering in cafés after the day of good clean fun their leaders had promised them. But whether they will be less eager another time is an open question. This generation of students remembers no Government but Franco's, and the Generalissimo has always found people who would march whenever he said "Gibraltar!"

Older members of the foreign colony here, whose memories go back at least as far as the years of cobelligerence with Hitler and Mussolini and the demonstrations over Gibraltar then, find nothing to wonder at in the revival of the old hue and cry—or in the double-dealing that the Spanish have recently been doing in Morocco. "Of course he would make trouble as soon as he felt himself strong enough," one Englishwoman remarked. (In Madrid "he" always means Franco; he is also called Paco.) And she added: "Didn't you Americans think of that when you started doing so much for him?" It also appears that the Generalissimo's men are not above trying to make discord between their benefactor and its other allies. A well-connected Spaniard said to an American businessman during the fuss over Gibraltar and Morocco, "We know you can't say so, but we realize that you are on our side in all this."

No doubt Franco hopes to pull a fish from the waters his men have been troubling, but just when he hopes to land it is not as clear as is the species he is angling for. It is not very difficult to see that he is reasserting his claim to Big Brotherhood over the Arab world, which is entered by the Strait of Gibraltar. He has reminded the other western nations of this claim several times in the past decade, although they haven't paid much attention, and he used to shout about it in the days when there were other Big Brothers in Rome and Berlin. But what is perhaps most interesting about his recently assumed attitude is that he feels himself strong enough to assume it at all. Even though the Generalissimo sometimes overestimates his strength, he usually gets away with it.

Last Spring I went back to Spain after an absence of three years. It seemed like a different country. In the spring of 1950 the black-market peseta had fallen from forty to sixty to the dollar, pushed down by the desperate buying of dollars in the free market of Tangier. The government's gold reserve was almost gone, spent for wheat in three drought years when the country's yearly production was one million metric tons less than the pre-civil-war average. The countryside was bare and blowing away on the winds from the Sierras. Electricity for industry and household needs was off three or four days a week. The main road from France to Madrid was in such a state of repair that it broke an axle on my car, and on the railroad from Madrid to Lisbon a train jumped the track. Bread, olive oil, and other basic foods were rationed, and the black market in them flourished. Coffee was simply unobtainable.

The cost of living in 1950 had risen four hundred per cent since 1936, but wages had been raised only two to three hundred per cent. The workers, who of course had no right to strike, were grimly holding on. The Monarchists, who had discovered a tenderness for the poor, were saying that to get rid of Franco the United States had merely to offer a loan to a Government to be headed by Don Juan. Even some of Franco's generals were speaking out against him. At that time I wrote ["Franco—Fascism and Futility," *The Reporter*, June 20, 1950]: "It seems to have been the fate of General Franco to face a crisis about every five years, and his luck to settle his crises by doing nothing about them." I was partly right and partly wrong.

In the spring of 1953 almost all of this had changed. The peseta was stable again at about forty to the dollar. Spain had had two bumper harvests. Fields were greener than I had ever seen them, and I have been visiting Spain for over twenty years. Even in the desert-like northern part of Aragon things were growing, and where the earth was turned it had a dark, rich look. White bread was unrationed, as was everything else, and the olive oil had lost its rancid smell. River beds, long dry, were running, and young women in new bright-colored skirts showed that the cotton mills were working and that a good many people could afford to buy their output. Workmen no longer stopped Americans in the street to complain that they couldn't afford black-market cigarettes; there was no black market any more. Two years earlier the workers *had* struck.

The reasons for the change were several, and they had manifested themselves almost simultaneously. The first was the wave of "walk to work" strikes over most of northern Spain in the spring of 1951, starting in Barcelona, where the workers had simply refused to use the streetcars to get to work on time. In Catalonia many employers, and in the Basque Provinces many priests, gave aid and comfort to the workmen. In that spring of 1951 General Franco was in the depth of his crisis, and all his luck would not seem to be enough to get him through another bad year.

It was then that the late Admiral Forrest P. Sherman embarked on his well-publicized visit to Spain to open the aid-for-bases talks—talks that went on for more than two years, giving Franco ample time to exploit the thesis that the United States couldn't afford to let Spain go down. And it was then that another and greater Friend of General Franco, to Whom he frequently appeals, sent down the steady, nourishing rains that Spain had not enjoyed in years. The wheat grew, the rivers quickened, the generators turned, the mills spun, and the workers worked five days a week.

After so much had been done for him, General Franco at last decided to do something for himself. He got rid of his old friend Juan Antonio Suances as Minister of Industry and Commerce (but leaving him as head of the Instituto Nacional de Industria, which Suances founded) and split the Ministry into its two component parts. To the more important Ministry of Commerce he appointed a banker, Manuel Arburua, and Arburua set himself the task of eliminating Spain's greatest economic evil, the black market. To do this, he had to eliminate rationing and the "Tangier gap" in the peseta—the difference between the legal rate and the rate in Tangier's free market, which set the black-market price in Spain. By the end of 1952, Arburua had accomplished his task, with the help of God's good rain and of American loans, official and private. That is the gist of the story of Spain's recovery from economic disintegration.

In 1951 Spain produced four and a quarter million metric tons of wheat, and in 1952 four million. This was not quite up to the 1931–1935 average, but it was a good deal better than the three million average of the previous five years. The figures are even more impressive when one realizes that the country has twenty per cent less land in wheat than it had before the civil war. It could be that a lot of people lost their taste for bread when they couldn't get it, but it is more likely that a lot of them still can't afford to eat much of it.

In 1952 the government eliminated its compulsory quota system of buying wheat from farmers and set a higher price, which was a wise move because 1953, in spite of its bright beginning, turned out to be a dry year. The government had to buy nearly a million tons abroad, but Arburua refused to reimpose rationing. Instead, the price of white bread went up and the cheaper bread became browner. But Spain didn't have to dip again into its meager gold reserve of around $60 million. The money to buy its wheat came from the Export-Import Bank and from private American loans.

In the years of Suances' Ministry, the government used to give textile manufacturers permits to buy cotton *sin divisas*, which meant that the textile men had to raise their own foreign exchange. This they generally did by selling pesetas for dollars in Tangier, thus sending the peseta down. Since there was usually somebody in the Ministry willing to tip off a friend when a large batch of permits was given out, black-market operators did a good business buying cheap Tangier pesetas and selling them in Spain when the peseta recovered a bit. They probably made their final killing early in 1953, when the peseta made a spectacular recovery.

An important agent of the recovery was the World Commerce Corporation, the company founded by the late

Edward R. Stettinius to invest in backward countries. The company, which is now headed by Frank T. Ryan, made an arrangement with the government by which it pays for cotton in dollars and sells it to the manufacturers for pesetas. World Commerce then resells the pesetas—legally, of course—through five U.S. banks and in Madrid to legitimate users. The price has been fixed at 42.50 to the dollar, which is about three pesetas cheaper than the official rate and only a small fraction lower than the current Tangier rate. Tourists, relatives of Spaniards in other countries, foreigners doing business in Spain, and Spanish businessmen bringing their money home all help World Commerce to get its pesetas sold. Ryan's company has lent the government $25 million, some of which was used to buy wheat. The director of World Commerce in Madrid is an American citizen named Ricardo Sicre, who was born a Catalan and was on the other side during the Spanish civil war.

There are a good many Americans in Madrid this year, doing business of one sort or another or just hoping to do business. There are the official advisers and big private operators at the Ritz and the Palace; there are what a Virginian friend of mine calls "the carpetbaggers" at the Castellana Hilton; and in the more modest hotels are civilians with Air Force accents. They have behaved with much more circumspection than a like number of Americans would have behaved in, say, Paris or Rome during the two years they dickered over the terms of the deal. The Generalissimo's men impressed on the American negotiators that the Spaniards are a proud and sensitive people—as they are—and this intelligence appears to have filtered down. "We make suggestions about how things might be done," one American official said, "but we don't try to tell them." Or as an unofficial American put it: "After all the mistakes we made in France and Italy, we're trying to put on a model operation here. And what do we get for it? Not a goddam bit of thanks, and Paco starts making trouble."

General Franco has other reasons for feeling able to strike a pose. Last spring he made a tour of Andalusia (which may be one reason why the road to the south is being improved) and attended the Feria at Seville. It was the first time he had ventured to invite himself to this most social event of the Monarchist-minded aristocracy of the south. He was received, of course, but more, he was entertained with private bullfight parties and flamenco music into the small hours. He must have felt that at last he had made the social grade, and there isn't any doubt that the Monarchist opposition is currently moribund. The Duchess of Valencia, once his most vocal, if not his most responsible, critic on the Right, is reported to have said recently that he is a saint. (My informant also reported, for what interest it may have, that the Duchess keeps a pack of baby wolves chained beside her front door, but whether to keep visitors out or in, he could not say.)

The Generalissimo must also have been pleased by the bestowal upon him of the Vatican's highest secular decoration, the Supreme Order of Christ. The Vatican apparently considers Franco a permanent adornment of the Spanish scene.

His critics on the Left, mostly to be found in the liberal wing of the Church and in the lower echelons of the Falange, must have been appeased by a fifteen per cent wage increase just put in effect in most industries. On the streets of one of the provincial capitals, Republican in the civil war, men have been seen who were political commissars in the Republican Army. It appears that the General is at last showing mercy to those who can no longer hurt him.

And it appears that if he is not yet looked on with real affection, he does enjoy a distant popularity for the better times of the last three years. When he showed himself at bullfights last summer, the applause was no longer perfunctory and no longer confined to the more expensive sections.

Perhaps the current attitude toward Franco was best expressed by a family I know, Republican in politics, middle in class, and poor in worldly goods. For years they had dreamed of migrating to America. I met the whole family in their city's plaza one Saturday night. They were laughing and bound for the movies. "Oh, we've given up any idea of leaving Spain," the wife told me. "We still work hard, all of us, but we get enough to eat and we go to the movies once a week." And to my next question: "Him? Oh, we'll put up with him. There's nothing else to do."

254

All this does not mean that Spain's present prosperity is anything more than comparative—comparative to three or four years ago, not to the rest of Europe—or that it reaches all classes of people, or that it is bound to last. Spain has achieved about the degree of recovery (for Spain) that France achieved (for France) five years ago. To make another comparison, a foreign resident of long standing likens the condition of the people now to that of the early years of the Republic, when the depression in the United States was reflected here, rather than to their state of being under Primo de Rivera, from 1923 to 1930, when the United States was prosperous and so was Spain. Statistically, Spain's per capita income is $250 a year.

The businessman and the organized worker (organized, of course, by the Falange) have probably profited most from Spain's recovery; shopkeepers and independent farmers have profited somewhat; the professional classes and hired farm laborers have profited hardly at all. Among intellectuals the two-job system is still common. The Andalusian peasants still work seasonally—and when it doesn't rain—and are jobless the rest of the time. To cope with this problem, the Government would have to tackle the large landowners, whose support it needs. All through the south the poor are in the same rags they have worn and patched these many years. City streets still abound with beggars, especially in the south—perhaps a sign of liberality, since not so many years ago the police kept beggars off the streets.

In economic terms, the recovery has been most noticeable in capital goods, in replenishing inventories, and in imports. Yet Spain's industrial plant is still ten or fifteen years behind anything that could be called modern by European standards. A little new railway equipment has been imported, but the strain of greater production is wearing out the rolling stock faster than it can be replaced. The toy trains still creep across the countryside at twenty-five miles an hour. The roads have been improved, but not much. In another year or two the work now going on will produce wider and straighter roads, but they will probably not be much smoother, thanks to the Spanish custom of rough-finishing a road and then leaving it for the traffic to roll down.

The power shortage in Spain is chronic, except in very wet years. Last year in the north, electricity was cut back to sixty per cent and then to forty per cent of full flow, and Madrid is presently without electricity one day a week, not to mention the other days when it unaccountably goes off for an hour or two. Power is unevenly distributed; Madrid gets its electricity from far to the north, and Málaga's comes from Alicante, some three hundred miles away. The greatest need is for thermal units, to make up for the hydroelectric shortage.

The land still has that dark, rich look, nourished by the two good years of rain, but when the wind blows in the south the smell of dust is in the air, and another dry year would probably reduce the soil to what it was in 1950. Fertilizer is still in short supply, and although the decline has been checked, two-thirds of the country is still uncultivated.

Spain's unfavorable balance of trade is still about what it was in 1950—$120 million. The recovery since then has been due almost entirely to two years of good rainfall and enough American aid to get through one dry year—plus a little intelligent use of these assets.

In a sense the recovery emphasizes the previous inefficiency of a Government that let things get so out of hand, and even the present comparative efficiency is no guarantee that they will not go bad again.

In a good year Spain needs a little outside financial aid; in a bad year it needs quite a lot, because in the good years the country has not been able to build up the reserves that might put it on its own feet. General Franco will doubtless be getting dollars for quite some time to come. The rain is up to God.

The Thousand Faces of Spain

BY MARK VAN DOREN

The Cypresses Believe in God, by Jose Maria Gironella. Translated from the Spanish by Harriet de Onis. Knopf. Two Volumes. $10.

To read a novel about a war is almost certainly to learn something about that war one had not known, even if this be only the author's view of it, or at any rate his view of life in general. Gironella's long novel—it fills a thousand pages—is about the civil war in Spain, and who would not know more than he does about that dreadful event? It came near to taking one out of every ten lives in Spain; it was contemporary with similar events in China; it focused hatreds that finally expressed themselves all over the earth between 1939 and 1945. While it proceeded it was the occasion for many opinions, both as to its origin and as to its meaning, in the United States. Any American who ever had an opinion about it can afford to test that opinion by this book. He may or may not come out with the same opinion, but he will have had what he probably lacked before: experience of the people who fought the war, and of what they thought and felt as it descended upon them.

The book confines itself to the descent. Beginning in April, 1931, with the death of the monarchy, it stops in July, 1936, with the military uprising against the Republic, which in most American minds may be the first act in the tragedy rather than the last. Doubtless for Gironella it is not the last act either; it is the end of the beginning; but the beginning is what interests him, as indeed it ought to interest us. Out of what fuel did the fire come, and out of what all but unimaginable heat? Gironella is trying to tell us this, and trying as he does so to render the truth about every passion that burned among the Spanish people—every one of dozens or hundreds, or, as he suggests in a note to the American reader, of thousands. "There are in this land," he says, "thousands of ways of life." And he does not seem to refer merely to individuals. He means ideas, theories, prejudices, passions. It is of those that his book is full almost to the point of confusion, though he would say complexity.

In any case, what we have here is five years of thinking, feeling, and talking on the eve of violence, with just enough of the violence to give us a taste of the mutual massacre to follow. We have all this in one small city of Spain, Gerona in Catalonia. And we have it, furthermore, reflected in the lives of a single family in that city, the family of Matías Alvear, an anti-clerical Spaniard of the middle class who like his devout Basque wife, Carmen Elgazu, is not Catalan in origin and so can take a spectator's view of the fierce separatist leanings of those about him. Of their three children the eldest, Ignacio, is singularly free from anything like personal conviction, so that he can listen and learn as we do. But César, the second son, would have been a priest had he outlived the end of the story; he might even have been a saint. And the daughter Pilar has no politics, so that nothing prevents her from falling in love with Mateo Santos, organizer of the Falange in Gerona.

One naturally remembers the Rostov family in *War and Peace*, with which this novel has been compared. Tolstoy used that family, along with several others, to clarify and intensify our view of the war with Napoleon. Or did he? Or, more accurately, was that all he did? It is a fascinating question, for it has to do with the mysterious relations that exist between history and fiction, or as Aristotle put it, between history and poetry.

How true can a historical novel be—how true, that is, of an event that takes place in the background, or even in the foreground, of its characters' lives? Which should seem more important to us, the event or the individuals it affects? If the event, then why write fiction? If the individuals, why write historical fiction? The best answer seems to be that the event should of course engage us but that the people should engage us more, to the point perhaps of being all that we finally remember. Andrey, Natasha, and Pierre are more interesting at last than Russia and France. So are Achilles and Hector more interesting than the Trojan War, though it is terribly interesting too; and so is Falstaff, say, than the struggle between Henry IV and those who would dethrone him.

But what, then, has happened to history? And if Gironella has succeeded with his individuals—the Alvears and their friends—what has happened to the civil war concerning which we expected to learn so many things we didn't know?

Gironella, fortunately or unfortunately, need have no worry on this score. He has not written a *War and Peace*, an Iliad, or a *Henry IV*. His story of the Alvears has not extinguished his chronicle of what went on in all of Spain, or at any rate Gerona. The Alvears have their reality and their charm, but they never overwhelm their environment as the huge figure of Pierre, stumbling through Tolstoy's novel, blots Russia out. The explanation of this could lie in the very transparency of Ignacio Alvear's mind and heart. Without convictions of his own, he can be and indeed is a lens through which the reader looks at the innumerable parties of opinion among whose more articulate members he strolls, listening and arguing to the end not so much that we should see or believe him as that we should see and believe them. Pierre, for all his impressiveness, was less intelligent; in a sense he understood nothing. Rays of opinion, striking him in front, still left us with only his back before us, the shadow not of Russia but of himself. We hear the theories, but we remember him —and understand him better in the end than we do the theories.

Another explanation might be the sense Gironella gives us of having desired to make all of his persons representative of something. In the greatest stories people represent only themselves, though it is true that they belong to classes and have thoughts other people can have. Gironella is often lifelike and his people have their power to touch us. The devotion of Carmen Elgazu to her husband and children is immensely moving, like the big ears of César. But we cannot escape the suspicion that Gironella has schematized his human material. The difference between the devout Carmen Elgazu and the "radical" Matías is all too neat a case of at least one difference that split Spain down the middle. So is the reflection of this difference in Ignacio and César: the first a boy whose thoughts go everywhere and the second a boy whose thoughts go only to God.

So far there is nothing in the family to remind us of the Falangists and of the military leaders who in the end will together conquer Spain. But then Pilar's falling in love with Mateo does remind us of the Falangists. To round out the picture, Ignacio himself falls in love with Marta, daughter of Major Martínez de Soria, who will lead the military uprising in Gerona. So there it all is, along with such minor circumstances as that Ignacio works in the same bank with Cosme Vila, who will become leader of the Communists, and in that bank knows many another man who represents a party or a sect.

The temptation to make characters representative in this way must be very great for any historical novelist, particularly when he knows or believes that most of the opinions held about his subject are erroneous if only because they are oversimplified. Listen, he will say: Let me set some people before you who will demonstrate

259

how complex the true situation was, and how difficult to judge as you judge it.

An American might have said this after our Civil War, concerning which many Europeans had positive opinions but sketchy knowledge. Such an American might have proposed to demonstrate through the persons of an imaginary family not merely that brother could fight against brother or father against son, as everybody knew was frequently the case, but that the Democratic and Republican Parties had their factions, that abolition was an unpopular doctrine in portions of the North, that Lincoln himself was not an abolitionist, that Lee loved the Union as he understood it, that New York was a boiling mess of theories both friendly and unfriendly to the government, that civil liberties suffered on both sides, that Lincoln was denounced as a dictator, and so on and so on.

The American might have done this and still not have convinced us that his family was real as things in fiction must be real. Nor might that have been his primary objective. He was a historian, let us admit, more than he was a poet, and as such he did succeed in spreading on the record a host of matters commonly ignored, so that the subject at hand lost some of that glittering simplicity which had prevented Europeans from penetrating to its depths.

Here is the virtue, limited though it may be, of Gironella's novel, whose thousand pages impress upon us first of all the bewildering variety of Spanish opinion during the early 1930's. There were not two or three leftist parties; there were twenty-one. There was not one rightist movement; there were half a dozen, and each of them distrusted the rest. There were vicious rightists and there were noble ones, just as there were mad leftists and sane ones—or supersane ones, as the fanatics said who insisted that socialism was for children.

Meanwhile there was the Republic, despised or defended according to one's view of its vitality, and beyond that, of its desirability. The one question depended upon the other, and perhaps there were too few with enough confidence in the Republic to make it easy for them to dismiss its detractors, whatever the motives for their detraction were. Or was it not detraction but a plot, laid long before and skillfully concealed until the time came to execute it? Most of the persons in the novel appear to think otherwise, though they never deny the existence of a force that stands ready to move in whenever the country has become hopelessly divided. Let us stand together, they say, or else the Falange and the military will take over.

And there was the Church, which Ignacio cannot enter though his brother can and does. The Church alone has a thousand faces in this book. The majority of these may be attractive, but certain ones are not; and the political opinions of the clergy have great range. Gironella, though it is pretty clear that his own affection is for the Church, gives its enemies every chance to express themselves with lucidity and logic. And so with every other cause or institution. Ignacio likes Mateo but can say that in his experience Falangists tend to be bullies and smart alecks. Mateo's father accuses them of "a synthetic seriousness." There is always something suspicious about the quiet, intense way they dedicate themselves so they know not what; for they freely confess that the future of their organization is not blueprinted. They will do whatever they are called upon to do, but they still do not know or even seek to know just what this is. The people indeed may be quite right about them: They are waiting to walk in. And when they do—which is after the novel ends—they will have the same deadly bearing as now. Gironella seems to know this and not to like it very much—seems, for he never speaks in his own person. He is at least as impartial as Ignacio is; he is "implacably" so, if one may quote again his address to the American reader.

Gironella aims at implacable impartiality, and yet there may be no such thing. Our doubt that it exists absolutely in his case grows on us as we read. He will show the worst of every side, and creditably he does so. Yet there comes into being, implicitly if not otherwise, a relativity of worsts. Ignacio, as a part of his universal experience, at one time has two teachers who are Socialists. They remain the rational and generous persons they begin by being, but they never sound older than the children they teach. And while all of the parties have their vicious members, the Anarchist and Communist leaders outdo their rivals in a fashion suggestive of melodrama.

Not that Gironella needs to be thought of as having planned such a result. No one should accuse him of distorting what he understands to be the facts. It was a wild, insane, and cruel time for everybody. "Poor Spain!" cries Ignacio to himself as the novel nears its end; and yet that end was but the end of a beginning.

What *were* the facts about the Spanish Civil War, at the stage where Gironella considers it? Or what was the truth, if that is a better word? What *is* the truth—eternally, in God's mind as it were? Doubtless no man can say, not even Gironella with all his ambition to be exhaustive in his report. The truth about a great event is the sum of all the relevant opinions as to what it was. In the present case, since there were twenty million Spaniards, there must have been twenty million opinions, or responses, or participations, or whatever term will suit. Yet the meaning of all these is still another matter. Where is that to be found, and how is it to be judged? Gironella, ambitious as he is, has to limit himself to a few hundred persons in one city; he cannot tell us what everybody, literally everybody, did or thought. And if he had been able to do so, what would our conclusion be? A greater novelist would have concentrated his gaze upon fewer persons and given us perhaps more truth. But about those persons, not about the event. The problem, or the mystery, of historical fiction thus asserts itself again.

Meanwhile the reader of this novel, in so far as he has read it for the history that is in it, will have mastered one fact if no other. The subject was and is complex—not to say, in a perfectly respectful sense of the word, unintelligible. What possessed this people, so affectionate and yet so bitter, so ironical yet so fanatical, so wise and yet so wild, to behave as they did here? It is to the credit of Gironella that he asks the question rather than answers it. For no man's answer would be believed. César, dying as he wished to in the closing pages, kept his answer to himself. "He did not understand one word of what was taking place. . . . What was evident was that Spain had not had charity, and that someone must give his life to expiate this evil. He offered his." To what, or to whom? That also was César's secret. It could have been to whoever it is that understands everything: all the facts, all the persons, all the truth. History and poetry do all that they can do, but then there is the truth, which does nothing save exist. Often spoken of, it never speaks. In silence, and forever, it knows itself.

FOUR NATIONS

France: Politicians,
Pressure Groups, and a New Face

BY THEODORE H. WHITE

For six full years the chief whipping boy of the Atlantic alliance has been France. The indictment against France may be summed up, simply, as the real or alleged refusal of the French to make those decisions without which the progress of the entire Atlantic alliance is reduced to a crawl.

Rarely have the French and their Allies faced a situation that sets them so profoundly at odds with each other as they are at the moment. This winter the French must decide whether or not to begin the partial surrender of their sovereignty to the Union of Europe, conceived jointly by them and the Americans; this winter they must decide whether, how, and on what terms to put an end to the war in Indo-China, which is draining France dry; this winter they must again consider whether and how to arrest the economic blight that is reducing France season by season to the status of an industrial anachronism. And all these decisions must be made under the pressure of Allies so exasperated that they now care less what the results of these decisions are than that they be finally made, once and for all.

The exasperation of France's Allies has valid origins in the nature of French politics today. If a government can be compared to an intricate piece of machinery which translates crude popular pressures more or less smoothly into decision and program, then it may fairly be said that in France today though the motors hum, the gears do not mesh.

In the sense that our Republican and Democratic Parties (despite their internal divisions) translate American political emotions into government, or that the Labour and Tory Parties (despite similar internal divisions) translate British political emotions into government, France as a nation today lacks parties that can do the same.

No western country offers its electorate a more varied political spectrum: all shades of conservatism or reaction, all shades of socialism and social reform, all attitudes toward religion from outright hostility to downright servility. Yet, in practice, none of these parties offers voters more than a parochial set of prejudices and myths so narrow and mutually exclusive that, however they group themselves together in coalition, none can offer the French people a real choice of directions in which they can agree to move. Rigid, mechanically controlled, the old parties have almost entirely lost the ability to offer France either new faces or new perspectives.

It is these parties, gathered in all sorts of precarious coalitions, with which the western world has been dealing since 1947. Through this ever-changing, ever-constant leadership, France has expressed itself in the United Nations, underwritten NATO, launched European Union, signed and sponsored treaties. And the outer world's exasperation begins with its doubts, which are echoed in Paris, as to whether this political leadership can commit the French people to any historic course of action or in a crisis deliver anything more real than a majority of votes in the National Assembly.

During a third of a century of wars, depression, fear, inflation, and disaster, the French people have been divided and subdivided into a nation of closed and sealed groups far more akin to Mussolini's image of the corporative state than the shining community of democracy and representative government which the French insist their country remains.

The political government of France can harass these sovereign corporative entities with rules and regulations or plead with them, as citizens, to show responsibility. But it cannot crack down and curtail the rights of the few for the greater good of the many, impose discipline, dissolve cartels, deny subsidies. The French government does not so much administer its people as it negotiates with them, yielding to the pressures of the strongest or, when trapped, resorting to inflation to purchase the goods and services required for survival.

The crudest form in which these corporative groups present themselves is that of political-economic lobbies —far better organized and far more powerful in the state-dominated economy of France than in any other free and representative nation.

264

There is, for instance, the alcohol lobby, an unbreakable formation of winegrowers, beet growers, apple growers, and distillers whose members produce twice as much alcohol as the nation can consume each year and force the government to buy the surplus at a rate four times the world price. French vats are so full of unsalable government-owned alcohol that it would be cheaper now for the government to dump it all in the sea than try to store it. And Frenchmen are so full of alcohol that the expenses of the French Social Security System in care of alcoholics and diseases directly attributable to alcoholism are larger than all taxes paid by spirit and wine dealers. Yet the wine lobby must be subsidized and millions of acres must be kept in crops whose only yield is alcohol while the French economy screams for more meat, more milk, more fruit, more wheat.

There is a truckmen's lobby that has made a shambles of the economics of rail transportation by political jiggering with the nationalized railways' rate structure. There is a tobacco lobby, a steel lobby, a butchers' lobby, and a thousand more. Each of these groups negotiates with the government directly. Right-wing Governments such as those of Pinay and Laniel can occasionally wring half-hearted co-operation from some of the smaller sovereign corporative groups (as did Laniel in his famous compact with the Paris butchers to stabilize meat prices in the capital). Left-wing Governments alternately try to threaten and bribe them into compliance. But no Government of any kind controls them.

These vested economic interests—usually (and mistakenly) called cartels—are, of course, the most publicized separatist groups in the state because their methods have fossilized French industry into a structure roughly fifty years behind the times and paralyzed the nation's physical comfort and welfare. But they are not the only groups living a destructively independent life in a greater community.

French science and technology are compartmentalized in tight restrictive coteries because the exclusive senior academies of French higher education, for reasons that go deep in the nation's intellectual tradition, turn out only a fraction of the technicians, however brilliant, that the nation needs.

There are other communities of men bound together only by their interest in recovering payment for war damages from the government. Old-age pensioners, First World War veterans, Second World War veterans, and deportees all bleed the body of French politics as picadors do a bull. Colonists and colonial interests pursue objectives quite irrelevant to the destiny of France as a nation. The Second World War has created other groups: collaborationists pressing constantly on the Fourth Republic for forgiveness, resistance veterans who have splintered their past heroism into contentious factionalism.

Finally, the administrative machinery of France is itself a conglomeration of incorporated functionaries, vested interests with great power and prestige, some of which are not only totally unresponsive to political control but openly contemptuous of it. Thus during last summer's strikes of the underfed and underpaid lesser civil servants, France was simultaneously treated to the spectacle of powerful and entrenched colonial officials participating in a *coup d'état* in France's richest colonial domain, Morocco, without authority and without political guidance, an action almost certain to bring infinite sorrows in the future. Nor did the Government resist this group, as it did the lesser civil servants. Confronted with a *fait accompli,* it assented and draped the Morocco coup with ex post facto authority and legality.

The French political roulette wheel decreed that the Minister of Foreign Affairs who was forced to condone the Moroccan coup be Georges Bidault, the same man who had held that post in 1946 when another set of colonial functionaries in Asia flouted the political authority of Paris to plunge into the Indo-China war, which has since drained the nation white. So powerless was the Government that the mastermind of the Moroccan coup —Marshal Alphonse Juin, perhaps the most ambitious soldier in any army's uniform—could a few days later publicly sneer at the Presidency of France, stigmatizing that high office as one with more tedious chores and empty honor than real power, and declaring that his own political conduct was governed only by the superior interests of France.

Several things must be said to mollify the harshness of this picture. First, the people who defend their privileges with such bitterness do so not so much out of wickedness as out of fear. The selfishness of modern Frenchmen, which so saddens those who thrill to the glory of French culture, rises from the history of the past forty years of turbulence and inflation, which has taught them that survival is assured only to those who look out for themselves first.

Secondly, within the cells of the compartmented enterprises, French brilliance burns as brightly as ever. Its achievements in engineering, science, design, and even in some phases of local politics remain the peers of the best the modern world can offer. This brilliance is fragmented, unco-ordinated, hence wasted, but it persists.

Last, and it should be repeated over and over again, the divided and antagonistic groups and individuals of France have necessarily arrived at a tolerance of each other so great as to make liberty in France more complete both in expression and conduct than in any other western democracy. Which raises the ultimate questions: What price must be paid for this liberty? Can this total liberty be managed or restrained by efficient direction acting for the community as a whole without a ruthless new type of government? Or must it continue to the ragged edge of anarchy?

These are the people and this is the political structure that have been summoned to make decisions on which all western plans turn.

Neither the people nor the structure is, however, a static one. This summer two decisive, distinct but organically related events occurred in France. Together, they foreshadowed the beginning of a new national opposition to the present state of affairs, entirely different from the factional and partisan oppositions that the political parties have always hitherto displayed in the narrow arena of the National Assembly in Paris.

One event was the great wave of summer strikes (*The Reporter*, September 29). The summer strikes were simply the intrusion of labor—splintered, confused, and misled—upon French politics. All the postwar adjustments of burdens between the independent groups that make up French life and between these independent groups and the government have been made at the expense of labor.

267

Labor, divided between Catholic, Socialist, and Communist leadership in permanent rivalry, has not, since the war, been able to muster its vast ranks for more than an orderly retreat in defense of the rights and dignities it won in the unity of Liberation. The burdens of postwar France, as translated in taxes and inflation, have always rested most heavily upon the ordinary workingman, by now reduced to a state of permanent misery simply because his divided protest could never be effectively brought to bear upon the government. The spontaneous, grass-roots summer strikes simply warned the nation that labor, even divided as it was, could project France into anarchy overnight if goaded too far—and that it had been goaded as far as it could bear. If France was to be governed at all, if France was to bear the weight of global and international obligations, the strikes warned the nation that it could no longer be done by the pauperization of French workers. Something had to give, either internally or externally, or the meaning of France in the world would become a fiction —as it still may.

The second event of the summer, which preceded the strikes by some six weeks, was the presentation to the National Assembly of an alternative program and alternative leadership that proposed to reverse the entire course of French affairs since the war.

This program is called the Mendès-France Program, after its author, Pierre Mendès-France, a short, stocky, heavy-set man, jet-black of hair, broad of nose, and blue-black of jowl, who looks far more like one of the blue-trousered workers in the Paris Metro than one of the most eminent and scholarly intellectuals in French life.

The impact of Mendès-France and his program on French life, like so many phenomena in French politics, is all paradox. The current favorite of the non-Communist Left and the standard bearer of those who mumble of a new Popular Front, Pierre Mendès-France is, in almost every respect, a man of the Right—a hard-money, balanced-budget, orthodox economic technician and member of the businessmen's Radical Socialist Party. A man who declares in all sincerity, "I hate politics, I do not indulge in politics, I am not a politician," Mendès-France has proved himself the shrewdest long-range political strategist in France. Without patronage or powerful friends, his present position as one of the two or three dominant figures in French national politics is due almost entirely to his ability to translate his abstruse, intricate, scholarly researches into a few simple yet logical statements about the world. These he has repeated with such monotonous yet brilliant persistence that by now even the politicians who loathe Mendès-France must borrow from or pay lip service to them.

The entire Mendès-France program can be summed up in the three words which form the title he has given his latest political pamphlet, *Gouverner, C'est Choisir* ("To Govern Is to Choose").

France, as Mendès-France describes it, is a nation that can no longer see itself clearly. This France, still drunk with memories of old greatness, still clutching at the promises of Liberation, divided by recent history, each of its constituent groups terrified at any threat to its archaic and vestigial privileges, has forced on its government burdens far too great for French resources to support. To govern France effectively, the men who do so must decide that they will abandon profound obligations, both domestic and international, that they have managed to support since the war only by an inflation that corrupts and destroys all. The first duty of French government, says Mendès-France, is to choose what shall be given up, for only by abandoning part of its claim to global greatness now can France withdraw, regroup its forces and energies for counterattack, and then return to its rightful power.

In speech after speech, Mendès-France over the past three years has filled in this outline. His detail is both simple and specific. Those burdens Mendès-France would choose to abandon first are the war in Indo-China and the huge military obligations of NATO.

Not the slightest trace of anti-Americanism or softness to Soviet diplomacy can be discerned in Mendès-France's convictions. It is simply, as he puts it, that France cannot be strong everywhere at once—in Asia, in Africa, in Germany and at home. Mendès-France is neither an opponent nor an advocate of European Union. Indeed, in his speeches he seems curiously indifferent to it, though he voted to sustain the Schuman

Plan. What he seeks is that France, whether in or out of such a union, be strong.

Along with his abandonment of external burdens, Mendès-France would wring out the swollen Social Security System, strip away the hidden and direct subsidies to pressure lobbies, and reorganize the uncoordinated and misdirected nationalized industries.

Despite its opposition to heavy armaments, such a program would scarcely be sufficient to win for Mendès-France the acclaim of the Socialists, the Left Catholics, and other free-wheelers of the non-Communist Left. All these choices are negative ones. But in choosing to slash with unrelenting ferocity France's budgetary burdens, sacrificing thereby its current diplomatic obligations, Mendès-France proposes other positive choices. These concern not the outside world but France at home. They require the diversion of almost all that is saved by slashing the burden of arms and subsidies into vastly expanded public housing (for housing is easily France's most terrible social problem), into a new basic investment program both in industry and agricultural development, into much greater government support of technology and science.

To the Left, such a program is appealing. While it will not immediately lessen the burden on French workers, it will result eventually in new houses, new schools, and the promise of an expanding economy instead of the stagnant one that the workers now support without hope.

The third essential ingredient of the Mendès-France program is obvious. It is that the Assembly, once having accepted these choices, abdicate a huge share of its legislative prerogative and endow whatever Premier it chooses with power to jostle, shake, and discipline by decree the various special interests that now overwhelm individual Deputies and control their votes. Specifically, his program requires that the Assembly give a Government advancing such a program full powers to make any of these adjustments by decree within the frame outlined—and that such a decree become law immediately unless the Assembly by specific veto overrides it, and by so doing casts the Government out of power.

Such proposals and such programs have been talked about, largely because of Mendès-France's own writings and speeches, for several years. What was a vast importance this summer was that in the June crisis, for the first time the President of France proposed their author to the Assembly as Premier-Designate, and that 301 members of the Assembly voted for his appointment, while only 119, of whom 101 were Communist, voted against him. Mendès-France was defeated only because of the abstention of those eminent Deputies and their friends who have sat in France's Cabinets for the past eight years. Their abstentions left him just thirteen votes short of the constitutional majority necessary for investiture.

No reading of the portents and omens can forecast either the future of Pierre Mendès-France or of his country during the coming winter.

An earnest, serious, hard-working man (Mendès-France is mayor and departmental chairman of the Norman town and district he represents in Paris), his self-chosen role since the war has been to sit in the red-plush hemicycle of the Palais Bourbon and chant of doom like a Cassandra. He has refused every offer of a Cabinet post, saying, "One cannot cauterize a wooden leg." The melancholy satisfaction of seeing all his predictions come true for seven years has given him an almost fatalistic belief that his program (with or without him) will be accepted by the Assembly or that France will slowly decay and fall from the ranks of the great powers.

Mendès-France cannot back his convictions with either an organization or a machine of his own. No intrigue in the fashionable salons of Paris, where so many political careers are launched, made, and broken, operates in his support. No personal flair for bold, dynamic mobilization of masses of men in the streets tempts him to adventure outside those realms of scholarly monograph and speech that have made his views dogma among so many French journalists, intellectuals, and worried citizens.

It is perhaps the very modesty and restraint with which Mendès-France carries himself personally that has made his rise to influence over the past year so important. A possibly exaggerated symbolism has attached itself to him and to his program. He has coined the phrases that shape the current clichés of politics in

271

Paris. All these phrases can be summed up in a paragraph:

What the political leadership of France decides is not nearly so important as that it make some decision, some choice, no matter what. And, once having decided, it must do so clearly enough that the people of France can fuse, as a community, to support or oppose its decision. "To govern," in short, is truly "to choose."

No crisis in France is ever the last one. No long-heralded hour of decision since the war has ever produced the decision. Not even in this winter of over-bearing problems and demands can one be sure that the party coalitions in Paris will arrive finally at a decision on the great project of European Union, on the war in Indo-China, on the overhauling and recasting of its industrial system. All these problems have been part of the furniture of the French political stage for many years. What is new is simply a public discontent capable of an anarchic shrugging off of all present government forms, and the appearance of a program and leadership ready to remake and reshape these forms about a new policy. If this program and this restlessness fuse under new leadership that can capture a majority of the French National Assembly, then France may finally have that truly responsible and representative Government that her Allies have criticized her for so long for lacking. It is certain that the Atlantic Allies would find such new leadership less complaisant and docile than the political leadership they have dealt with in Paris hitherto. But it is well that France's Allies, which have heaped so many and such thankless burdens on her, be prepared for the event.

Sir Winston Orders a Bomb

BY ALASTAIR HETHERINGTON

London

The decision that Britain is to build its own hydrogen bombs, its own long-range bomber force, and its own guided missiles was announced in Parliament on February 17. It amounts to something like a Declaration of Independence from the United States.

Britain is going to duplicate or supplement a large

part of the American effort in strategic air power and thermonuclear weapons. The Government thus hopes to make its voice more audible both in Washington and in Moscow and hopes to restore the United Kingdom to the status of a great power, less dependent on American protection. The Government does not say this; it prefers to emphasize the vital importance of the "Grand Alliance" and its strong wish to continue close co-operation with the United States. But the decision would never have been reached if co-operation had been closer in the past.

Sir Winston Churchill explained the decision to the House of Commons in a speech that was profoundly moving to those who heard it. He said that the Soviet Union at present had neither hydrogen bombs nor the means of delivering them on North American targets. But in three or four years it will have them. That gives the western alliance an interval in which to prepare its defenses. Britain must reinforce with its own hydrogen weapons the great power of the United States Strategic Air Command. It was a speech packed with information and asides, but here is the essential theme:

"There is only one sane policy for the free world in the next few years. That is what we call defense through deterrents. This we have already adopted and proclaimed. These deterrents may at any time become the parents of disarmament, provided that they deter. To make our contribution to the deterrent we must ourselves possess the most up-to-date nuclear weapons and the means of delivering them."

In a later passage he discussed whether Britain could have left the effort in bombs and bombers to the United States alone, limiting Britain's share to comment and criticism of American policies. Of this course he said:

"Personally, I cannot feel that we should have much influence over their policy or actions, wise or unwise, while we are largely dependent, as we are today, upon their protection. We too must possess substantial deterrent power of our own."

Nowhere in the Prime Minister's speech or in the Government's annual White Paper on defense is there a word of criticism of the United States. Quite the reverse. The Government is thankful for the American share in NATO and SEATO, for the financial grants to Britain, for

273

the exchange of information on new weapons, and for the protective shield now provided by U.S. air power. The gratitude is genuine. It is shared by millions of people in Britain, ordinary men everywhere from London to Wigan and Wick. We British well know that without the American alliance, Britain might not have survived as a free country. Do not be misled because our newspapers use their freedom to speak plainly, even harshly, about particular American policies. We know who our friends are and we like them.

That, of course, is one reason why there has been criticism of the Government's decision. Why duplicate the American effort? Why spend vast sums when American strategic air power protects us? If we must, then why not share the fruits of our research with the United States and ask for the same in return? Can we afford the cost when Britain already carries proportionately one of the heaviest defense budgets in the world? Is it not piling Pelion on Ossa (or Ben Nevis on Mount Whitney)? These questions are being asked and will be asked increasingly in coming weeks, although outright opposition to the Government's decision is not common.

The Government's answers to these questions—some given with formal authority and some informally—are revealing. Sir Winston told the House that Britain must have a direct share in the supreme deterrent to war. He and the Cabinet are convinced that thermonuclear weapons are so important as a deterrent that Britain cannot be left out. The Government sees these weapons as having hopeful implications: Because they make the power of retaliation so tremendous and so terrible, they "significantly reduced the risk of war on a major scale," in the words of the White Paper. British atomic scientists have no doubt that they can make hydrogen or lithium bombs—and what's more, make them more cheaply than the United States can. The Government has ordered them to go ahead.

Will the British weapons add to the existing American deterrent? The Government says "Yes" and the critics say "No." The Government says that the weapons will help persuade the Soviet leaders that war would be madness. The critics say that if American air power hasn't persuaded the Soviet leaders already, then the

British weapons will make little difference. The critics question whether Russian calculations will be altered if, for example, four hundred British bombers are added to twelve hundred American, or if 250 British bombs are added to a stock of 850 American nuclear weapons. Presumably what matters in the Kremlin's reckoning is the certain knowledge that Kiev and Leningrad would be hit. Whether they are hit by British bombs on the second day of a war or by American bombs on the tenth day is relatively unimportant. That, at least, is what some critics have said, but the Government believes the difference might be important indeed.

But there is a second and more significant factor—uncertainty about American strategic plans. The R.A.F. and U.S.A.F. do not always see eye to eye, nor are they fully informed of each other's intentions. Neither knows exactly what the other plans to do in the event of war. The British view, expressed in the White Paper, is that we must "so organise . . . as to enable us to survive and to defeat the enemy if all our efforts for peace should fail." In other words, we must be ready for what would happen if we cannot come to agreement with the Soviet Union and if the strategic deterrent to war does not succeed. In that event Britain must be ready to prevent a devastating attack with hydrogen bombs on the British Isles. As the White Paper says, "A prompt and overwhelming counteroffensive with the most powerful weapons available offers at present the surest means of limiting the scale of such attacks." In particular, we must eliminate at once the enemy airfields from which a thermonuclear attack on Britain might be launched.

To do this, we British cannot rely on the U.S.A.F. The Prime Minister made the point in a carefully worded passage:

"There are scores of airfields from which the Soviets could launch attacks with hydrogen bombs as soon as they have the bombers to carry them. . . . Unless we make a contribution of our own—that is the point which I am pressing—we cannot be sure that in an emergency the resources of other powers would be planned exactly as we would wish or that the targets which would threaten us most would be given what we consider the necessary priority, or the deserved priority, in the first few hours."

275

The Government's belief is that the U.S.A.F. would want to protect its own bases in England but would have numerous other tasks at the outbreak of war. For Britain's survival, as the Prime Minister has said more than once, it is essential to destroy the Russian air bases "in the first few hours of the war." A maximum of twenty to thirty hours has been mentioned. The U.S. Strategic Air Command might eventually deal with them, but perhaps not for some days. Its planning is said to give highest priority to the attack on enemy cities—to disrupting government and destroying morale, as at Hiroshima and Nagasaki. Whether terror raids would have quite that effect on a country not ready for surrender, as Japan was, is questionable; there is also the doubt, which inwardly worries some people in the R.A.F., whether such a strategy can be justified morally. Of course, the ideas of the U.S.A.F. may be changing. But meanwhile the British Government has decided that it must build its own strategic bombing force.

It has been asked how the R.A.F. could quickly locate the enemy bases to attack, especially as they may be deep in Russian territory. Although no public answer can be obtained, the problem is evidently one the R.A.F. thinks it can solve. It has also been asked whether a first Russian blow on Britain—an atomic Pearl Harbor—might not prevent the R.A.F. from even starting its counteroffensive. Some answers to that question have been given. Not all the British bomber force would be at home stations, since Cyprus and other points eastward would be available; fighters and anti-aircraft missiles of Britain could probably stop much of the first Russian flight; and with proper radar and other preparations the British bombers ought to be in the air before the first Russian flight arrives. It is axiomatic, of course, that a major war will never start unless the Russians begin it by striking first.

The Government decision has met little opposition in Parliament, the press, or the country. The lack of opposition has taken the Government itself by surprise. Sir Winston spoke of the risk of "panic," but people have responded well to the Government's appeal for "no flinching." Perhaps many have not yet been able to grasp fully what it all means. The prospects of hydrogen warfare are so terrible as to be almost beyond normal
276

imagination. It is notable that one of the most widely quoted passages in Sir Winston's speech was where he asked poignantly, "Which way shall we turn to save our lives and the future of the world?" and wondered what would lie before "little children playing their merry games . . . if God wearied of mankind." Here he woke a responsive echo in many minds.

In Parliament only about eight Members declared themselves directly against the decision—eight out of over six hundred. The Labour Party did not question it officially. The majority, led by Mr. Attlee, definitely supported it, but Mr. Aneurin Bevan used the opportunity to challenge the official party leaders more openly than for months past. Not even he, however, came out plainly against building hydrogen bombs and long-range bombers. He simply tried to make an issue—and here he succeeded—whether hydrogen bombs would be used against any aggression in Europe, however small. He gathered less than seventy Members into his minority group.

The majority within Labour raised two particular points of criticism. Could Britain not work in closer partnership with the United States, and could it afford the cost of so great a program? The first point was raised by Mr. Denis Healey, speaking second for Labour, and the other by Mr. John Strachey, the former Secretary for War. Both points have also been mentioned in the press —cautiously by the *Times* and critically by the Manchester *Guardian*.

It is, of course, a pity that Britain cannot work in closer partnership with the United States. The duplication of effort seems senseless. Each country is carrying out a vast program of research, development, and production in isolation from the other. Knowledge is not being shared. As one Member unkindly put it, the purpose of Britain's hydrogen bomb is to blow up the McMahon Act. True, the Act was modified last year, but we are still very far from pooling our knowledge and resources. American laboratories are closed to British scientists, and they can get no nearer the testing grounds than Las Vegas. As a result, British laboratories and firing grounds like Woomera are closed to Americans. There is no sharing of nuclear discoveries, no co-ordination of research. Each country is going its own way, even in the less sensitive fields of aerodynamic and electronic research, although collaboration on guided missiles has been greatly improved.

One cannot tell, of course, where British research is ahead of American or vice versa. Secrecy prevents governments as well as the public from knowing. But a few points may be suggested.

There are reports that Britain's thermonuclear bomb will use a lithium isotope as its fuel instead of tritium. Lithium is said to be cheaper and easier to handle. The British bomb, in fact, is to be a "poor man's bomb"—but none the worse for that. Sir William Penney's team of scientists is said to be well forward with work on this weapon.

In the field of guided missiles British authorities hope by 1958 to have weapons far ahead of anything American. British comment on the American Nike anti-aircraft missile is uncomplimentary. It is supposed to be good for training and for persuading the citizens of New York, Washington, Chicago, and other cities that they are well protected, but no good for operational service. The Russian aircraft it would have to meet are supposed to fly at forty to fifty thousand feet and at five to six hundred miles per hour; they would probably come not in ones and twos but in groups; and missiles in equal numbers ought to stop them thirty to forty miles from the target. It is said that Britain will have such missiles within three years, and that nothing else with a lower performance is worth putting into production so far. This may be a tall story to camouflage failures of production, but it may be true, and British research may actually be gaining a lead in this field.

The Vulcan bomber, with its vast triangular wing, may look ungainly, but it is said to be an aerodynamic marvel. What is more, the R.A.F. hopes to fit the Vulcan with a device that will let it reach its target without interference from enemy anti-aircraft missiles. This is said to be at a very early stage of experiment, but if successful it would be vital.

A new British radio-navigation and bomb-control system was mentioned briefly by the Minister of Supply during the Parliamentary debate.

It is unfortunate that the United States should not be given the benefit of these discoveries. It is also unfortunate that Britain should be unable to harmonize its bomb and bomber programs with that of the United States. Fuchs, Burgess and Maclean, Pontecorvo—these names provide one reason. But there have been American security cases also. Does mere possibility of risk of loss through turncoats outweigh the very real and very present loss through isolating research and development in our two countries? That is for people in Washington to decide. In the absence of a decision the British Government, following America's example, has decided to "go it alone" in thermonuclear affairs.

A great gain from sharing would have been in saving money. As it is, the cost of Britain's program is causing concern. The White Paper gives figures only for the coming financial year, and they are slightly lower than this year's. That is thanks to cuts in the Army and Navy (cuts very unwelcome to those services). But costs for 1955–1956 are only the beginning. Thermonuclear weapons are only at the stage of experiment, not production. Two of the three new long-range bombers (the Vulcan and Victor, the third being the Valiant) are still under test, and full production costs have yet to be met. The guided-missile program similarly faces mounting costs two or three years hence. The Government has announced that there is to be an important expansion of fundamental research facilities; part of the cost will be borne by private industry, but much must fall on the taxpayer. The main measures of civil defense for cities— mobile rescue and relief columns, evacuation, shelters, and so on—have been deferred until more is known about radioactive fallout, so that is another account to be awaited.

What will all this cost four or five years hence? Already the British defense budget is astronomical by prewar standards. British taxation is among the heaviest in the world—heavier even than that in the United States. Members of Parliament and private citizens hope that the Government will soon give an estimate of the eventual cost of the new program. It will be a heavy price to pay for making Britain's voice heard more clearly in Washington and Moscow, but if it must be borne, it will be—in spite of ructions in the House of Commons—for Sir Winston Churchill is not alone in wanting to restore Britain's status as a great power.

Two comments I have heard in the past few days are

relevant. One was from a British officer of high rank, who said: "When we put our views on strategic problems to the Pentagon two or three years ago they had a tendency to ask, 'Who's talking? What have you got to fight with?' They don't do that so much now." The other was from a printer who rarely offers political comment. He said something like this: "So we're to have these B-2 bombs. Maybe we can make both sides see some sense and keep a bit quieter. They might even do a bit of disarmament, you know."

How long will it take to build up Britain's thermonuclear weapons, long-range bombers, and missiles? No official answer has been given. Unofficially the period is put at a minimum of three or four years, and perhaps longer. It is a gradual process. Valiant bombers, with the performance slightly better than the American B-47, come into service this year and will carry British atomic bombs. The Vulcans, which can deliver hydrogen or lithium bombs, will not be ready in numbers before 1958 or 1959. The White Paper contents itself with a limited statement:

"Because of their extreme complexity and novelty, the time taken to put the newer types of weapons through all the various stages of research and development into production tends to be very much longer than in the past. It can be dangerous and misleading to ignore this fact. It is a mistake to assume, because it is announced that nuclear weapons, guided missiles, and supersonic aircraft, for example, are under development, that they are practically ready for use in operations. This applies to all other countries as well as to the United Kingdom."

The last sentence is the most important. The British plans assume that the Soviet Union has no long-range bombing force ready. It has jet bombers that could reach Britain, but none yet that could reach the United States in effective numbers. Not until 1959 is it thought that the Russians will have large numbers of jet bombers able to reach the United States and return home. And until they can reach the main American bases in Florida, Texas, and Arizona, the United States will have a great advantage—so great that the Russians would be unlikely to risk war. In the interval Britain has a certain amount of time to build up its own strategic air power.

Geography is heavily on the side of the United States and against Russia. Moscow is only 1,500 miles from East Anglia, Kiev 1,600 miles from Algiers, and Rostov less than 1,000 miles from Cyprus. Omsk, in the heart of central Russia, is 2,800 miles from East Anglia, 2,400 miles from Cyprus, and 3,200 miles from Okinawa. Dallas, deep in the United States, is 5,700 miles from Warsaw, 5,100 miles from Murmansk, and 4,100 miles from Anadyr, a remote and icy place near the Bering Strait. From the polar regions, where air refueling of Russian aircraft might eventually be possible, New York City is 3,500 miles, Chicago 3,400 miles, and Dallas 4,000 miles. The prototype of a heavy bomber with swept wings was seen over Moscow last May Day, but if it first flew in 1954, production in quantity is unlikely before 1957 or 1958. From its size it seems likely to carry fuel for some twelve hours' flying, which at six hundred miles per hour would give it a maximum radius of 3,600 miles. This means that even with refueling in flight near the Pole, it could barely reach New York or Chicago, and could reach Texas and Arizona only on a one-way mission. Until the Russians have a large number of these aircraft, war strategy based on one-way missions would be a wild gamble.

Clearly, however, the continental defense of North America against such one-way raids is as important to Britain as it is to the United States. If we are to have time to build up our strategic air power, it is vital that the United States and the main bases of its bomber force should remain invulnerable in the interval. Even if the British and American estimates differ on the current strength of Soviet air units, the importance of American continental defense is in no way disputed. It is vital to the whole alliance.

After 1960, what? Britain will have its bombs and bombers, with bases dispersed but individually vulnerable. The Soviet Union will be in the same position. So will the United States, except that its main bases will be rather less vulnerable. By then we shall have reached the "saturation" stage of which Sir Winston spoke. Each side will be able to inflict crushing or almost mortal injury on the other. In every country guided missiles will be increasingly important, although it seems improbable that any country will by then have developed an effective intercontinental missile capable of carrying a nuclear warhead. That, at any rate, is the British expectation.

Unless universal disarmament has been accepted—something to be sought strenuously but not counted on—the advantage after 1960 will go to the country with the best scientific resources. Each side will be straining after new devices and counterdevices. More and more, it seems to interested people in Britain, we shall come to regret the lack of complete partnership in research between Britain and the United States.

West Germany, the Precarious Miracle

BY MYRON M. COWAN

Ten years ago, Americans who entered old Frankfurt-am-Main to take up occupation duties found a city whose heart had nearly been leveled into rubble. Today, Frankfurt's rebuilding has gone so far that recently its city council received a request to leave one block of ruins in a state of devastation in order to remind Frankfurt citizens that there had actually been a war.

All West Germany is the scene of such phenomenal revival out of dust and ashes, and today the Federal German Republic, Europe's newest sovereign nation, is also its most booming one. With a population of fifty million, it is producing at almost double the rate of Hitler's Reich of seventy million. There has never been so swift a resurgence. Yet there remain several uncertain factors that neither Germans nor their western neighbors can safely overlook.

A German banker remarked to me, "When you start from the bottom, you have nowhere to go but up." Particular forces and men, however, determined what road this course would take. The start of the way up occurred not immediately at the end of the war but a few years thereafter, and the decisive impetus toward it was given by the United States. The Founding Father of the Federal Republic, as well as its economic prime mover, was none other than General Lucius D. Clay, our military governor for Germany in 1946-1949.

Prior to the economic and political reforms initiated by General Clay in 1948, flattened West Germany lived on the "cigarette economy," in which the American cigarette replaced the inflated Reichsmark as the yardstick of value. The food ration was set at 1,500 calories daily, a substandard diet, and even this often sank to 1,200 calories daily. Lack of food, housing, and consumer goods, plus a worthless currency, resulted in a stagnating industry. Steel production in 1946 limped along at 2.6 million tons. There was little incentive to work. Membership in the Communist Party of West Germany began to climb.

By the summer of 1946, General Clay and his aides had become disillusioned about the intentions of the Soviet Union. They were fully aware that the Kremlin was going to push its sphere of influence as far west as possible. A negative, punitive policy toward Germany only played into the hands of the Communists. Besides, the U.S. Army had to spend $1 billion in relief funds to feed the hungry Germans and to provide vital necessities for their economy. The Army wanted to get the Germans "off the U.S. taxpayer's back."

So General Clay persuaded the British to join in forming "Bizonia"—an economic fusion of the two occupation zones under a German administration designed to coordinate and restore the trade and industry of this area. "Bizonia" (which later became "Trizonia" with the French co-operating) was a step toward German government.

But this was not enough. General Clay again took the lead. He realized that a West German government must be formed to give it a political identification and that West Germany must be made economically viable if it were to become a barrier against the westward spread of Communism. It was General Clay who carried with him not only the British and French but also the reluctant political leaders of West Germany to establish the Federal Republic in Germany.

The Kremlin saw that General Clay's program was a direct challenge to Soviet foreign policy. To halt the Americans, the Russians imposed the Berlin blockade, thereby facing the United States with a supreme challenge. General Clay cabled the Pentagon on April 10, 1948: WE HAVE LOST CZECHOSLOVAKIA . . . WHEN BERLIN FALLS, WESTERN GERMANY WILL BE NEXT. IF WE MEAN . . . TO HOLD EUROPE AGAINST COMMUNISM, WE MUST NOT BUDGE. . . . IF WE WITHDRAW, OUR POSITION

IN EUROPE IS THREATENED. IF AMERICA DOES NOT UN-
DERSTAND THIS NOW, DOES NOT KNOW THE ISSUE IS CAST,
THEN IT NEVER WILL AND COMMUNISM WILL RUN RAMP-
ANT. I BELIEVE THE FUTURE OF DEMOCRACY REQUIRES US
TO STAY.

And stay we did, along with our Allies. With an effective airlift, we induced the Russians to raise their blockade. Today in east Berlin there is a Stalinallee; in west
Berlin a Clay-Allee. The former is a street name imposed
on the Berliners by their Red conquerors; the latter was
given by grateful Berliners to honor the man who saved
them from Communist domination.

On the economic side, meanwhile, the metamorphosis of
West Germany began with the currency reform of June,
1948. At one stroke, ninety per cent of the liabilities and
securities (in Reichsmarks) of individuals and corporations were wiped out; one new Deutsche mark was paid
out for every ten of the old. To meet the squeeze of
current expenses, shopkeepers as well as big businesses
had to put their hoarded stocks on the market. For the
first time in years, Germans could buy a pair of shoes, or
a dozen eggs, or a piece of wearable cloth. The "D.M."
was accepted quickly as valid money—replacing the
American cigarette—because it could purchase goods.
So the happy cycle started: Money spent to buy goods
provided funds for business to produce more goods.

The success of the D.M. was helped by $3.5 billion
of Marshall Plan aid coupled with extensive U.S. Army
dollar help. It was these billions that effectively primed
Bonn's economic pump, once German officials had
brought themselves to realize their potentialities for free
enterprise. Under their initial controls, West German
Administrations had first sought to channel money into
economically or socially beneficial projects such as housing. But in December, 1948, Professor Ludwig Erhard—
Bonn's Economics Minister—lifted these controls. Erhard
was the leading exponent of free enterprise, which he
preached with all the fervor of a modern Saint Paul. He
argued that if people were free to use their money as
they saw fit—to open a restaurant, a movie theater, or
even a beauty parlor—they were actually benefiting the
economy as much as by building houses. And he was
proved right. For his measure further strengthened the
D.M. and provided the required stimulus to the conva-

lescent economy by giving Germans freedom to do business unrestricted by government red tape.

The result of this has been that in the short space of half a dozen years, free-enterprise capitalism starting out from wreckage has revealed its superior vitality as against socialist or Communist methods in a demonstration unequaled elsewhere.

Still, after the 1948 currency reform there was literally no German investment capital left. How to meet this crucial need? This was done in numerous and ingenious ways.

The Bonn government was required to match every Marshall Plan dollar—usually in the form of raw materials such as gasoline, cotton, grain, and sulphur—in local currency as counterpart funds. The Bonn government then formed the German equivalent of our old Reconstruction Finance Corporation, which loaned out these funds to industry for rebuilding and modernization. The German "RFC" has completed its task and is now in the process of liquidation.

West Germany then set up perhaps the highest tax schedule in the free world, making it prohibitively expensive for an industrialist, big or little, to take his profits for his personal use. Taxes on a 100,000-D.M. income came to 80,000 D.M.

But the government provided special incentives whereby a German business man could escape heavy taxes. If, for example, a German invested his profits in state bonds or state housing, such profits were tax exempt. These state bonds provided fresh funds that were loaned back to industry and business for rebuilding and modernization.

Perhaps the most striking success for this scheme was registered in shipping. The Bonn government permitted a tax exemption to anyone who invested profits in shipping or shipbuilding under clause "7-d" of the tax law. It attracted over $300 million of German money out of the $500 million that went into the postwar rebuilding of a merchant marine, and made West Germany the world's second largest shipbuilder.

The German automotive industry provides another example of how the "up-by-the-bootstraps" technique has worked out through financing out of profits and depreciation. Heavily damaged by the war, the industry

285

is now at more than three times its 1938 level of production, and the Volkswagenwerke, producing a thousand cars per day, has become the fourth largest individual automobile manufacturer in the world, following General Motors, Ford, and Chrysler.

Today, in spite of foreign debts that include the major portion of $822 million reparations to Israel for Nazi crimes, the Bonn budget is in balance, and a major tax cut is going into effect. The Bank Deutscher Laender—Germany's equivalent of our Federal Reserve system—now has a comfortable gold and foreign exchange reserve totaling $2.7 billion, earned from exports. Bonn has become the largest creditor in the European Payments Union. Together with the British, it is working to make its currency freely convertible with the dollar. In spite of the fact that it has had to absorb approximately ten million refugees from the east—a large percentage of whom are elderly or handicapped—West German unemployment last December was 1,288,000 in a nation of fifty million.

Unquestionably, this is a brilliant record of revival. One must take in account also the factor that until only yesterday, West German scientists, technicians, and industrialists had been working under Allied restrictions in many fields such as arms and aircraft production and atomic energy, in which they are only now free to begin to catch up with western technology. "The industrial boom in Germany is continuing and still gaining momentum," said the Bank Deutscher Laender in a recent survey.

Still, under the glittering surface there are elements of insecurity. While West Germany's economic spurt has now given it almost an embarrassment of riches, orders have gone down from Bonn to various government agencies to play down the "economic miracle" in all contacts with Germans or foreigners and to stress instead Germany's continuing problems and weaknesses.

One of Germany's basic weaknesses is its failure to develop a substantial domestic consumer-goods market. Top priority had been given to build up foreign trade. A second weakness—but not admitted publicly—is the continuation of Germany's "cartel mentality." This hinders the growth of a more viable domestic economy. The cartel mentality is not solely confined to big business.

Surprisingly enough, Germany's Socialist Party and the Trade Union Federation—representing six million workers—have also come out in support of what they call "good cartels." It is German dogma that a cartel provides more economic security for all—worker as well as employer—than unhampered free enterprise.

A third potential weakness is the impact of the planned West German remilitarization, whose cost is estimated at a minimum of $10 billion, on the German economy. German politicians and businessmen have been blithely maintaining that it will have no adverse effects. They are selling themselves the old thesis that one can have guns and butter too.

However, in Zürich hardheaded Swiss bankers are expressing doubts about this German attitude. They say the Germans are only fooling themselves and that their rearmament program cannot be accomplished for even $10 billion (plus American supplies of heavy equipment) and this initial capital outlay cannot help slowing down the booming economy.

Meanwhile, the German capital shortage that still persists, according to the "poor-mouth" talk of German bankers and industrialists, has in effect made the Deutsche mark "work overtime." The margin between national solvency and bankruptcy is thin indeed. For example, approximately sixteen and a half times the capital of German banks is out on loan today. Of this amount, more than six times the capital is committed in loans of four years or more, almost twice the capital in loans from ninety days to four years, and the balance in short-term (ninety-day) loans. For a country allegedly without a substantial pool of capital funds, this is a great gamble. But then, the whole postwar reconstruction of West Germany has been one big gamble.

In charge of the game are such skillful, conservative men as Wilhelm Vocke, director of the Bank Deutscher Laender; Herman J. Abs, an international financier and the "Jesse Jones of Germany"; Fritz Schäffer, Bonn's Finance Minister, who balances the national budget; Robert Pferdmenges, private banker, intimate friend and adviser of Dr. Adenauer; and Professor Ludwig Erhard, the apostle of free-enterprise capitalism.

But this is not the only gamble West Germany faces. Its political scene, which has outwardly shown growing

287

pro-western stability and strength, also exhibits undercurrents of increasing uncertainty. Chancellor Adenauer, openly committed to a pro-western and pro-American policy, is lucky in that his legislative branch is one of the few in western Europe that have no Communist Deputies. They were eliminated in the September, 1953, election and the Chancellor's coalition enjoys a two-thirds majority in the Bundestag. Nevertheless, in spite of Bonn's recent ratification of the Paris mutual-defense agreements, his coalition Government is showing serious signs of coming apart at the seams. The Free Democratic Party, spokesman of big business and industry in West Germany, is charting a new course, seeking "normal diplomatic and economic relations" with the Communist bloc. Adenauer is distinctly against this—at this time. The Socialist Party, Adenauer's principal Opposition in the Bundestag, has him on the defensive in the question of German rearmament. Dr. Adenauer made substantial concessions to the Mendès-France Government on the Saar problem to get agreement in Paris for German sovereignty and rearmament. These concessions have been bitterly contested, both inside and outside the Bonn government. And the "Saar solution" remains far from being that.

Under the West German Constitution, the Chancellor remains in office for four years, and can be removed only if the Bundestag first agrees upon and elects a successor by majority. This would be highly unlikely to happen to Adenauer. However, while the aged Chancellor is a strong man and on the economic side has been fortunate to be advised by similarly vigorous brains, on the political side he has not surrounded himself with strong men. The most uncomfortable fact about the Bonn Administration today is that American foreign policy is firmly tied to the life expectancy of this seventy-nine-year-old statesman. If he should die or leave office, both his Government and his pro-western policies probably would be shattered in a struggle for power by a group of political mediocrities.

In the rival pulls on them to link their fortunes either with the West or East, the Germans recognize that they are caught in the very front line of the political and economic struggle between the two camps, and self-interest has made them consider certain facts in between.

First, individually and collectively the Germans—at least the West Germans—are governed by an instinctive desire for personal and national security. They want to regain political and economic equality among the nations of Europe.

Also, there is widespread antipathy in West Germany toward "remilitarization" of the country. Whether a majority of West Germans are in favor of rearmament or against it is still hard to say. But there is certainly enough evidence of German unwillingness to rebuild an armed force to provide grounds for doubt. Chancellor Adenauer himself showed his awareness of organized labor's opposition to the rearmament program when he made a highly publicized visit to the Düsseldorf home of Walter Freitag, head of the German Trade Union Federation, to appeal for support—a gesture comparable to President Eisenhower's journeying to Detroit to visit the AFL's George Meany to gain backing on a key issue.

But not only does German labor show reluctance to support rearmament. Big business and industry have been hanging back as well, affected by hard material facts. The order books of the German steel industry are filled to capacity for months to come. Demand for consumer goods is growing in Germany and this is affecting business thinking as a whole. "Why interfere with this boom for the sake of a rearmament program that will cut down production and sales of consumer and industrial goods, both abroad and at home?" asked a Ruhr industrialist.

Much more interesting to the business world is the possibility of increased trade with the Communist bloc—especially Red China. The Chancellor may focus his attention on the West, but the Ruhr is looking eastward. German businessmen see the British, French, Dutch and Belgians making trade agreements with the Communist bloc, and they now want the same rights.

The prospects of trading with Red China are particularly tempting to many Germans, possibly because distance lends enchantment. German exporters see in Red China's industrialization a great new market for a wide variety of heavy capital goods and equipment such as steel mills, rolling stock, bridges, telephonic and other communications systems, machine tools, rails, pipelines, cement factories, and electrical supplies.

It must also be remembered that a ruling impulse of Germans whose country is split by the Iron Curtain is to reunite it, and Bonn knows that this can be done only by making some kind of a deal with the U.S.S.R., master of the eastern territories.

Finally, the development of the hydrogen bomb by both America and Russia has frightened the Germans, as it has the British and the French. The presence in the Rhineland of "Atomic Annie," the new 288-millimeter U.S. atomic cannon, is very unwelcome. The Germans have pondered information handed out by the U.S. Army that "Atomic Annie" has a firing range of twenty miles, and feel that in the near future Russia too will bring up atomic cannon. If American and Russian atomic cannon should fire at each other, a lot of German real estate would disappear in smoke and dust. This fear dampens any enthusiasm for a close military alliance either with the East or the West that would involve Germany as a belligerent.

In attempting to evaluate German thinking today, I believe the term "Stalingrad vs. Detroit" sums up much of it. The German would like to avoid being attached or subjected to either. Stalingrad, the place where 300,000 of Hitler's men were annihilated at the turning point of the war, stands as the symbol that the Red Army today, and probably for generations to come, is militarily the dominant force on the European continent. "Detroit," equally thought-provoking, stands for America's great industrial and technological superiority. Twice within living memory, America has meant to Germany the difference between winning or losing a war. With its infinitely greater resources, America could make life unpleasant for a hostile or pro-Communist Germany. Could Germany risk offending the strongest single world power?

It may seem unrealistic in Moscow, as it certainly does in Washington, to think of a "third force" between Communism and the western world. Yet the idea of such a force—which does not imply the defenseless neutrality of the impotent or weak—is clearly gaining ground in Germany today. The Federal German Republic, for all its upsurge, stands in need of peace and time to consolidate its gains. Its achievements are brilliant, yet its position remains precarious. The one thing it cannot afford is to be a battleground again. Its dream, instead, is to become the fulcrum of an East-West balance of power.

The Crucial Hour for Italian Democracy

BY CLAIRE STERLING

Rome

The Italian Communists lost Fiat at the end of March. The vote among the employees of Turin's great auto works was 32,487 for the non-Communist unions against 18,921 for the Communist-controlled General Confederation of Italian Labor (CGIL)—almost exactly the reverse of the vote last year. For the first time since the war, the Communists were thoroughly beaten on their home ground, in the city where their party was born and among the most militantly revolutionary workers in the country.

The Communists have been blaming everybody but themselves for their defeat in Turin—the management for intimidating the workers and turning Fiat into a "half-fortress, half-prison," and the Americans for threatening to cancel $32 million worth of offshore procurement contracts if the CGIL won. But it isn't very likely that the toughest trade-unionists in Italy could be intimidated so easily by management pressures. Nor is it probable that the Americans could do, in a few months with $32 million, what they haven't been able to do in ten years with the $5 billion they've sent to Italy. It was neither fear nor blackmail that defeated the CGIL at Fiat; it was loss of faith in the Communist Party.

Italian workers have been faithful to the Communist Party longer than any others in Europe, and because of this popular support the Communists have come closer to winning a free national election here than anywhere else in the world. But it looks now as if the party has over-reached itself. The political machine that has run so efficiently for so long is beginning to sputter.

What happened at Fiat is not an isolated case. True, the CGIL still has an over-all majority in the big northern factories, but the trend in all recent trade-union elections has been going against it.

The party itself still has more than two million dues-paying members of voting age. Its yearly income

amounts to $40 million, perhaps $50 million; it has 365,-
000 employees—one to every six members—on its payroll; and it numbers among its thousands of publications
the newspaper *L'Unità*, with the largest daily circulation
in Italy.

Nevertheless it's losing what Italians call *mordente*,
or bite. Not long ago, an organizer for an anti-Communist union couldn't even walk into Fiat without running
the risk of a beating. It wasn't long ago, either, when
industrialists in the northern third of Italy didn't hire a
worker, let alone fire him, without the CGIL's approval;
when a general strike call on any issue from wages to the
Atlantic pact or the Rosenbergs' execution was an order,
strictly enforced by the party's private militia; when
landowners and priests didn't dare to appear on the
streets after dark in the region of Emilia, where the
party has its greatest strength; when all but leftist newspapers were burned on arrival at some Emilian railroad
stations. The photographs of six Emilian workers who
died in a riot in Modena still hang on the walls of the
Modena public library—they are shown in their coffins
with pictures of Party Secretary Palmiro Togliatti in their
folded arms. The Modenesi come to party headquarters
as usual on Sundays. But they come halfheartedly, for
only a few minutes, and only after they've been to the
movies or finished an outing into the countryside on the
family Vespa. Neither in Modena nor in Bologna nor
anywhere in Emilia do the landowners any longer need
police protection.

This softening is evident all over the north. During the
past year, industrialists have applied unprecedented
pressures in CGIL strongholds from Bologna to Turin to
Milan's industrial suburb of Sesto San Giovanni. All
union activity has been forbidden on factory premises.
Signs reminiscent of a former era have appeared, saying,
"This place is for work, not for politics." Armed plant
police have been increased to an average of one for
every fifty workers. Employees affected by American offshore contracts—about 150,000 in Italy—have been told
bluntly to vote against the CGIL or lose their jobs. All in
all, some seven thousand CGIL shop stewards have been
fired.

Not only has the CGIL failed to get these shop stewards reinstated; it has scarcely put up a fight for them.

Its answers to the new pressure tactics have been meek indeed: Letters of protest have been sent to management, and signatures have been collected for petitions; in many cases where American offshore contracts are involved, agreements have been reached with management to let the anti-Communist unions win—in at least one case, after $20,000 had changed hands; CGIL strike calls have been few in number and have usually been only for token demonstrations of three or four hours; strikes over political issues like European union have been a flat failure.

Other sallies have been made against the party lately that would have been unthinkable a few years ago. Last December Prime Minister Mario Scelba announced a ten-point program to curtail some of the party's extralegal privileges, block some of its major financial sources, and rid the government service of those who fail to "give a sure guarantee of loyalty to the democratic state." Scelba had all the power he needed to do this same thing as Minister of the Interior—a post he held almost uninterruptedly from 1947 to 1954—but apparently he wasn't sure he could get away with it until recently.

Scelba's program has brought some results. The government has taken back 187 of the 200 state-owned buildings, formerly used as headquarters for Fascist organizations, that the Communists had occupied at the time of the Liberation. A few weeks ago the government took advantage of the relaxed atmosphere in Emilia to take over Bologna's Communist-run hospital system. A two-month inquiry had shown that the administration had run up a deficit of $200,000; that it had added a private pavilion to one hospital and furnished it, through public funds, with individual serving trays and night-table lamps costing $20 each and rugs costing $100 each; that several directors of the city hospital administration had been living in this pavilion rent-free.

All this is just a beginning. It would take years to investigate the financial dealings of the 1,048 towns and cities run by Communist mayors or of the ten thousand co-operatives from which the party is probably siphoning off funds. Moreover, short of a total embargo on all trade with Russia, the satellites, and China, no government could hope to catch up with all the front men and dummy corporations doing business for the party at an estimated profit of $20 million a year.

Simultaneously with Scelba's program, an organization called Pace e Libertà (Peace and Liberty) has been flooding Italy with wall posters and magazines calling attention to the Communists' corruption. Among other things, the posters have announced that many or most of the top party leaders were once informers for Mussolini's secret police; that party bureaucrats ride to work in expensive custom-built cars; that Togliatti's former wife once embezzled $5,000 from the party treasury; and that both Togliatti and others in the party secretariat keep mistresses—or "concubines" as Pace e Libertà puts it—who wear costly jewelry and furs.

Pace e Libertà claims much of the credit for the Communists' current decline. But as far as anyone knows its propaganda has not caused major defections among the Communist rank and file. Rather, according to those who know the Communists well, it has tended to revive a flagging sense of solidarity. Italians who join the Communist Party don't think it is the Salvation Army anyway. "There isn't much to be gained," says the ex-Communist writer Ignazio Silone, "in telling people who've lived through Fascism, the war, and the German occupation that all men are corruptible, and that Communists are no different from other men. The question isn't whether party leaders are scoundrels, but whether they're capable and effective scoundrels."

That seems to be the big question. The northern workers have withstood any number of pressures in the past, including mass excommunication by the Vatican, mainly because they have believed that the party leaders—scoundrels or not—would lead them to the revolution.

But the revolution hasn't come.

There's no doubt that this is at the bottom of the Communists' crisis. For a brief moment it came out into the open in a singular document circulated at the party's national conference in Rome last January by a group calling itself Azione Comunista (Communist Action). While the document is known to have been written by somebody outside the party bureaucracy, it clearly reflects views that are common among northern workers; it seems also to have reflected the views of Pietro Secchia, who was Togliatti's second in command until he was demoted just after the conference was over.

Why, asks Azione Comunista, didn't Italy have its revolution back in 1945, when, as Secchia said in the Senate at the time, the big industrialists were "dying of fear and full of servility"? Why, when Togliatti was Minister of Justice—and there were Communist Ministers of Finance, Public Works, and Transport in the Cabinet until 1947—did the party do nothing to change Italy's reactionary social and economic structure? Why, when the Communists have controlled more than a third of Parliament since 1953, have they been incapable of preventing the government from moving toward the Right? And why, when the Party's numerical and electoral strength has been going up, should its ability to defend the working class be going down?

The answers are listed, in the best party jargon, as "parliamentary cretinism," "bureaucratic centralism," "satrapism," and "class collaboration." There are obviously other reasons, but short of confessing that he hasn't really been leading a revolutionary movement all along, Togliatti can't give them.

Togliatti hasn't taken a revolutionary position since April 1, 1944, when he returned to Italy from his Moscow exile bearing orders to collaborate with everybody —the King, the provisional Badoglio Cabinet, the Catholics—to win the war. It has become fashionable these days to blame the late President Roosevelt for inviting Togliatti into the Government at that time, thereby putting him on the road to power. Indeed, this has become one of Premier Scelba's favorite clichés. But the party had so many armed followers in 1944 that there was really no choice but to take Togliatti in, and actually he has been playing the role of the perfect democratic parliamentarian ever since.

It is now generally believed that Stalin didn't really want the Communists to take over Italy in the early postwar years: He had no desire for another Greek civil war in Europe and no objection to letting the United States rather than the Soviet Union spend the $5 billion needed for Italian reconstruction. What he wanted, then and later, was simply to have Italy neutralized by its own unresolved difficulties in the interests of Soviet foreign policy.

He couldn't have found a better instrument than Togliatti. After some dangerous flirtation with deviationism when he was in Moscow at the time of the great purges, Togliatti became a model Stalinist—later Malenkovite, and now Bulganinist. He is infinitely adaptable, cautious, and patient—ideally suited, with his professorial speech and the manner of a good bourgeois, to soothe apprehensions about firebrand Bolsheviks in the minds of a fearful middle class.

Togliatti's first concern, on his return, was to reassure this middle class. "We do not intend," he announced in 1945, "to ask for the bureaucratization of any part of the national economy . . . or to fight capitalism in general. . . . Even if we were alone in power today, we'd appeal to private initiative to help in the reconstruction, because we know that Italy isn't yet mature enough for certain tasks."

Togliatti then set out to build a large and relatively loose party, designed to hold the workers without frightening off all the other Italians he needed for his two major purposes: the manipulation of Italian foreign policy through public opinion and parliamentary influence; and, since force was ruled out, a long-term program of bringing the party to power through the ballot.

The policy had inherent risks. Such a party couldn't screen its recruits very carefully or give them the rigorous ideological training a tough revolutionary movement requires. Moreover, it would have to make embarrassing compromises with the Church in a country that is ninety-five per cent Catholic. And it would repeatedly have to sacrifice not only the workers' political energies but also their interests for larger considerations.

The strategy hasn't prevented Italy from joining the Atlantic alliance or ratifying the Paris pacts. But it worked well enough to prevent the consolidation of a stable democratic majority in the 1953 elections. Having advanced that far, however, Togliatti has found himself, like Hannibal, standing at the gates of Rome but unable to get in; and like Hannibal's, his legions, not caring to be wasted on secondary objectives, are beginning to desert.

Having failed to win by constitutional means, Togliatti has begun to lose his attraction for the lawyers, doctors, dentists, notaries, salesmen, small businessmen, and small landowners who want radical changes but not a revolution. He has also lost most of his appeal for the workers, many of whom do, or at least did, want a revolution.

Where can Togliatti go from here? Not back to the revolution. Even while the storm was gathering over his head at the national conference last January, he was inflexible in his determination to carry out the party's mission as an adjunct of Soviet diplomacy. When Secchia spoke of trouble ahead and urged "an all-out fight for freedom in the factories," Togliatti replied: "The essential thing today is the fight against the imperialist warmongers. This is the theme of our party, and no question can be posed separately from this." Three months later, the party had gathered sixteen million signatures for a petition to outlaw the atom bomb—and Fiat had fallen.

It is becoming more and more evident that the northern workers don't share Togliatti's absorption with foreign affairs and imperialistic warmongers. They certainly don't care enough to submit cheerfully to the systematic destruction of their job security and their unions.

It is only in recent months that either the Catholic Italian Confederation of Labor Unions (CISL) or the Social Democratic Italian Labor Union (UIL) has been able to catch these workers' attention. But many workers are now beginning to feel that the CGIL has neglected their needs for so long that it has forgotten how to defend them. A union that refuses to be "provoked" into striking for the reinstatement of a shop steward, while it insists on striking against German rearmament, is no longer behaving like a union.

Last summer, CISL and UIL signed a national contract for the so-called *conglobamento,* a package wage increase that would benefit three million workers. The increases weren't big, but they were increases, a rare event in Italy. The CGIL refused to sign the contract.

It is doubtful whether Togliatti and his 143 Communist Deputies yet realize that the working class they've been speaking for in Parliament also has to be answered to. The Communist leaders follow the principle of *tanto peggio, tanto meglio*—"The worse things are, the better they are." They are convinced that any swing to the Right, any return to anything like Fascism, would be bound to send thousands, perhaps millions, of democratic Italians into a Communist-guided Popular Front. No wonder that the workers who still have bitter memories of the "worse" under Fascism are inclined to question the wisdom of Togliatti's program. Many of them are beginning to feel that as things stand now, the Communist Party isn't so much a protection against Fascism as an invitation to it.

Whether this mood is temporary or permanent, it gives the democrats—in whatever non-Communist party they may be found—their first real break since the Liberation.

The immediate possibility is that Pietro Nenni's Socialist Party might finally be induced to reclaim its independence. Whatever his private thoughts—about which the rumors are endless—Nenni has so far refused to split with the Communists, mostly because he has believed that if he went, his workers wouldn't go with him. Many of these workers, however, don't seem to be as sold on the formula of working-class unity as they used to be.

Their restlessness can be measured by the results at Fiat, where UIL, with several "independent" Nenni Socialists among its candidates, came out with double the vote—from 5,889 to 11,613—it got last year. A better measure, though, is Togliatti's visible distrust these days of his once unshakable ally. As early as last October, the Communist Central Committee took over direct handling of the CGIL's finances, so as to control the amounts doled out to the few Socialists it still tolerates on the CGIL staff.

By this March, the party had become so distrustful that it cut the Socialists' usual ration of funds to a trickle for the Fiat elections, assigned a nominal role to the CGIL, and handled the campaign itself. So the party itself, not just the CGIL, suffered defeat.

Most observers feel now that Nenni's party can be won over in the foreseeable future, if not from the top then from the bottom. It is to the Socialist workers, the rank and file of Nenni's party, as well as to the left-of-center white-collar class that Giovanni Gronchi, the new President of the Italian Republic, has addressed his appeal. The hope that Nenni would bring the Socialist workers over to the democratic side has been lingering for years among democratic politicians in Italy. Now there is a new hope: that the Socialist workers may bring Nenni over to the democratic side.

Widespread fears have resulted, from rather different quarters. The prospect of Nenni and his workers somehow crossing the great divide is equally abhorrent at Communist Party headquarters on Via delle Botteghe Oscure and at the American Embassy.

Can Nenni be trusted? For years the destiny of Italian democracy has been revolving around this question. Now since Gronchi's election the chance that democratic politicians may take the risk of trusting Nenni has increased remarkably—particularly since the risk seems to be underwritten by a growing number of workers in Nenni's own party. On the other hand, there is a danger that the anti-Communist but leftist trend which has been visible in Italy since Gronchi's election may receive a severe setback if the Sicilian elections of June 5 indicate a further growth of the extreme Right and the extreme Left. To compensate for its losses in the north, the Communist Party has been pouring money and agitators into the backward rural south. It is said to have invested $10 million and five thousand activists in the Sicilian campaign; such an investment can undoubtedly bring returns from a peasantry that is still living in abject poverty and is still unaware of the fact that the party's revolutionary glamor is wearing off in the north.

Both the prospects of Communist gains in Sicily and the fact that the Communist trade unions are losing in the north are keeping the national leaders of the anti-Communist trade unions rather fidgety.

The danger, as one UIL official has put it, is that the same industrialists who were once compelled to put up with everything in their factories will now refuse to tolerate any unionism at all: "They may make the mistake of interpreting the CGIL's growing weakness as an opportunity to take revenge on all the workers for the 'Big Fright' of the postwar era." The danger could become particularly great if the "Big Fright" is reawakened by the results of the Sicilian election.

Italy is worth watching these days. With the Communist Party declining in the north and threatening from the south, with a new President who despite his limited powers seems determined to cut some of the Gordian knots of his country's politics, a decisive hour for Italian democracy may be at hand.

DISSIMILAR

A Great Book

BY MAX ASCOLI

Dialogues of Alfred North Whitehead, as recorded by Lucien Price. Little, Brown. $5.

There have been memorable philosophers whose thinking has not been tempered by wisdom or by charity. Sometimes the power of reason can be as reckless as a force of nature. Western civilization has paid a very high price for Hegel's system, from which both the idolatry of the state and Marx's historical materialism have stemmed. Seldom has a philosopher's creative thinking been sustained by so much wisdom as in the case of Alfred North Whitehead.

The book that Lucien Price has written brings those already acquainted with Whitehead's thinking into a respectful intimacy with the working of that extraordinary mind; the uninitiated will find here the best introduction to Whitehead. These "Dialogues" show him firmly in possession of his formidable ideas, always kind, always true to himself, with a nearly universal range of interests, from mathematics to religion to literature to music to politics, and yet ultimately concerned with a very few basic issues—perhaps with only one. Alfred Whitehead was a true monotheist.

He had a horrible fear of arteriosclerosis of the mind, no matter whether it shows itself in the way young people are educated, or in the hardening of dogma, or in the stiffening of political institutions when they become intolerant of novelty and dissent. "Teachers should be acutely conscious of the deficiencies in the matter taught. What they are teaching may be quite lacking in the necessary ingredients of nutriment. They should be on their guard against their materials and teach their students to be on their guard against them. Once learning solidifies, all is over with it." "The vitality of thought is in adventure. *Ideas won't keep.*" "A hundred thousand years ago—or sometime—nobody knows when—there came a turn in the development of man which brought about a very rapid advance. It was man's capacity for origination, his capacity for novelty, his curiosity, his liking for investigation. My fear for humanity is that they may lose it. One of the few places where it is still free is here in the United States."

The theme recurs over and over again: "It is the rigid dogma that destroys truth; and, please notice, my emphasis is not on the dogma but on the rigidity." For he knew that philosophy has to be dogmatic, and he himself brought into existence a philosophical system with built-in anti-rigidity checks. He knew how to shape finite concepts of crystal-clear purity without ever losing the sense of the infinite and the humility that the sense of the infinite imposes on all our circumscribed concluded achievements.

He had a religious respect for the infinite potentialities of human beings that can be stunted when the state or political authority tries to confiscate the whole of the human person. Talking of Woodrow Wilson, he said, "Only a part of the man was acting, as President, because only a part of man is organized in the state."

He believed in God: "God is *in* the world, or nowhere, creating continually in us and around us." Of this creativeness, that spark of the power of God which was Whitehead gave faithful evidence throughout the eighty-seven years of his life. Born in England, the son of a minister, he spent the last and most productive years of his life in Cambridge, Massachusetts. He came to Harvard after having lost his son in the First World War, and ever since the start of the Second, until he died in 1947, he never stopped dreading what this unending war would do to men. "One of my anxieties about this war has been lest a rigid system be imposed on mankind and that fragile quality, his capacity for novel ideas, for novel aspects of old ideas, be frozen and he go on century after century, growing duller, more formularized until he and his society reach the static level of the insects." And again: "I have often thought that this war might be determining [man's] future one way or the other. The momentum, the impetus of independent thought is so easy to lose."

Throughout this book, Whitehead develops his ideas in conversation mostly with his wife—a woman worthy of him—and with Lucien Price, who recorded what was said and submitted the text he had prepared to the Whiteheads. The dialectics of these dialogues is that of conversation—different, therefore, from the more ponderous one of systematic reasoning, and even more from that which plods along by sorting out and—sometimes—analyzing facts. (Once, when asked "Which are more important, facts or ideas?" Whitehead reflected awhile, then said: "Ideas about facts.") The dialectics of conversation, as evidenced here, is a simultaneous attaining of intuition and ideas on the part of three exceptionally noble human beings, profoundly attuned to one another. Truly, they play with ideas as Mozart played with his themes.

Thanks to Lucien Price, the performance of this trio has been transcribed to enrich our lives.

A Note on Santayana

BY GOUVERNEUR PAULDING

My Host the World: Vol. III of Persons and Places, by George Santayana. Charles Scribner's Sons. $3.

It was always a farewell to everything, not just to arms. The first farewell was to Avila, where he might have become a canon of the cathedral, a canon who doubted his faith, or a lawyer occupied with endless litigation about the fields beyond Avila's walls, a lawyer skeptical of the law. His second farewell was to Harvard, escaping, he thought, from obvious danger: The perennial supply of youth provided by the better private schools would have forced him to observe the effects of age upon his own person rather than upon that of others.

But there was no escape. Oxford proved as perilous, because of the dons. Each year at Harvard young men came in, but four years later they went out into the world, where at least they progressed into senility out of Santayana's sight; the dons at Oxford were students who, never having gone out into the world, irritatingly grew old *in situ*, as the archaeologists would say, gluttonous or dull or religious. Santayana fled Oxford.

As long as he was saying good-by to places, no harm was done, for he kept places in his mind, with all their essential qualities, and here in this last volume of his memoirs the places are safe from all possible destruction. Avila is safe in his prose, as Toledo is safe in the Greco painting, and Rome, Boston, Oxford are safe—in the sense that Nineveh and Tyre are safe, in a cold and perfect abstraction.

It is Santayana's farewell to persons in this book that is disturbing, because he could not make it a gracious farewell or even a farewell at all. He betrayed all his friends: He fled them because they could not remain forever young; yet they stayed with him, insistent reminders, horrid reflections perturbing this Dorian Gray to the end. One need not mention names: Here is a friend of his, an old man now, sitting in an English garden busying himself with embroidering a large design in gold thread; he has lost his figure, his money, his malice, and his wit. Here again is an English gentleman, married often and unwisely, and Santayana, after all the years, is still gossiping about him in the pantry. "People do not grow better when they grow older. . . . No: we are no longer charmed by their virtues or interested in their vices."

It is a wonderful thing to achieve serenity, terrifying to achieve it in emptiness of heart.

The Last, the Very Last

BY RAY BRADBURY

This was the museum and this was the special room in the museum and this the mummy exposed unprotesting to the moving drifts of dust in the sunlit morning air. The mummy was almost but not quite the right color and almost but not quite silent and it did not lie in a hewn marble chest. It sat, rather, in the center of a velvet-portiered parlor surrounded by families of worn blue-velvet chairs all wearing antimacassars. Beyond the curtained areaway, in some far part of the tea-colored house, the museum attendants were murmuring, tinkling the breakfast dishes. Now, moving forward into the golden dust that tumbled down the spring light, a shadow half the size of a man snuffed out the blazing roses in the carpet.

And then, during a period of five minutes, the mummy, mouth half open, its October face crooked back against a green velveteen cushion, became slowly aware of the shadow snipping the roses, one by one, became slowly aware of the stranger standing there for a long while just looking and looking.

"Well," whispered the mummy.

"Colonel Bisttram," said the boy, "I'm James Kneale."

"James." The Colonel nodded faintly.

The boy licked his lips nervously. "I sneaked in. The other boys wanted me to find out. Is it true, what they say? Everybody's talking. They said you used to make speeches on Memorial Day, eight years back. I was only four then. I don't remember. Is it true?"

"So you came to ask that?" whispered the old man, not moving. His large aquiline nose sighted at the chandelier. The nose was as delicately white as a tea-cup, sunlight glowed through it, very fine, very fine. "Yes," he said at last, a bit louder, "it's true."

"You were in the Civil War and saw Mr. Lincoln and Jefferson Davis both?"

"Yes."

"And you're one hundred and eight years old and you're the last, the very last, there aren't any more anywhere in the world, North or South, veterans of the Civil War?" The boy stopped, breathlessly.

"All of it," whispered the old man, shutting his eyes, "true."

"Nobody anywhere else, *nobody?*"

"I," said the old man, opening his eyes again, "am the last."

"Gosh," said the boy. "No wonder they're so careful!"

"Don't go!" cried the old man softly as the boy turned to run.

"I shouldn't be here. They tell about you being afraid of colds."

"No," said the Colonel. "After one hundred and eight years a man can face anything there is to face. It would be worth a cold to talk to someone so incredibly young. We make a fine pair. You so new I can't even imagine it, and me so old you can't imagine me. Please . . ." He twitched one finger on the armrest. "Sit down."

The boy sat.

"Is it true about the President of the United States flying to see you, Mr. Bisttram, Colonel?"

"That's what they say. This being Memorial Day, they thought they'd better do it now. Next Memorial Day may be a bit late. I don't quite know why they're coming. I'm nothing but an old man."

"Sure, but the last one, the last one!"

"It could've been somebody else. It just happens to be me. They didn't pay much attention before. Not that I wanted them to. Oh, they had me do the Gettysburg speech every year until I got too brittle. Even now I still do the speech every Memorial Day in the courthouse square. They put my voice on a record and they play it. I don't read well, but it always struck me there's no bad way to read that speech. Anyway, I retired from saying it in person years ago. And now, sudden-like, this week, the government took a surprised look around and found I'm the final model in stock, their only remaining one-hundred-and-eight-year everlasting clock, James. And now this house is an antique shop, everyone peeking in the windows. Want to know how it feels to be an everlasting clock, boy?"

"Yes, sir."

"God's truth, Jim, as long as I just sit here, and don't look down at these two liver-spotted hands that don't belong to me, I'm fine. I'm ten, eleven, twelve years old."

From beyond the plush curtain came a soft swell of voices and footsteps. The boy half rose from his seat in panic. The voices subsided; the boy sat down, breathing quickly.

"They say the President's flying here from Washington in an hour. You going to wear your uniform, Colonel?"

"I had them burn it forty years ago. No, don't look that way," said the old man. "I said then, I say now, it doesn't matter whether the uniform was blue or gray. Now, more than ever, since I'm picked to be the last, I'm going to be the last with a vengeance. I'm the last man in blue and the last man in gray and when I die they both die and that's the way it should be."

"Yes, sir. But which side *did* you fight on, Colonel?"

"It's gotten hazy. An old man forgets. Colors, they begin to run on you. I see soldiers with me, but a long time ago I stopped seeing color in their coats or pants. I was born in Illinois, raised in Virginia, married in New York, built a house in Tennessee, and now, very late, here I am, good Lord, in Ohio. You see why the colors blend and run so?"

"But heck, you remember *battles!*—you remember which side of hills you was on! I got to tell the kids. How about the sun? Mornings, I mean. Did the sun come up on your left side or right? That'd help. And did you march toward Canada or the Gulf of Mexico?"

"Well, Jim, it was a mixed-up argument. Seems some mornings the sun came up on my good right hand, some mornings over my left shoulder. We marched all directions. It's 'most a hundred years since. You forget suns and mornings that long past."

"You remember winning, don't you? a battle won somewhere? The boys'd like to know!"

"No, I don't remember winning," said the old man, quieter. "I don't remember anybody winning anywhere anytime. War's never a winning thing, Jim. You just lose, you just lose all the time, and the one who loses last is the one who asks terms. All I remember is a lot of losing and sadness everywhere and nothing good but the end of it. The end of it, Jim, that was a winning all to itself, having nothing to do with guns. But I don't suppose that's the kind of victory your boys mean for me to talk on."

"They told me, ask about battles. Antietam, they said, ask him Antietam."

"I was there."

The boy's eyes grew bright. "Bull Run, ask him Bull Run, they said."

"I was there." Softly.

"Shiloh. What about Shiloh?"

"Yes, Shiloh. There's never been a year in my life I didn't think what a pretty name and what a shame to see it only on battle records."

"We got Shiloh, then, and Bull Run, *and* Antietam. Fort Sumter?"

"I saw the first puffs of powder smoke." A dreaming voice. "So many things, so many things come back, oh so many things. Songs. I remember songs. There was one that went: All's quiet along the Potomac tonight, where the soldiers lie peacefully dreaming; their tents in the rays of the clear autumn moon, or the light of the watchfire, are gleaming. Remember, remember. After the surrender, Mr. Lincoln came out on the White House balcony and asked the band to play, Look away, look away, look away, Dixie Land . . . a long time ago . . . And then there was a Boston lady who one night wrote a thing will last a thousand years: Mine eyes have seen the glory of the coming of the Lord; He is trampling out the vintage where the grapes of wrath are stored. Late nights I feel my mouth move. I hear me singing back in another time. Yes, we'll rally round the flag, boys, we'll rally once again, shouting the battle cry of freedom, we will rally from the hillside, we'll gather from the plain, shouting the battle cry of freedom. So many songs, sung on both sides, so many, sung both ways, blowing north, blowing south on the night winds. Tenting tonight, tenting tonight, tenting on the old camp ground. Hurrah, hurrah, we bring the Jubilee, Hurrah, hurrah, the flag that makes you free. . . . When Johnny comes marching home . . ."

The old man's voice faded.

The boy sat for a long while without moving. Then he blinked. "Wait'll I tell this to the kids."

"Yes, tell them. Tell them for me."

"What's the President going to say to you this morning, Colonel?"

"I've thought for a whole week now. Here's the President sitting where you sit now. I see his lips move, but I can't hear what he says. What is there to say? When an old century stops and a new one starts, you fire skyrockets and pinwheels. When a man retires from business you hand him a solid-gold Ingersoll. But the President can hardly be coming to give me a watch, eh, Jim? or light a pinwheel? I imagine he's having as much trouble making up his speech as I'm having with mine."

"You going to make a speech?"

"Not a long one." The old man laughed drily. "Mr. Lincoln kept it short and right at Gettysburg. You want people to remember, don't take up their time. All last night I lay thinking, how can I put in a little handful of words the way I feel? I wrote it out in my mind and corrected it this morning. A handful of words, Jim, I pared my speech down to that."

"I can't hear you," said the boy.

"Bend close," whispered the old man.

"Don't go to sleep, sir!"

"Jim," whispered the Colonel, "I'm not going to sleep."

"Don't go to sleep, Colonel!" cried the boy, afraid.

"Quick." There was only a kind of cool air moving in the old man's motionless lips. "I'll tell you the words. Bend down. I thought I could wait, but . . ."

"You got to wait, sir!" cried the boy. "I'm sorry I bothered you. I'm sorry!"

"Don't think that. Close, now. Listen . . ."

"Colonel!"

The old man gave a convulsive clench of one hand, which caught the boy in a blind, vising grip. "You listening, Jim?" said the faint bellows.

The boy could only nod and swallow.

The Colonel's lips moved. "Jim, you got to remember. It's just a little bit, a little bit, you got to remember. Here are the words, now, here. Repeat after me: *As of this day . . .*"

The boy repeated the words and cried, "Colonel, Colonel!"

"I'm still here. Now the rest of it. Don't ever forget it, boy, don't ever forget. Listen . . ."

The boy poised, trembling, over the thrown-back head, the pale hawk face, the whispering and the coldness, to hear the words; while outside, in the spring sky, an airplane flew over.

The door of the Colonel's house burst open, the boy ran, the boy fled into sunlight, sobbing, one hand to his face, stumbling blindly, then running on.

Without seeing them, he ran into a crowd that was advancing upon the house with flags and pennants and a silent brass band ready to start. They caught hold of him running and crying and heard him wail and still held onto him and heard him repeat the few words again and again.

"It's over," he sobbed, "it's all over."

Some of them asked him what was over.

"The War," said the boy. "That's what he said! *The War, it's all over now!*"

The crowd stood back away from the boy and turned to look for a long while at the silent house. Only the flags moved in the soft May wind over their heads.

WHERE WE STAND

This Liberal Magazine

BY MAX ASCOLI

It is proper for a publication to restate from time to time what it believes in and reassess its aims.

Chance may have led each of our readers to stumble upon *The Reporter,* but the relationship with these readers is no longer accidental. Indeed, it has proved an enduring one, in which more and more people are joined in reciprocal confidence. The time is well past when *The Reporter's* beliefs and purposes could be considered the private, tentative bond of a group of writers united in a publishing venture. Reader response proves that there is nothing tentative any longer about *The Reporter.*

Our belief is in liberalism. In the last few years there has been a distinct tendency in our country to use this word with qualifying adjectives or to quarantine it within quotation marks. Yet it is still difficult to find someone who, no matter how committed to the far Right or Left, withstands the temptation to call himself a liberal in his own sense of the word—once he has made sure that he has escaped being confused with people who are called or call themselves liberals. Few other words, if any, have been so blurred by the "yes, but" treatment. Meanwhile, the idea of liberty is paid constant tribute by American politicians of both parties as a disembodied principle so secure in the high heaven of abstraction as to require no effort to be made operational. Yet what is a liberal, if not a man who gives all he has to make liberty operational, and develops the highest possible degree of skill this vocation demands?

The Reporter's liberalism is based on the belief that liberty, far from being an ethereal thing, is always identified with and related to specific and present situations. In our day and country, for instance, freedom of the press or of information needs defense not against the enemy of past times—censorship—but against the peril of the present that is the oversupply of news. The point has been reached where freedom of the news, to be effectively operative, requires to be counterbalanced by a certain degree of freedom from the news. This is the specific situation in the publishing field to which *The Reporter,* this liberal publication, has applied itself. It manages to be quite selective in its handling of the news; it does not believe that all news items are born free and equal with a built-in or innate right to get into print. Other publications feel differently, but *The Reporter* sticks to its rule: It endeavors, as best it can, to sort out the meaningful and relevant from the trivial and gossipy, the natural-born, honest-to-God news from the synthetic facsimiles concocted in public-relations mills.

The oversupply of news is by no means the least cause making for the ever-spreading apathy and indifference that plague the public mind. In a remote way, everybody worries somewhat about the A- or H- or U- or C-bomb; no one relishes the idea of being vaporized. But who can do much about it all; who can prevent war from coming? *The Reporter* believes that there are quite a number of things that can be done, and that there are a definite number of men who can do these things, men with well-known responsibilities, addresses, and telephone numbers. These men must not be allowed to get away with high-sounding slogans, like instant retaliation—whether "massive" or "measured." The issues the men in power must cope with are well within the grasp of the American public, if the effort is made to give us not soporific slogans or slanted news but the truth. It is never easy to get at the truth, but according to the liberal belief there is such a thing, and—at great cost—men can reach it and be saved by it.

Liberalism is an exacting creed, and no wonder so many people are satisfied with paying lip service to the blessings of liberty and to the inevitable victory of the free world over the slave one. Of all political isms, liberalism is the only one that does not prescribe any ultimate goal to be pursued as an end in itself. Neither can such a goal be found in the particular exigency with which freedom happens to be identified. We cannot pursue anti-Communism as an end in itself, and yet there is no greater threat to the human race than the consolidation and spread of Communism. We should know by now what a price we paid and are still paying for having pursued victory over Nazism as an end in itself.

Freedom is never unalloyed, and were some metaphysical laboratory ever to produce "pure freedom" it would not be worth having. Its unique, unsurpassable worth depends entirely on the way in which it is alloyed with specific interests and exigencies. The way to make freedom prevail over Communism is to prove that industrial production under democracy, with competing political parties and predominantly private enterprise, can ultimately give material comfort and spiritual well-being to an ever-increasing number of men. But the places where this ought to be proved are to be found in some of the spots near the Communist orbit where economic misery and political disorder increase the Communist temptation. Men are so made as to prefer sometimes a purposeful slavery to an aimless freedom.

The first condition for making freedom prevail and defeat Communism is to avoid pursuing either goal for its own sake. Liberalism is definitely intolerant of anything considered as an end in itself—including liberty. What can be said of life can be said of liberty: We cannot live life, but we can live, as fully as we are able to, that fragment of life which is ours. A liberal, a man who cultivates the skills that make freedom operational, is always a man on special assignment.

Because of its devotion to freedom, this magazine is always on special assignment.

This is a fortnightly of facts and ideas, or perhaps it would be better to say—gratefully borrowing from Whitehead—of ideas about facts. Being a liberal publication, it endeavors to harmonize the two, avoiding the promiscuous collection of news on the one hand and the reiteration of predictable, opinionated opinion on the other. News and opinion is the journalistic currency —frequently manipulated—by which facts and ideas are given circulation. Liberalism means an unending search for the right operational balance and, in the case of this publication, this means the right balance between facts and ideas. The two must check and control each other so that the facts are scrutinized and the ideas tested. Facts—largely products of man's willfullness or negligence—must be reckoned with, for the moment is always likely to come when, no matter how stubborn and irrefutable, they may be overruled or refuted.

This liberal publication, of necessity, must be always

objective and never impartial. Objectivity means a rounded, conscientious study of facts, so as to determine their causes and their weight. But this scrupulous care implies no detached reconciliation with their existence. Moreover many alleged facts, under close scrutiny, turn out to be phony. So, in facing such an issue as that of Formosa and Quemoy, this magazine has never lost sight of the human beings directly concerned, the Formosans—the most important conditioning fact in the whole picture. In no way should they be considered mere accessories to an international real-estate deal.

This magazine had no qualms in applauding the President when it was possible to think that he was earnestly trying to disengage our nation from the fanatical pressure of our Communist enemies and of his rightwing Republican friends. Maybe he is still trying, perhaps he may still succeed, provided our allies are firm enough. The President is past master in the art of letting necessity force his hand—a necessity over which he can claim to have no control. But when the strategic importance of Quemoy and Matsu was advanced as fact, *The Reporter* did not hesitate to call that fact a phony.

Because of its liberalism, *The Reporter* is truly independent—independent, that is, of both political parties. One of the blessings of the way the two-party system is organized in our country lies perhaps in the fact that American liberalism has never been seriously tempted to become a party. On the other hand, it must be admitted that like our two parties American liberalism has been singularly leery of defining its own theoretical principles, the set of ideas by which its operations are guided. This has greatly contributed to the lack of commonly accepted standards even in the most articulate liberals.

Liberalism in our country has developed into an instinct, to be sure, exemplified by some of the noblest characters in public life. But this particular condition has been a very heavy handicap on liberalism lately, when it has had to withstand two different yet equally demanding tests. The first was the assault of ruthless, seditious demagoguery. The second was the task of presenting the American case to the outside world. Useful as they are, our political parties cannot do this job. It can be done only by liberals, assigned to this particular task. So far, unfortunately, the language of American liberalism has proved to be strictly for internal consumption.

Yet the need for ideas is urgent—and not only for communication with the outside world. For this reason, this magazine has had to indulge in more "think pieces" than it would have liked. The need being great, it has had sometimes to be satisfied in a hurry, without any chance of protracted reflection in an ivory tower—*Satisfaction While U Wait.*

In one respect, *The Reporter* has not lived up to its liberal creed. It still has too much politics. For a liberal, approximately only half of a man is a political animal— Caesar's half. For this I plead guilty, adding as an extenuating circumstance that the temptation has been too great—or perhaps the emergency. In the year to come *The Reporter* will prove, I hope, that the other half is not forgotten.